ABRAHAM-LOUIS-RODOLPHE
DUCROS
A SWISS PAINTER IN ITALY

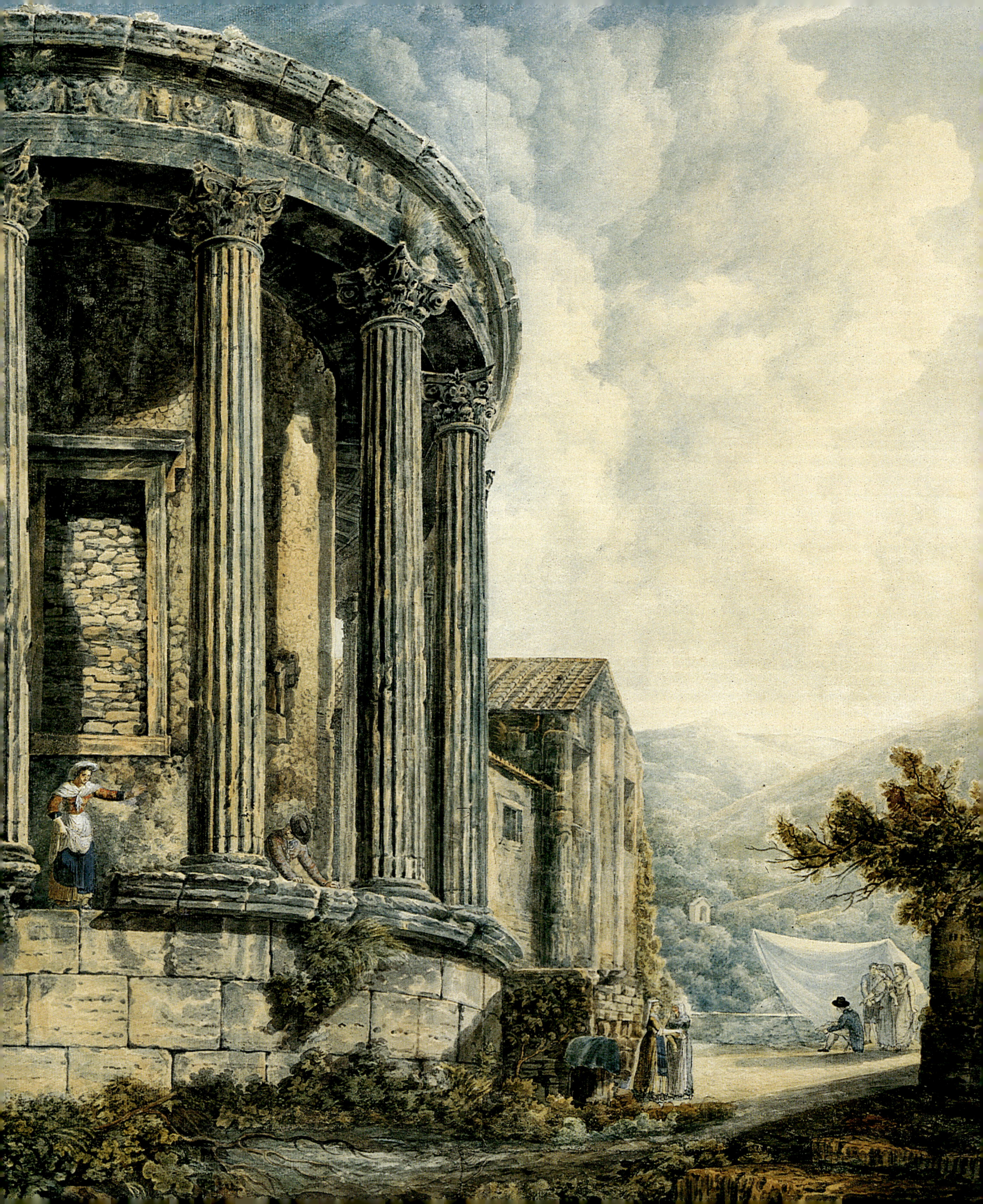

ABRAHAM-LOUIS-RODOLPHE DUCROS

A SWISS PAINTER IN ITALY

NATIONAL GALLERY OF IRELAND

Published on the occasion of an exhibition at
The National Gallery of Ireland
11 June – 31 August 2003

This exhibition catalogue is sponsored by

PRO HELVETIA
Arts Council of Switzerland

in association with

Embassy of Switzerland
Dublin

Distributed by National Gallery of Ireland

This catalogue is a translation of the 1998 catalogue
edited by by Jörg Zutter
Coordinated by Sergio Benedetti and Fionnuala Croke
Edited by Elizabeth Mayes
Translated by Charles Penwarden

Design by Jason Ellams
Printed in the E.U. by Snoeck-Ducaju & Zoon

ISBN 1904288-03-0

Cover illustration: Louis Ducros, *Eruption of Vesuvius and Shipwreck*, *c.1800* (cat. 36)
Frontispiece: Louis Ducros, *The Temple of Sibyl, Tivoli, c.1783* (cat. 15)

CONTENTS

PREFACE

After Lausanne, Quebec and Norwich, the work of Abraham-Louis-Rodolphe Ducros (1748–1810) comes to the National Gallery of Ireland. This exhibition in Dublin is especially welcome because it brings these works by the famous Swiss watercolour painter, one of the most prestigious holdings of the Musée cantonal des Beaux-Arts de Lausanne, to an institution whose internationally renowned collection reflects the strong interest of Irish art lovers for landscape, and particularly for the *vedutisti* of the eighteenth and nineteenth centuries.

Links between the two institutions will be further strengthened in autumn 2003, when Lausanne hosts the exhibition *Prospects on Paper: Landscape Art in Ireland*. This will give Swiss visitors the chance to discover some of the masterpieces in the collection of the National Gallery of Ireland.

The importance of Ducros in the history of European landscape painting is well established. Still, it is worth briefly recalling the originality of his position at the end of the eighteenth century. Forced into exile – as were most French-speaking Swiss artists of the day – by the lack of an art-buying public at home, Ducros made his career in Italy, where, one might say, he imported the tradition of the Swiss *petits-maîtres*. His first topographical watercolours, executed during a journey to Sicily and Malta, show the influence of Claude. Nevertheless, his singularity soon emerged in the works of his "Roman period", notably in the variety of techniques he employed for his landscape compositions. That Ducros had learnt from Piranesi is evident in the freedom with which he manipulates and idealises the various elements and in his treatment of scale: human beings are always very small in comparison to nature and the ancient monuments. Technical limits combined with the need to produce in sufficient quantity so as to meet the demand of tourists stimulated Ducros to invent new procedures. The prints that he produced with Volpato made the most of what could be learnt from the artisanal Swiss practice of coloured engravings. As the format of the watercolours grew, so it became necessary to glue several sheets of paper together. In his efforts to compete with oil painting, the mature Ducros used all kinds of technical tricks, highlighting his watercolours with gouache and oil, and varnishing selective areas in order to heighten the effects of depth. There was a marked change in his iconography, from the sunny landscapes and colourful landscapes of his first period in Rome and its environs to the darker and more tormented compositions of his years of exile in Naples and Malta, after 1793. By 1800 or thereabouts, his universe was becoming a pre-Romantic one, in osmosis with the current sensibility and taste for the sublime and the catastrophic, sometimes even evoking the Gothic novel. Here were volcanic eruptions, shipwrecks, storms, night scenes in the moonlight and emphatic chiaroscuro.

The Musée cantonal des Beaux-Arts de Lausanne originated with the ensemble of Ducros's watercolours; this, as the customary expression here has it, was its "primitive collection". We are delighted that this collection is now being exhibited in Dublin, and would like to warmly thank our colleagues at the National Gallery of Ireland: Raymond Keaveney, Sergio Benedetti and Fionnuala Croke, who initiated this project.

Yves Aupetitallot
Director
Musée cantonal des Beaux-Arts de Lausanne

FOREWORD

The availability of a modern, customised special exhibitions space in its new extension has made it possible for the National Gallery to establish a programme of special shows which introduce its public to a wider experience of art. At times this will involve a focus on the great masters, admired by all, and alternatively it will mean introducing lesser known talents, whose work is nonetheless fascinating and worthy of our attention. In managing such a schedule the Gallery will be reliant on the support and cooperation of sister institutions around the world.

Ducros – a Swiss painter in Italy is a typical example of the fruits of this new initiative, bringing to its Dublin audience a selection of some fifty works by this extraordinarily talented artist who, outside of a specialist community of admirers, is little known beyond the confines of his native Switzerland. Whilst the name Ducros might not be instantly recognisable, his images and his subject matter have universal appeal, representing as they do the splendid and seductive attractions of the Italian peninsula, attractions which were at their most potent in the late eighteenth century, the age of the Grand Tour. It was as a supplier of images to travellers to Italy that the artist established his reputation, a reputation which not only pleased collectors, but also impressed painters and topographers who were astonished at his revolutionary use of the technique of watercolour painting which in his hands aspired to the quality of oil painting in its scale, range and complexity of effect. Later this year, in acknowledgement of this special event, the National Gallery of Ireland will arrange for a selection of Irish views by Irish artists to travel to Lausanne.

We are most grateful to our colleagues at the Musée cantonal des Beaux-Arts de Lausanne, and particularly to Yves Aupetitallot, Director, and to Catherine Lepdor who assisted with the preparation of the exhibition. At the National Gallery of Ireland, special thanks go to Sergio Benedetti, Fionnuala Croke, Susan O'Connor, Sara Donaldson and Niamh McGuinne. The National Gallery appreciates the support of the Embassy of Switzerland in Ireland and Pro Helvetia – Arts Council of Switzerland in making this event possible.

Raymond Keaveney
Director
National Gallery of Ireland

ABRAHAM-LOUIS-RODOLPHE DUCROS (1748–1810)

PIERRE CHESSEX

1748

Abraham-Louis-Rodolphe Ducros (or DuCros, as he would sign himself in his Italian glory years) is born on 21 July in Moudon (Pays de Vaud, Switzerland). His father, Jean-Rodolphe, teaches writing and drawing.[1]

1750

The Ducros family is living in Yverdon, where Jean-Rodolphe is a *régent* (schoolmaster). Two more sons are born: Louis-Guillaume-Samuel in 1750, who will follow in his father's footsteps and make his career in Yverdon, and, in 1751, François-Barthélemy, who will become a pastor.

1761

Jean-Rodolphe Ducros buys the burghership of Yverdon.

Fig.1 Pierre-Louis De la Rive, *Presumed portrait of Ducros*, pencil and crayon, 13.8 x 12 cm. Musée cantonal des Beaux-Arts, Lausanne

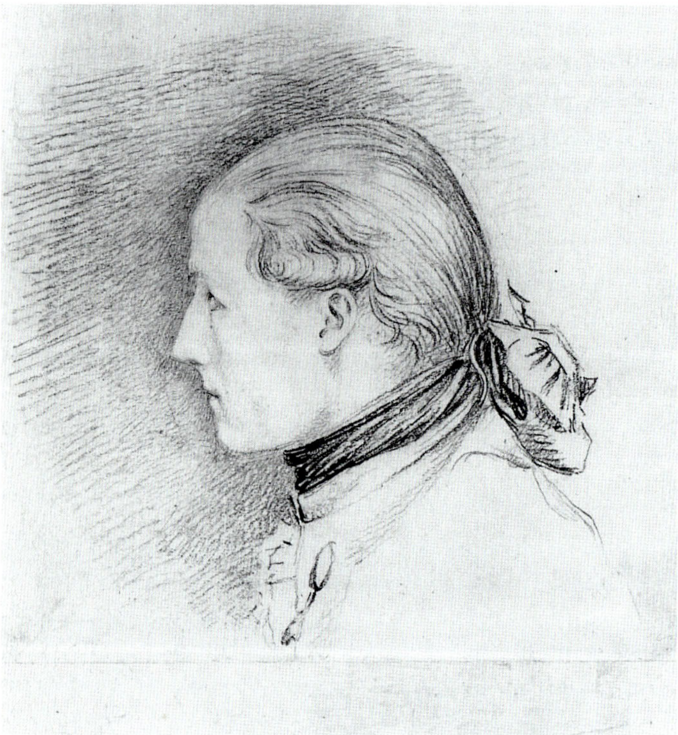

1764

Death of Jean-Rodolphe Ducros. Abraham-Louis-Rodolphe, his oldest son, takes up his position at the school. In spite of their youth, his widow has the inheritance passed on to her sons.

1765

'The older Ducros, son of the late S. Ducros, *Régent*, who, jointly with his brother, had been entrusted with the *régence* of the third class, expressed the wish to withdraw elsewhere for his own greater benefit, to which the Council consented.'[2]

1768–70

Although it is said that Ducros at first worked in commerce, 'he was a born painter; he could only be a painter: first he used the moments stolen from his daily occupations to draw; soon, he was full of disgust for commerce: he left his counter in Geneva and travelled through Italy to the sanctuary of the arts.'[3]

In reality, Ducros started taking lessons at the private academy of the Chevalier de Fassin (Nicolas-Joseph Fassin, 1728–1811) in Geneva in 1769, making numerous copies of Flemish and Dutch painters.

1771–72

Ducros is reportedly travelling in Flanders with his master, 'but after leaving him, it was in Geneva that he found friends and all the support he needed.'[4]

1773–75

In Geneva he copies Wouwerman, Nicolaes Berchem, Jan Both and Jacob van Ruysdael in the company of his friend, the young painter Pierre-Louis De la Rive (1753–1817) (fig. 1). From the latter we know that they also paint many watercolours in the Geneva countryside and Savoy.[5]

1776

'Now, tired of copying, Ducros decided to make the journey to Rome.'[6] He sets off with Isaac-Jacob La Croix (1751–1782), an engraver who has worked in the Basel workshop of the famous

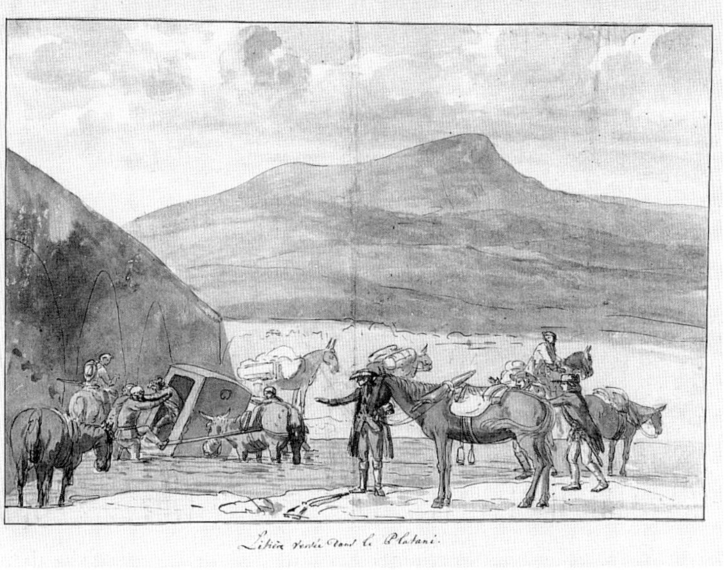

Fig. 2 Louis Ducros, *Litière overturned in the Platani, 1778*, watercolour, 30 x 41.5 cm. Rijksprentenkabinet, Rijksmuseum

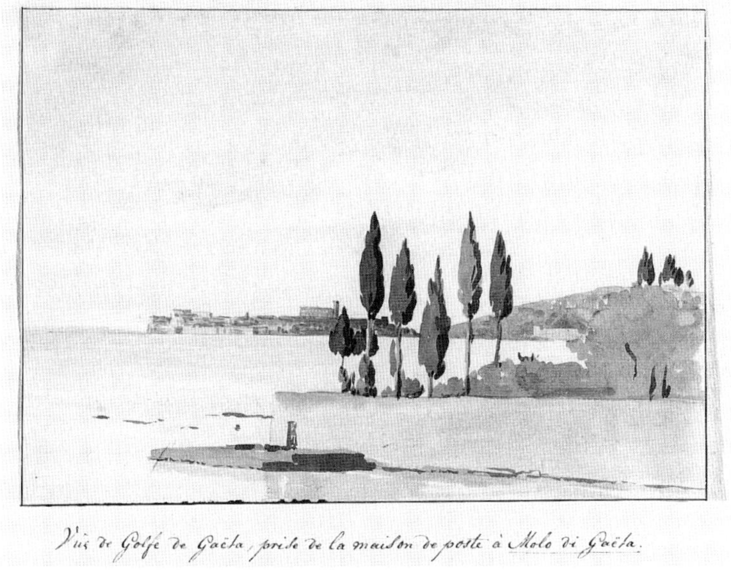

Fig. 3 Louis Ducros, *View of the Bay of Gaeta, 1778*, watercolour, 18.1 x 25.2 cm. Rijksprentenkabinet, Rijksmuseum

Christian von Mechel (1737–1817). After the traditional stops at Bologna and Florence, the two young men reach Rome at the end of the year. Ducros is twenty-eight.

1777

Ducros takes lodgings in the Campo Marzio quarter, comprising the parishes of San Lorenzo in Lucina, Santa Maria del Popolo and Sant'Andrea delle Fratte, all centring around the steps of the Piazza di Spagna. Between now and 1793, his name appears almost every year in the *stati d'anime* of the parish of San Lorenzo.

1778

Ducros and his fellow countryman La Croix are boarding with the painter Fortunato Vercelli on the Strada delle Carrozze.[7] In March, Ducros is hired by the Dutchman Nicolaas Ten Hove to accompany him on a journey to the Kingdom of the Two Sicilies along with three gentlemen from The Hague: Willem Carel Dierkens, Willem Hendrik van Nieuwerkerke and Nathaniel Thornbury.[8] They leave on 10 April. After stopping at Terracina and Gaeta, (fig. 3) the travellers arrive in Naples on 12 April and stay for five days. There they meet Sir William Hamilton (1730–1803), Extraordinary Envoy of the King of England to the Kingdom of the Two Sicilies from 1764 to 1803, who will become one of Ducros's most faithful patrons (fig. 4). This Scottish aristocrat, a great collector of art and antiques,

Fig. 4 David Allan, *Portrait of Sir William Hamilton, 1775*, oil on canvas, 228 x 181.2 cm. National Portrait Gallery, London

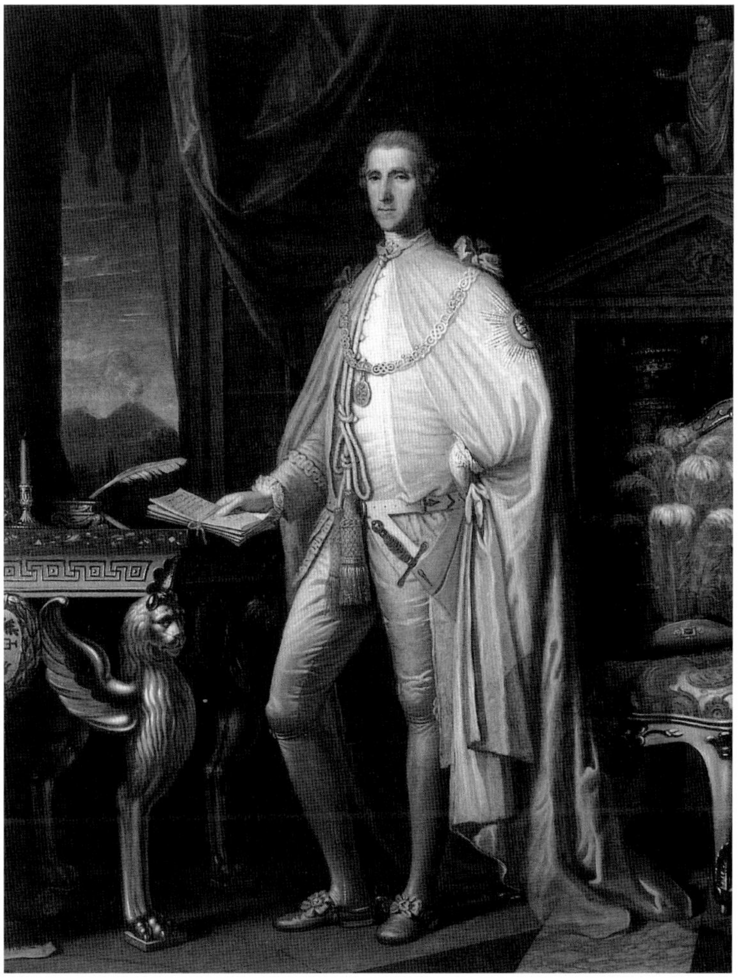

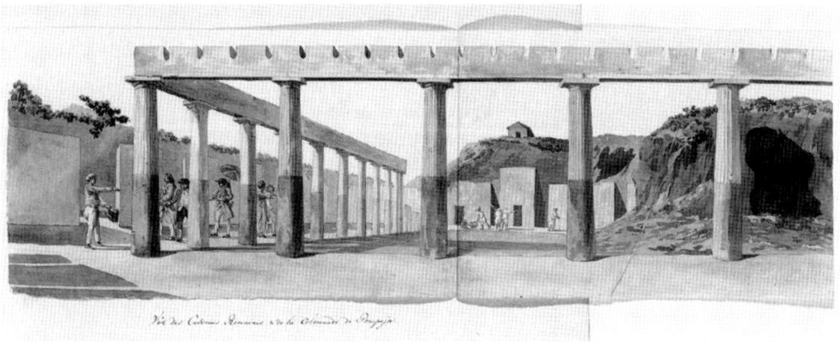

Fig. 5 Louis Ducros, *The colonnade and the Roman barracks, Pompeii, 1778,* watercolour, 22.3 x 69.3 cm. Rijksprentenkabinet, Rijksmuseum

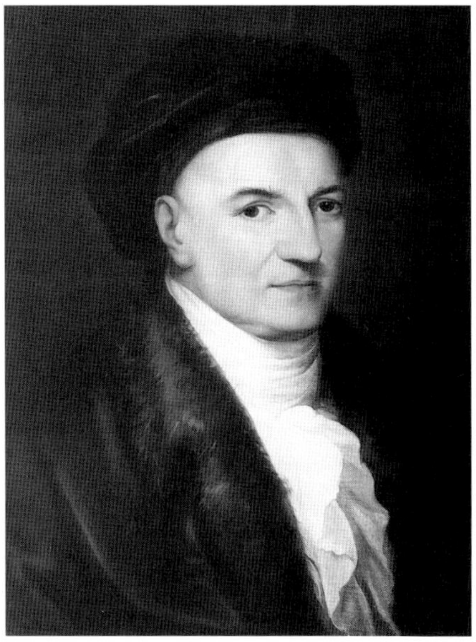

Fig. 6 Francesco Antonibon, *Portrait of Giovanni Volpato*. Museo civico, Bassano

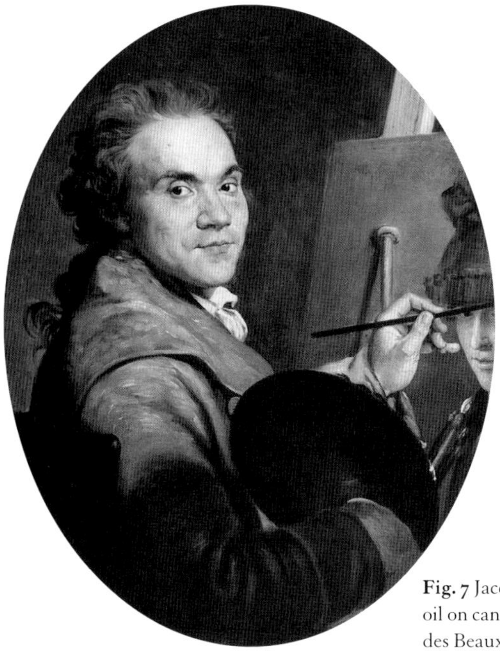

Fig. 7 Jacques Sablet, *Self-portrait,* oil on canvas, 75 x 64 cm. Musée cantonal des Beaux-Arts, Lausanne

is fascinated by the scientific observation of Vesuvius. He supplies them with letters of recommendation for the South (fig. 5). Leaving Naples on 18 April, the travellers make stops at Avellino, Paterno, Canossa, Barletta and Trani, resting at Bari on 25 April. There Nieuwerkerke notes that: 'The painter travelling with us, highly skilled and with an indefatigable zeal for his art, went out early in the morning to do a few views of the town. [...].'[9] On 28 April, the coaches sink into the mud on the way into Brindisi, a mishap related by Dominique Vivant-Denon, who gets caught at the same time as Ducros and his companions.[10] On 3 May they are at Casalnuovo, where they visit the ruins of the ancient city of Manduria before going on to Taranto.

On 7 May they hire boats with lateen sails which set off via Reggio Calabria and leave them at Messina a few days later (fig. 2). The four gentlemen and their painter make leisurely stops in various Sicilian towns: seven days in Messina (14–19 May), where they meet the Genevan merchant Jean Brechte, the Dutch vice consul and then consul there; four days in Taormina (20–23 May); eight in Catania (with an excursion to Etna between 28 and 30 May); four days in Syracuse (1–5 May); three days in Agrigento (25–28 June). In between these stays they sail to Malta on *speronari* (small boats) on 6–7 June. Contrary winds force them to spend a few days on the island (8–16 June) and they take the opportunity to visit the island of Gozo. A French brig (*L'Heureuse Marianne*) takes them to Agrigento on 25 June. From 29 June to 15 July they stay in Palermo for the festivities of Santa Rosalia. They make an excursion to Segesta. From 16 to 20 July they make the Palermo-Naples crossing on a French brig. Back in Naples, they are invited on several occasions to the *casino* of Sir William and Lady Hamilton on Mount Pausilippo. They climb Vesuvius on 26 July. They are back in Rome on 12 August.

The 300 watercolours made by Ducros during this journey are put together in three large in-folio albums that will remain in the Ten Hove family until 1948, when they are acquired by the Department of Drawings at the Rijksmuseum in Amsterdam.

1779

La Croix returns to Switzerland after working as an engraver with Giovanni Volpato (1732–1803) (fig. 6) and Jacob-Philipp Hackert (1737–1807).

Ducros begins collaborating with Volpato. Some of his large-format watercolour views of Rome (75 x 50 cm) reach Switzerland (the home of the Guiguers in Prangins). A number of these are for British patrons.

1780

Ducros is living on the Corso.[11] In association with Volpato, he publishes *Twenty-four Views of Rome and Environs*. Their main novelty lies in the fact that they are contemporary views and in a very large format.

1781

Still at the same address on the Corso,[12] Ducros takes on Peter Birmann (1758–1844) from Basel as his assistant. At first Birmann draws for him but then falls out with his master over money matters and goes to work in Volpato's studio.

'Mr Ducros of Yverdon, who has earned himself an excellent reputation in Rome, is working in collaboration with Mr Volpato on a collection of illuminated views of Rome, of which he has finished twelve in the same format as *The School of Athens*, and another twelve of medium size.'[13]

1782

Ducros has moved to the Strada della Croce. His lodgings there will now serve as both studio and shop for the next ten years. Here he will sell his own works and the prints illuminated in collaboration with Volpato, Jacques Sablet, (fig. 7) and Raffaele Morghen, as well as coloured prints by other artists (such as Louis-Jean Desprez and Francesco Piranesi). This year he shares his dwellings with his fellow countryman Sablet.[14] Ducros produces wash-style prints of twelve Italian costumes based on Sablet's drawings[15] (fig. 8). He paints two large oils for the Grand Duke Paul Romanov, *The Grand Duke Paul and the Grand Duchess Marie at Tivoli* and *The Grand Duke Paul at the Forum*, executed during the newlyweds' travels in Italy.[16]

1783

Jacques Sablet has left the lodgings on the Strada della Croce and moved in to the Casa al Mosaico (Via Margutta) with the Genevan painter Jean-Pierre Saint-Ours (1752–1809) and several other Protestant artists.[17]

In March and April Ducros accompanies Pope Pius VI Braschi to the Pontine Marshes. Judging by a letter written to Charles Bonnet on 7 July 1783, he is in favour with the Sovereign Pontiff. 'His Holiness has showered favours on me in the different audiences he has granted me and, after the first visit, when I was taking my leave, called me back and invited me as obligingly as could be to be his guest and come and eat during his stay at Terracina at his main table with the prelates and people of his court. I chuckled to myself to see a child of Calvin, a heretic,

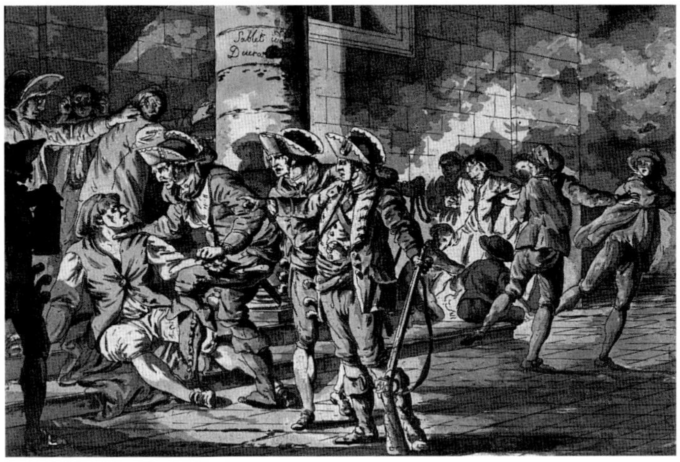

Fig. 8 Louis Ducros after J. Sablet, *The Peelers, 1782*, etching and aquatint, 17.7 x 25.4 cm. Rijksprentenkabinet, Rijksmuseum

under the flags of the Church, eating the ambrosia and drinking the nectar intended for the Saints [...] I found these handsome courtiers to be mere machines moved only by the strings of interest. Oh, how I prefer to be in Tivoli under the waterfalls at sunrise. Newton would have broken down light there without a prism [...].'[18]

The painter makes frequent stays in Tivoli and in the Sabine Mountains. Paints numerous watercolours in Umbria, near Narni and Terni and in the Nera Valley.

In a diary entry dated 29 March 1783 John Ramsay records visiting Ducros's workshop with the Scottish landscape artist Jacob More (1740–1793) and greatly admiring his watercolours. He also relates his visit to the home of Lord Breadalbane, where he meets Sir William Hamilton and James Byres. All present admire Lord Breadalbane's new acquisitions, Ducros's *Pantheon* and *the Temple of Antonine and Faustina*.[19]

An almanac for the year indicates that Ducros's renown has reached his native land. It states that he 'has published coloured prints of different views of the capital; most notably, he renders antique ruins with striking truthfulness.'[20]

1784

Ducros is still on the Strada della Croce.[21] At the end of his stay in Rome, King Gustav III of Sweden visits Ducros in his studio, as reported by the *Diario Ordinario* on 24 April. It is thought that Ducros was considered for the position of 'commissioner for antiquities' to the Court of Sweden, but in the end the more renowned Piranesi was chosen. Gustav III had a passion for antiques and had paid several visits to Volpato who, in addition to his print workshop, had since 1779 been carrying out

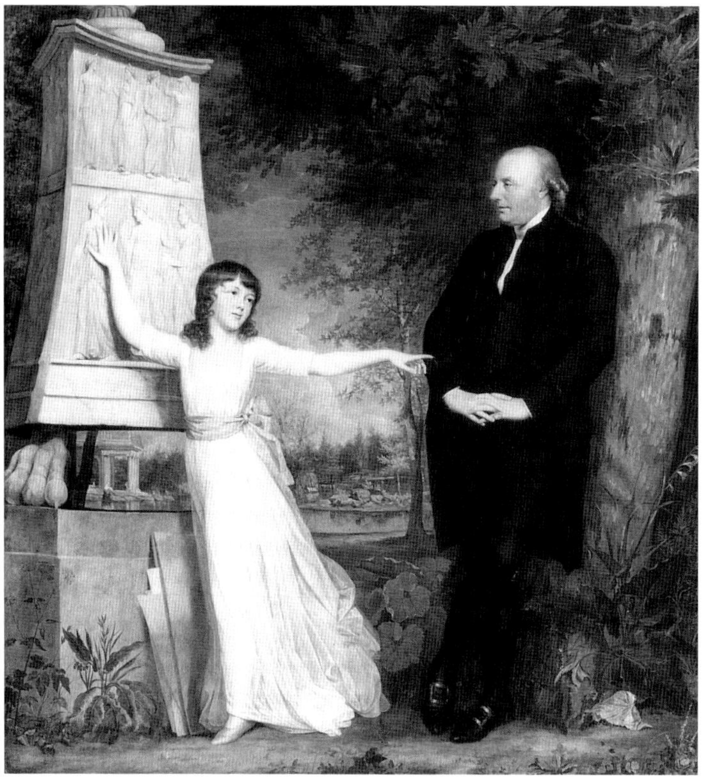

Fig. 9 Hugh Douglas Hamilton, *Frederick Hervey, Bishop of Derry and 4th Earl of Bristol with his grand-daughter Caroline Crichton in the gardens of the Villa Borghese, Rome, c.1790,* oil on canvas 224.4 x 199.5 cm. National Gallery of Ireland

Fig. 10 Samuel Woodforde, *Portrait of Sir Richard Colt Hoare and his son Henry, 1795–1796.* Stourhead, Wiltshire

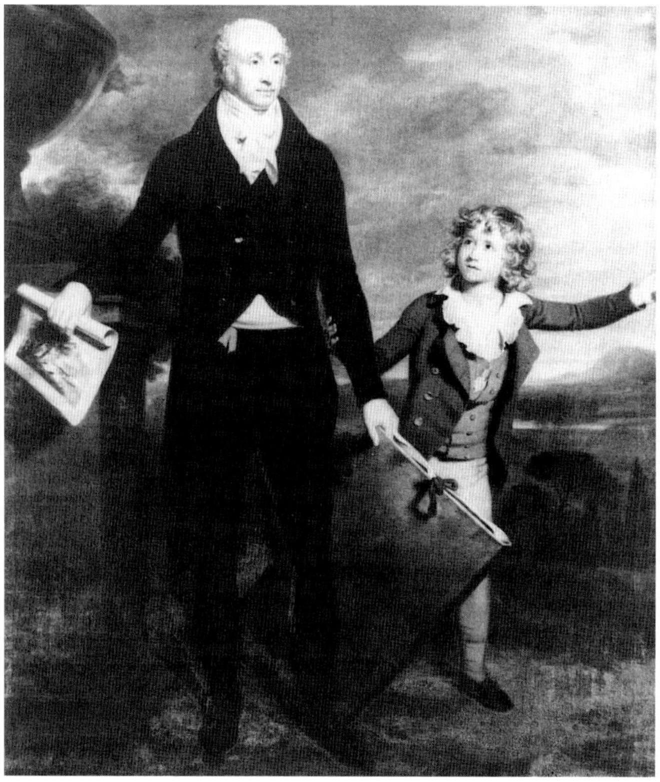

archaeological excavation work authorised by Pius VI at Frascati, the Baths of Caracalla, and other sites. It was probably during these visits that the King acquired the many views from the Ducros/Volpato series that are now distributed between the castle at Drottningholm, the Royal Palace and the National Museum in Stockholm.

Frederick Augustus Hervey, 4th Earl of Bristol (fig. 9), commissions Ducros to paint a *Cicero Discovering the Tomb of Archimedes at Syracuse,*[22] which work he is executing in late 1784 when he is visited by his fellow countryman Auguste Pidou, the tutor of Lord Grey, the future Duke of Stamford, who he is conducting on his European Grand Tour.

1785

On 10 April De la Rive writes to the Genevan collector François Tronchin: 'There are here some very skilled landscape painters [...], they all have a noble, elevated style. I believe that this country almost imposes it on them: you cannot think small thoughts in Rome. [...] I must, however, say a word about Ducros, who has made extraordinary progress, leaving all us minor landscape artists far behind.'[23]

Ducros paints *Waterfalls at Terni* and at *Tivoli* for Lord Breadalbane. Lord Grey of Wilton notes in his journal that they greatly admire the works of Ducros.[24]

The April issue of the Roman journal *Memorie per le Belle Arti* mentions these various commissions and sings the praises of Ducros's landscapes. Four watercoloured prints by Ducros and Volpato are purchased by James Byres on behalf of William Constable. Thirty-four watercoloured prints (eighteen large ones, eight medium-size ones and eight small ones) are bought by Baron Carl Sparre, the Swedish senator who accompanied Gustav III on his journey to Italy. The transaction is carried out through Piranesi.

Ducros sends a painting to his protector during his Geneva years, the naturalist Charles Bonnet, who thanks him in a letter dated 20 August 1785. This is also tells us that Catherine II was also a buyer of Ducros's work: 'Your fine painting, which reached us in very fine packing, was applauded by all connoisseurs and is one of the chief ornaments of our drawing room. I must also thank you for the repeated tokens of esteem that you have received from the Sovereign Pontiff. These would lead me to presume that he appreciates the value of the Fine Arts and that he knows how much they can adorn a reign. The Semiramis of the North knows it to, and it was a great pleasure to hear from your brother that your works have travelled as far as she.'[25]

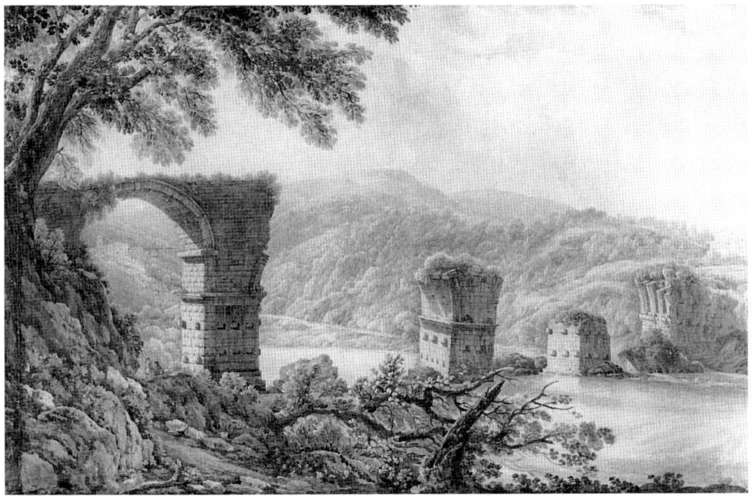

Fig. 11 Louis Ducros, *Augustus bridge, Narni,* watercolour, 77.5 x 113 cm. Stourhead, Wiltshire

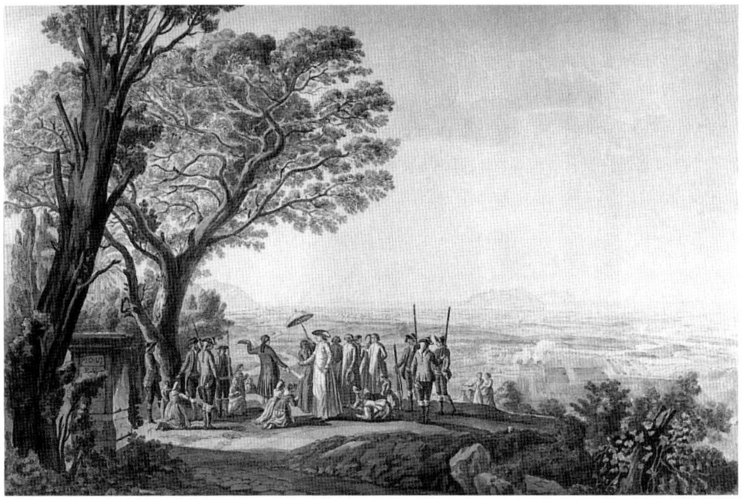

Fig. 12 Louis Ducros and R. Morghen, *Pius VI visiting the drainage works at the Pontine Marshes, c.1784–1785,* coloured etching, 24.8 x 25.8 cm. Goethe Museum, Düsseldorf

1786

Ducros is still noted at the same address as the previous years.[26] The painter makes the acquaintance of the English collector Sir Richard Colt Hoare (fig. 10), who will become a fervent admirer and his greatest patron. Colt Hoare's passion for classical antiquity and topography are fully engaged by the Swiss painter's work, in which each view can be appreciated in terms of its relation to a mythological or historical event. Colt Hoare lived in Italy from 1785 to 1791 and would take fourteen works purchased from Ducros (twelve large watercolour views and two watercoloured prints) back to his stately home in Stourhead, Wiltshire (fig. 11), which he inherited from his grandfather Henry Hoare. It was the latter who created the famous classical-style landscape garden.[27]

Ducros signs a large painting representing *Pius Visiting the Pontine Marshes*[28] to celebrate the improvement and drainage work undertaken by the Pope from 1777 onwards. There is another large oil painting[29] on the same theme which was reproduced in a widely published print signed by Ducros and Morghen[30] (fig. 12).

1787

The painter is still on the Strada della Croce.[31] He is mentioned in the list of painters living in Rome in 1787 by Aloes Ludwig Hirt: 'Du Cros from Lausanne, in his fortieth year, has the very great merit of enhancing with watercolour drawings done directly from nature. The truthfulness of his waterfalls, the brilliance of his ruins and a certain vaporous transparency in all his landscapes could not, in this genre, be raised to any higher degree, nor could their price, which can be as much as 25 to 30 *louis d'or*. Over the last few years he has become remarkably wealthy.'[32]

A Dutch traveller, Hendrik Fagel, has the same impression: 'Of the landscape artists, few have so high a reputation as the Swiss-born Ducros, the same man who went on the journey to Sicily with my cousin Ten Hoven and uncle Dierkins, and whose drawings are owned by my cousin Ten Hoven. This painter is so much in demand that he can sell a single watercolour painting for 300 to 350 florins. It is certainly true that there is nothing more perfect or more beautiful, but that is still a lot of money for a painting.'[33]

On 3 January, one of Ducros's fellow countrymen, Philippe Secretan, notes: 'Leaving the inn I went to Ducros's place. He was surrounded by paintings. Two Englishmen were perfuming him with their praises. I was hoping to engage with a fellow countryman but I found only a cold maker of pictures busy selling gouaches to the English.'[34] A few days later Secretan goes back to see the painter and, this time at last, finds a 'frank, cordial and kind man. This was definitely my fellow countryman. He showed me a very handsome painting in gouache of the Temple of the Sibyl at Tivoli.'[35]

Ducros is mentioned in a dictionary for the first time: 'Ducros and Volpato; these two artists are publishing in Rome coloured views of different shapes and sizes: *View of the Temple of Minerva,* in colour.'[36]

1788–89

At Easter Ducros is still in his studio on the Strada della Croce, where his presence is indicated by the priest charged with

to leave his position. He withdrew to Naples, where he is at the present time.'[53]

1799

French troops occupy Naples and Ferdinand IV takes refuge in Sicily. Ducros's financial situation is difficult. At the start of the year he writes to the new government of the Helvetian Republic, as attested by an excerpt from the minutes of the *Directoire Helvétique* dated 6 March 1799: 'The citizen Begoz will recommend Louis Ducros to the Minister of Foreign Relations of the Roman Republic, and will ask that he recommend him to the authorities in Naples, so that he may obtain justice on the subject of a bankruptcy that made him lose his fortune. He is living in Naples at the house of Louis Reymond, the banker.'[54]

Taking advantage of the presence of French troops almost throughout Europe, on 1 April Ducros addresses a long letter to the Directoire in Paris in an attempt to get back what he lost when he was expelled from Rome. This document is important because it constitutes one of the few autographic – and partially biographical – letters by this Swiss painter. On 10 June, a son is born in Naples: 'Luigi Raffaele Gaetano, figlio de Luigi de Gros e Anna da Daychè, coniugi domic. nelle case di Puoti, battezzato dal reverendo Don Gioacchino Zanca coadiutore (delegato), levatrice Antonia De Luca' (Luigi Raffaele Gaetano, son of Luigi de Gros and Anna da Daychè, husband and wife resident in the houses of Puoti, baptised by reverend Don Gioacchino, coadjutor (delegate), midwife Antonia De Luca).[55]

But the return of the Bourbons forces Ducros to leave Naples, where the architect Pietro Martorana has denounced him as a Jacobin. A note found in the Neapolitan archives speaks of 'A Swiss artist of the first order, named Louis Du Cros, of whom the town of Naples is now deprived, because Martorana accused him of Jacobinism, and who is now in Rome.'[56]

Fig. 16 Louis Ducros, *The launching of a warship in the shipyards at Castellamare di Stabia near Naples, c.1794–1796*, watercolour heightened with gouache and varnish, paper laid down on canvas, 70 x 106 cm. Coughton Court, Alcester, Warwickshire

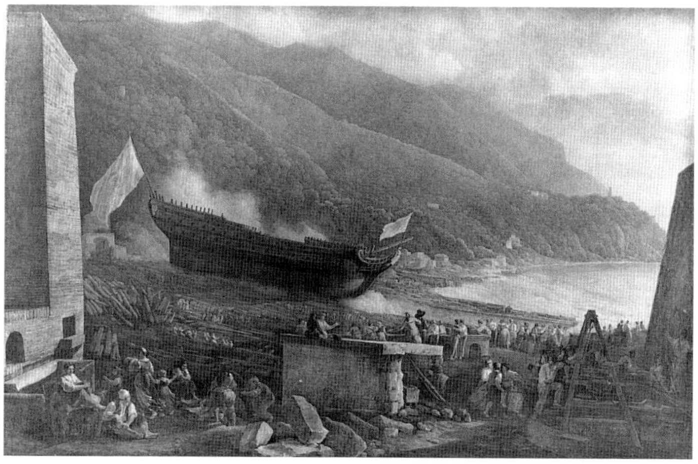

1800–01

On 5 and 6 June the collection of Lord Cawdor is sold in London. It includes twelve watercolours by Ducros, no doubt bought by John Campbell during a trip to Italy in 1784 or in 1786–88.

From November 1800 to May 1801 Ducros stays in Malta. 'I now find myself transported to Malta to execute views for General Graham, who has conquered the stronghold.'[57] Thomas Graham (the future Lord Lynedoch) was sent to Malta with the English garrison of Messina in November 1799 to blockade the port of Valetta, now occupied by the French. The blockade lasts until 4 September 1800. After the surrender of Bonaparte's troops, Brigadier General Graham leaves the island for Messina on 15 September. Since Ducros says that he arrived in early November, we must, in view of the commissions that he received, conclude that the two men meet in Messina in the second half of September, or in October.

Numerous watercolours of Malta and a very large *Panorama of Malta, View from the English Headquarters at Gudia*.[58]

1802

In a piece dated 1 May, Jean-Louis-Philippe Bridel writes in the *Etrennes Helvétiennes* that 'Ducros is in Naples where I plan to go and see him.'[59]

1804

On 18 March, in Naples, Ducros receives an invitation from the pastor Daniel-Alexandre Chavannes in the name of the Société d'Emulation de Lausanne to return to his country in order to found a drawing school.

1805

On 8 January Ducros writes from Naples to Conseiller Lambert asking him to obtain from the government of the Canton of Vaud a house where he can gather together 'all the precious drawings, paintings and plasters cast after the antique models that I possess, and also set up a small academy of drawing.'[60]

The government authorises M. Lambert to reply to Ducros in a letter dated 9 February 'that the government will be pleased to see you return to your country so that your gift for painting may be of benefit to your fellow citizens, and that they will provide you with a room in the school at Lausanne to store your plasters, drawings and paintings, and that in general all help will be given to your undertaking.'[61] Ducros apparently does not take up this offer. We do not know why.

In the summer August-Wilhelm Schlegel informs Johann Wolfgang von Goethe of Ducros's presence in Naples: 'S. Denis [and] Ducros are sojourning in Naples, another source of natural beauties. [...] Ducros draws inspiration from his travels in Southern Italy, Sicily and Malta for his large and attractively novel watercolour compositions representing ruins, seascapes and cliffs.'[62]

1806

Ducros is back in Rome. In volume II of his *Memorie enciclopediche romane* [1807], Giuseppe Antonio Guattani devotes a very long article to 'Signor Luigi Du Cros, painter of landscapes in watercolour, a genre of which he can be claim to be the father and propagator in Rome.' He mentions the recent works that he has seen in his studio and in particular the ones commissioned by Prince Friedrich von Sachsen-Gotha: *The Lucano Bridge* and *The Grotta dei paggi, Malta.*

Guattani's article is followed by a letter from 'Monsieur Du Cros a Helvetian landscape painter, in Rome, 5 September 1806', in which the painter tries to demonstrate the superiority of watercolour painting.

At the same time, in London, Farington mentions a debate on the respective merits of watercolour and oil in which Ducros's works are cited as an example.[63]

1807

Ducros leaves Rome in the spring. He makes a long stopover in Bologna, where he enters into relations with the Marquis of Malvasia. He then stays in Milan, where he visits the Accademia. He is back in his homeland by the end of the summer. At first, he lives at the home of his brother, François Barthélemy, who is a pastor at Nyon, halfway between Geneva and Lausanne. On 28 October, Ducros obtains exemption on the toll for 'two chests weighing 975 pounds, filled in part with studies and sketches and white drawing paper for his own use that he has sent through the Simplon and then by water from Vevey to Nyon.'[64] The rest does not reach him until the summer of the following year: 'the paintings from my office which are on their way are now in Milan', he writes on 22 June 1808.[65] He makes his first contacts in Geneva, where he tries to establish friendly relations with the artists De la Rive, Saint-Ours, Massot and Toepffer, as well as with families that are close to artistic circles (Eynard, Châtelain, Chavannes et Duval). This is evident from the several letters from this period kept in Geneva.[66]

On 30 November the Société des Arts in Geneva makes Ducros an honorary member at the same time as Madame Vigée-Lebrun and the Baron de Strogonoff. The *Gazette de Lausanne,* reporting the event, notes that, 'At his home can be seen various fine collections of views of Rome, Naples, Malta and Sicily; last summer he painted several themes from these beautiful lands, which he will show here this coming spring.'[67]

1808

Ducros addresses several petitions to the government asking them to provide him with the resources to open a drawing school. In the summer, he moves to Lausanne (fig. 17), where he hopes to be more successful. He obtains only a small amount of aid to give individual painting lessons in his studio.[68] A few ladies come to paint at his premises, along with an important local figure, Sigmund Effinger von Wildegg, who takes fifty lessons between December 1808 and December 1809[69] and who makes copies of several Ducros paintings (keeping careful record of these in his notebook). These copies will subsequently turn up in various Swiss collections, attributed to Ducros.

Ducros continues to solicit the government and on 5 November 1808 even prints a *Mémoire* that is nothing less than an artistic manifesto in which he proposes to establish and direct an Academy of Painting and Sculpture.[70]

1809

Ducros is wearied by the resistance that meets his projects and, after the death of his friend Saint-Ours on 9 April 1809, he writes to the painter De la Rive: 'Geneva never knew this great man

Fig. 17 Louis Ducros, *The Cathedral of Lausanne and the Old Hospital, 1808–1809,* pen and crayon, watercolour and gouache on paper laid down on canvas, 82 x 149 cm. Musée cantonal des Beaux-Arts, Lausanne

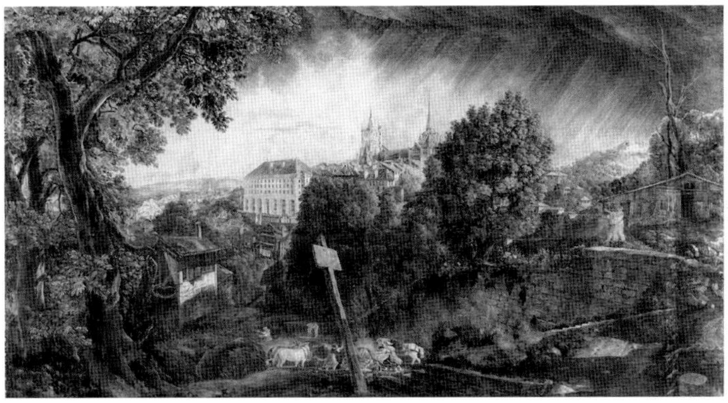

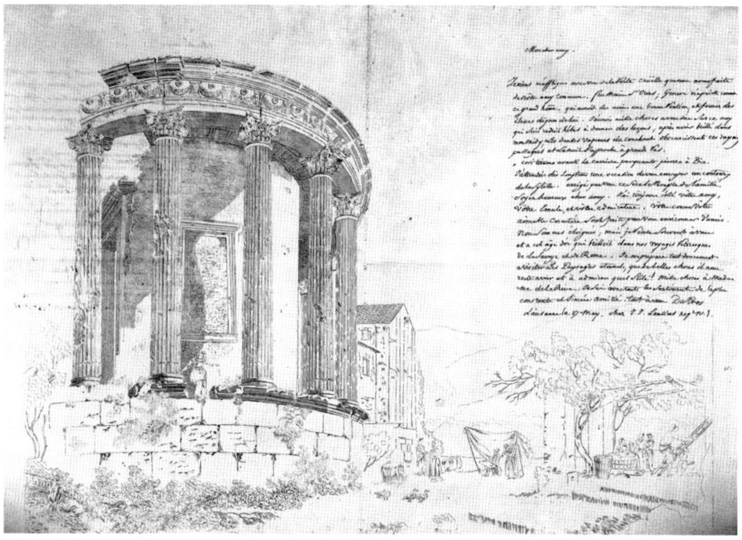

Fig. 18 Louis Ducros, *Temples of the Sibyl and Vesta with inscription written by De la Rive, 1809,* etching. Bibliothèque publique et universitaire Genève

who should have had a good pension and taught students who were worthy of him. There are a thousand things I could tell you about this, I who am reduced, alas, to giving lessons, after having shone in the South; the gentle vapours of sunset darken these fleeting rays and night is approaching at speed [...] I think often of you and of that golden age that shone in our picturesque travels in Savoy and Rome. Little by little, I am getting ready to visit eternal landscapes.'[71]

Over the summer Ducros has a very successful exhibition in Bern featuring works he has brought back from Italy. In this town he enjoys the support of the collector and art dealer Sigmund Wagner, who speaks of his enthusiasm to David Hess.[72]

His success is so great that the authorities of Bern decide to invite the painter to their city and make him a professor of painting at the Academy.[73]

1810

Having accepted this appointment with great joy, Ducros is due to take up his functions on 1 April. But he is struck down by an apoplectic fit and dies in Lausanne on 18 February at the age of sixty-two. A few months later, his large format watercolours are exhibited in Bern in one of his first Swiss exhibitions.[74]

1 This revised and corrected biography is based on the more detailed one presented in three different versions of the Ducros catalogue for the retrospective exhibition shown in 1985–87: exh. cat. London 1985, pp. 10–16; exh. cat. Lausanne 1986, pp. 11–24 and exh. cat. Rome 1987, pp. 13–20.
2 Register of Yverdon Council, 13 April 1765.
3 Bridel 1790.
4 *Journal de Genève,* 1789.
5 De la Rive 1832.
6 *ibid.*
7 AV, S. Lorenzo, 1778, kl 45/v.
8 Niemeijer, De Booy, Dunning 1994; exh. cat. Florence 1994.
9 Niemeijer, De Booy, Dunning 1994, p. 120.
10 Abbé Jean-Claude Richard de Saint-Non, *Voyage pittoresque et description des royaumes de Naples et de Sicile*, (Paris 1781–86), vol. III, chap. 3, p. 52; Niemeijer, De Booy, Dunning 1994, pp. 122–123.
11 AV, S. Lorenzo, 1780, fol. 66/v.
12 AV, S. Lorenzo, 1781, fol. 65.
13 J.G. Meusel, *Miscellaneen artistischen Inhalts*, 9, Heft, (Erfurt 1781).
14 AV, S. Lorenzo, 1782–83, fol. 27.
15 Exh. cat. Nantes 1985, nos. 76–87.
16 These paintings are now kept at Pawlowsk, near Saint Petersburg.
17 AV, S.M. del Popolo, 1783, fol. 46.
18 BPU, Ms Bonnet 37.
19 National Library of Scotland, Ms 1833.
20 Bridel 1783.
21 AV, S. Lorenzo, 1784–85, fol. 32/v.
22 This painting has not been located.
23 BPU, Archives Tronchin 191, letter 15.
24 Journal, 16 March 1785, Manchester City Art Gallery.
25 BPU, Ms Bonnet 76.
26 AV, S. Lorenzo, 1786, fol. 32.
27 These works are still at Stourhead (Hoare Collection, The National Trust), cf. exh. cat. London 1985, nos. 68–73, exh. cat. London 1996 (1) nos. 256–259 and exh. cat. London 1996 (2), pp. 284–285.
28 Now at the Museo di Roma, Palazzo Braschi.
29 Now at Pawlovsk, near Saint Petersburg.
30 Published 1784–85. A version is kept at Goethe-Museum in Düsseldorf, cf. exh. cat. Lausanne 1986, no. 42 and fig. 41.
31 AV, S. Lorenzo, 1787, fol. 32.
32 Quoted in Eckardt 1979.
33 Journal, 6 January 1787, The Hague, State Archives.
34 BCU, Fonds Pellis, Is. 4350, fol. 32; Giacomotti 1995, p. 33.
35 BCU, Fonds Pellis, Is. 4350, fol. 61.
36 M. Huber, *Notice générale des graveurs ...*, (Dresden/Leipzig 1787), p. 42.
37 AV, S. Lorenzo, 1788, fol. 26/v.
38 Exh. cat. London 1985, pp. 36–39 and 80–82; ex. cat. Bassano 1988, nos. 351–364.
39 Bridel 1790. On Bridel cf. Barghouth 1995, pp. 34–353.
40 *Notice des tableaux et des portraits exposés dans le Salon de la Société des Arts*, (Geneva 1789), nos. 27, 29 and 37 respectively; Chessex 1986.
41 AV, S. Lorenzo, 1790–9l fol. 32/v.
42 Knight 1985, pp. 54 and 57.
43 AV, S. Lorenzo, 1792, fol. 28/v.
44 *Notice des tableaux, miniatures et dessins fait par des Genevois, exposés au Salon de l'Académie*, (Geneva 1792), nos. 11, 12, 18 and 19 respectively; Chessex 1986, p. 365.
45 ACV, Private Collection, Hennezel.
46 Journal of Visits made by His Royal Highness, Bernadotte Royal Archives, Stockholm.
47 Letter to the Directoire, Naples, 1 April 1799, Ministère des Affaires Etrangères, Paris.
48 J.G. Meusel, *Neue Miscellaneen artistichen Inhalts*, (Leipzig 1797).
49 Exh. cat. London 1996 (b), pp. 124–125.
50 *Neuer Teutsche Merkue*, 1798, p. 182.
51 Gerning 1802, II. Teil.
52 Exh. cat. London 1985, nos. 77–79. It has not been possible to locate the paintings owned by Sir William Hamilton, cf. exh. cat. London 1996 (b), p. 284.
53 December 1796
54 BCU, Fonds Frédéric César de La Harpe.
55 Parrocchia di S. Giuseppe a Chiaja, Registro dei battesimi 1799.
56 Report by Duca di Campochiaro, minister, about the architect D. Pietro Martorana, 12 July 1806, Archivio di Stato di Napoli.
57 Lettre from Ducros to Sir Richard Colt Hoare, 22 December 1800, Wiltshire Record Office.
58 Now at the Musée National Suisse, Zurich.
59 Bridel 1803.
60 ACV, Plumitif du Conseil d'Etat et Onglets du Département de Législation, 4 and 6 February 1805.
61 *ibid.*, 9 February 1805.
62 A.W. Schlegel, 'Schreiben an Goethe über einige Arbeiten in Rom lebender Künstler in Sommer 1805', *Sämtliche Werke*, IX, (Leipzig 1846–47), p. 257.
63 Farington Diary, March 14, typed copy kept at the British Museum (Prints Collection).
64 ACV, Plumitif..., 28 October 1807.
65 ACV, K XIII/63.
66 BPU, manuscripts department.
67 Dated 18 December 1806.
68 Hugli 1983, pp. 21–28.
69 ACV, Sévery Papers, notebooks of Effinger von Wildegg.
70 Hugli 1983, pp. 104–106 ; Barghouth 1995, pp. 338–344.
71 BPU, 17 May 1809, Ms 2399, letter concerning a print of the Temple of the Sibyl.
72 *Neujahrsblatt* 1889.
73 AEB, *Manual der Akademischen Kuratel,* 9 September 1809.
74 *Schweizerische Kunst-und Industrieausstellung,* Berne 1810, nos. 37–43.

LOUIS DUCROS: FROM TOPOGRAPHICAL VIEWS TO THE SUBLIME SPECTACLE OF NATURE

PIERRE CHESSEX

The advent of the Helvetian Republic two hundred years ago marked the emergence of modern Switzerland. Although short-lived (1798–1803), this government was very important in that it put an end to the old Confederation and its regime of *seigneurs*, *bailliages* and subjects. For the first time, too, an attempt was made to establish a national cultural policy. To this end, in early 1799, the Minister for the Arts and Sciences, Philippe-Albert Stapfer, launched an appeal, inviting the Confederation's artists to formulate their grievances. He decried the lack of initiative shown by governments of the *ancien régime*, which had forced renowned artists abroad in pursuit of their career. Citing the examples of Fuseli in England and Ducros in Italy, he concluded that 'All the European nations were a home to Helvetian artists, apart from Switzerland itself.'

To what extent did these words reflect the reality of the age? What was the situation like for painters in the old Confederation in around 1770, when Ducros was starting out? How did he manage to become sufficiently known towards the end of the century for Minister Stapfer to consider him a renowned artist? In what sense can his works be seen as significant in the history of art? I shall attempt to provide a few answers to such questions below. These answers will be partial insofar as the available information on Ducros is itself very incomplete, with only rare archive documents, the occasional letter, addresses in Roman registers, newspaper articles, travel writings and the works themselves, most of them neither signed nor dated. These are scattered between Amsterdam, Rome, Saint Petersburg, Stockholm, Frankfurt, Valletta, London and Naples. Fortunately, the Musée cantonal des Beaux-Arts in Lausanne still holds some five hundred pieces, which the painter brought back from Italy in 1807. These watercolours, drawings and prints were saved from dispersion by the vigilance of a handful of enlightened citizens who, in 1811, after Ducros's death, started up a public subscription in order to buy the collection. The works are not dated but, when analysed in relation to the assembled documents pertaining to the artist's Italian career, they do give us an idea of the considerable corpus of watercolour landscapes produced within a definite time frame (between 1778 and 1810) and geographical ambit (Italy, Sicily, Malta and a few sites in Switzerland). They also allow us to formulate a number of hypotheses concerning the evolution of Ducros's style and the technical devices that he used in his search for an original language.

BECOMING A PAINTER IN SWITZERLAND IN 1770

Generally speaking, conditions for art-making in the then Confederation were not propitious: there was no institutional infrastructure (drawing schools, exhibitions, museums) and ambitious artists were forced to leave the country in order to learn their trade and seek opportunities in European capitals. As one of the first historians of Swiss art observed in 1774:

'Es ist ausgemacht, wenn der schweizerische Künstler sein Glück nicht in grossen Residenz-Städten sucht und findet, oder zu Hause aus eignen Mitteln leben kann, so muss er bey seiner Kunst verhungern.'[1] (A Swiss artist who does seek his fortune in a principality or who is without independent means must starve by his art.)

Exile was a necessity, certainly, but also a tradition. The custom of 'formative travel' had existed for centuries, ever since Montaigne, and the 'Enlightenment' had taken travel as its ideal

Fig. 19 Louis Ducros, *Painter and Roman peasants in the Colosseum,* watercolour and crayon on paper laid on board, 37.5 x 52.9 cm. Kunstmuseum, Bern

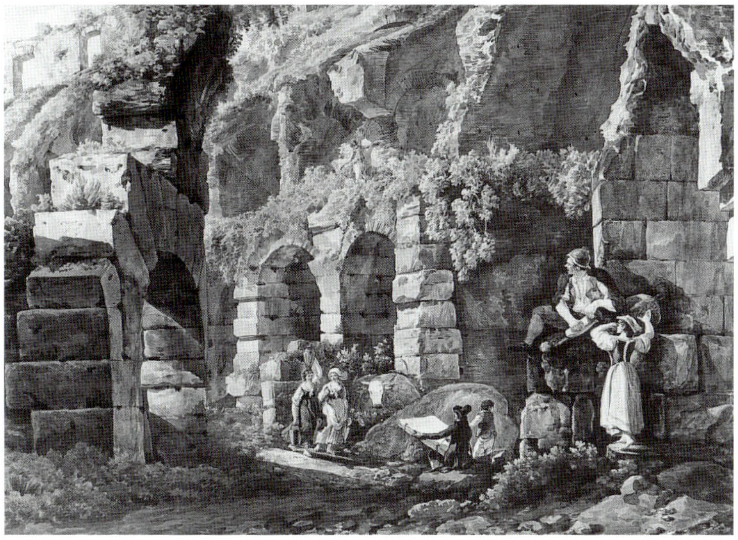

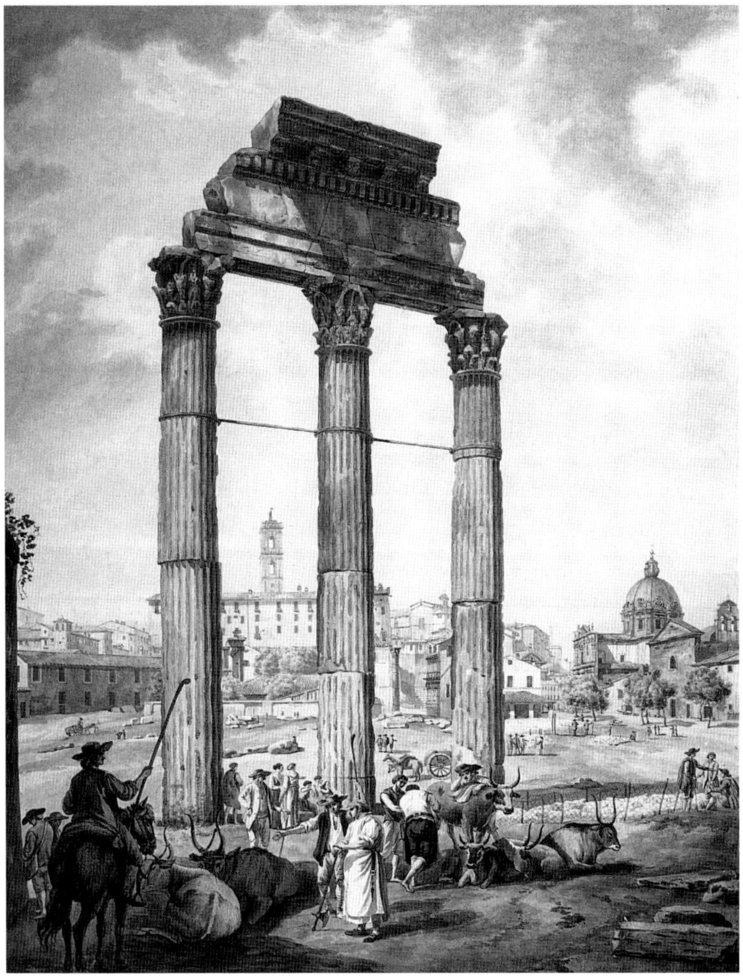

Fig. 20 Louis Ducros and Giovanni Volpato, *The Roman Forum with the Temple of Castor and Pollux, 1780,* etching and watercolour, 74.3 x 51.4. Cabinet des Dessins, Louvre

because it illustrated Man's vocation for mobility, discovery and knowledge. Taking a quick look at the history of Swiss art in the eighteenth century, we will see that the 'great names' remembered by posterity were all 'travellers': apart from a few brief stays in Geneva, Jean-Etienne Liotard was constantly moving between London, Paris, Istanbul, The Hague and Vienna; Johann Heinrich Füssli sojourned in Rome from 1770 to 1778 then settled in London, where he became known by the name of Henry Fuseli; Anton Graff was a portraitist to the German courts; Angelika Kauffmann first lived in London then become a fashionable portraitist to distinguished travellers in Rome; Jacques-Laurent Agasse painted in Paris then settled in London; Caspar Wolf travelled regularly around Germany, went to Paris and Belgium and died in Heidelberg; Jean-Pierre Saint-Ours was trained in Paris then sojourned in Rome from 1780 to 1792 before returning to Geneva; Jacques Sablet studied in Paris then spent the rest of his life travelling between Italy and France. Note that I have mentioned only the best-known painters, and none of the sculptors (Alexandre Trippel, for example, travelled from Copenhagen to London and then on to Paris before settling in Rome) or architects who, by tradition, often work outside their homeland.

Artists who stayed in their native land had no choice but to content themselves with earning their keep on such tasks as engraving reproductions for printers: the Yverdon *Encyclopédie*, for example, required more than 1260 engravings, while Zurlauben's *Tableaux pittoresques de la Suisse* featured 270 etchings and Charles Bonnet's *Œuvres*, a work of natural history, included 55 plates. Others worked in the studios of *petits-maîtres* engraving and illuminating prints for the many wealthy travellers who, after the end of the Seven Years War (1763), encouraged by the improvements in the stagecoaches, made the journey across the Alps.

This is the context that we must bear in mind when considering Ducros's rather obscure beginnings as an artist. It is quite possible that he worked with the printmaker Christian von Mechel in Basel or, more probably, with Balthasar Anton Dunker in Bern. In any case, he was certainly familiar with engraving and reproduction techniques and had contacts with the craftsmen who worked in these studios: his travelling companion when he left for Italy in autumn 1776 and his fellow tenant during his first year in Rome was Isaac-Jacob Lacroix de Morat, a specialist in these fields who had worked for Mechel and Dunker. Such, then, was Ducros's cultural background, but there is another component that also needs to be mentioned, that is, the years Ducros spent in Geneva, where he made the acquaintance of various collectors as well as the banker François Tronchin, a painter of Flemish origin, the Chevalier de Fassin, with whom he is said to have travelled in northern Europe, scientists, the naturalist Charles Bonnet, who would champion him throughout his life, and young Genevan painters who cherished similar dreams of travelling to Italy. One of these, Pierre-Louis De la Rive, would become Ducros's closest companion.

A few lessons with Fassin, much copying of the Old Masters, watercolour sketches from direct observation, a few rudiments of etching technique – such, broadly speaking, was the experience that this self-taught painter had acquired when he set out for Italy in 1776.

HONING TECHNIQUES AND SKILL: ITALY 1776–81

Ever since Dürer's travels south of the Alps, the journey to Italy had been a well-established artistic tradition. As prints spread knowledge of the discoveries made at the excavations in Herculaneum and Pompeii, and with the proliferation of archaeological drawings in Italy from the mid-eighteenth century onwards, Rome consolidated its position as 'capital of the arts', a magnet for artists who wished to take part in the debate on Antiquity. Ducros was one of the scores of painters from all over Europe who converged on the Eternal City. The atmosphere was stimulating, but the market was crowded: Aloïs Hirt has calculated that there were 400 Italian artists and 163 foreign ones in Rome[2] in 1787. Producing only landscapes, still considered a minor genre, and without access to the major religious commissions, which were given only to Catholic painters, Ducros understood that his best hopes lay with passing foreigners with an appetite for 'souvenirs' of Rome and picturesque views of Roman Campagna. He had the good fortune to be taken on in early 1778 by the brother-in-law of Belle de Zuylen, the future Madame de Charrière, who was making his way to the Kingdom of the Two Sicilies and Malta with a number of fellow Dutchmen from The Hague. The young painter's journey to southern Italy, Sicily and Malta in the company of these patrons was to constitute his own Grand Tour. There he discovered the landscapes of the Mediterranean and its ancient monuments and tried his hand at topographical views. The three hundred-odd drawings, washes and watercolours that he made during this journey, and which are still in the collections of the *Rijksprentenkabinet* in Amsterdam,[3] constitute a repertoire of picturesque scenes that he would subsequently put to good use (figs. 2–3, 5, 21, 32–34). These documents were among the first views of southern Italy, of regions in which numerous scientists, travellers and artists were now taking an interest: Sir Richard Payne Knight, accompanied by Charles Gore and the German painter Jakob Philipp Hackert, organised an expedition to Sicily exactly a year to the day earlier; Jean-Pierre-Laurent Hoüel travelled there between 1776 and 1779 and his sketches were used to make the aquatints for the *Voyage pittoresque des îles de Sicile, de Lipari et de Malte* (Picturesque Journey to the Isles of Sicily, Lipari and Malta). As for the team of French painters travelling with Dominique-Vivant Denon, preparing the Abbé de Saint-Non's famous *Voyage pittoresque*, they were in the area at the same time as Ducros and his companions. Indeed, the two groups did actually meet when their carriages were bogged down in the mud at Brindisi.

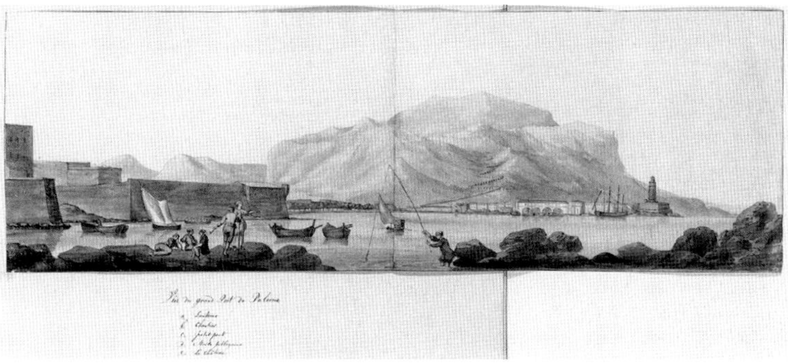

Fig. 21 Louis Ducros, *View of the port of Palermo, 1778,* watercolour on paper, 25.1 x 74.5 cm. Rijksprentenkabinet, Rijksmuseum

These topographical views were still infused with the harmonious vision of the universe that characterised the Swiss *petits-maîtres*. Very soon, however, as is manifest from Ducros's first known Roman works, around 1780, we can see that the young painter was responsive to other tendencies. He endowed his images with greater dynamism by drawing on the techniques used in Piranesi's engravings, choosing, for example, a lateral viewpoint and exaggerating the scale of the monuments in relation to the human figures. He also kept in mind the lessons of Claude Lorrain regarding the distribution of the trees and detailing of the leaves (200 engravings after Claude were published in 1777 in the two volumes of *Liber Veritatis*). He also made frequent use of the rules of classical landscape, using lateral elements to form a *corridor*, a tradition that Salomon Gressner brought back into fashion in his *Lettre sur le paysage*, published in Zurich in German in 1770, then immediately translated into French and, eight years later, into Italian, when it was published in instalments in the *Antologia romana*. But while Ducros borrowed various methods from his predecessors, he never set out to paint like Piranesi or Claude Lorrain. Ducros assimilated these techniques in order to make them a part of his own vision (fig. 20).

The series of *24 Vedute di Roma e dintorni* published with Volpato[4] from 1780 onwards give a good idea of the diversity of methods used by Ducros to compose his landscapes: some of the prints take their inspiration from Piranesi (*the Arches of Titus and Constantine*, *the Basilica of Saint Maxentius*, while others take a very different direction, *the Arch of Septimius Severus, the Temple of Saturn, the Temple of Virile Fortune,* and *the Capitol*). While the latter views are still 'oblique', the space in the foreground is now more distinct, being used to present figures in proportion to the ancient ruins, composing the kind of genre scenes that catered to growing public interest in the popular costumes that would be

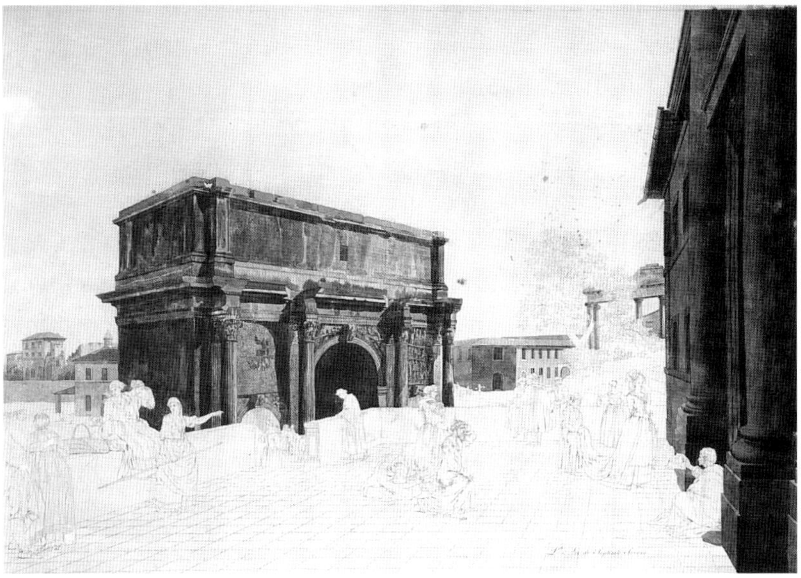

Fig. 22 Louis Ducros and Giovanni Volpato, *The Arch of Septimius Severus, Rome, 1780,* etching partially watercoloured, 51.2 x 74.7 cm. Öffentliche Kunstsammlung, Kupferstichkabinett, Bâle

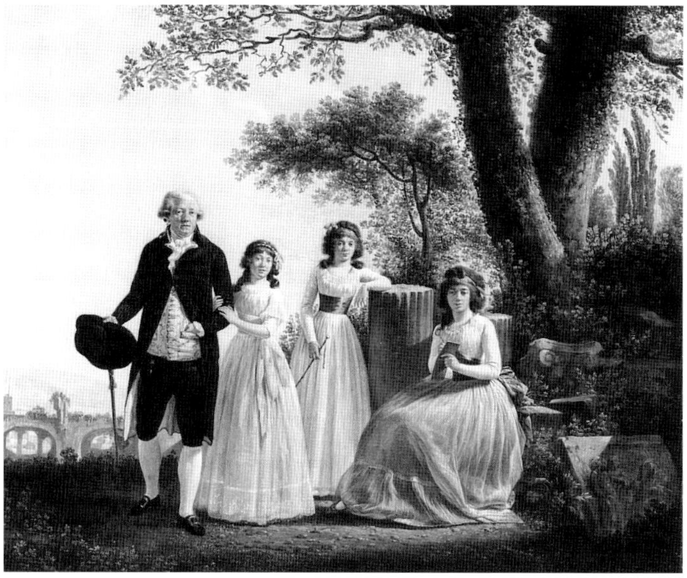

Fig. 23 Jacques Sablet, *Family portrait with the Basilica of Maxentius, 1791,* oil on canvas, 60 x 72 cm. Musée cantonal des Beaux-Arts, Lausanne, on loan from the Fondation Gottfried Keller

the glory of the prints produced by Bartolomeo Pinelli in the early nineteenth century. This orientation is particularly evident in the etchings and aquatints '*en manière de lavis*' (*Scènes et costumes italiens)* published by Ducros and Sablet[5] in 1782. However, it was the large illuminated prints of ancient monuments, inspired by Piranesi, that really marked the end of Ducros's years of apprenticeship and brought him his first success. His partnership with the Italian engraver Volpato, who enjoyed considerable prestige for his engravings of Raphael's *Stanze*[6] and had the patronage of Pope Pius VI, gave him access to Roman society. Their etchings with watercolour highlighting won the two artists renown for successfully uniting the tradition of large-format reproduction engraving, to which Volpato was the heir, with the artisanal practice of coloured engravings 'in the manner of Aberli', which Ducros had introduced into Italy. In his letter to the Directoire, Ducros would mention these 'collections of coloured views which were an important source of revenue for my establishment. It was like a line of business that I had added to my other activities.'[7] These 'other activities' were 'highly significant painting commissions.' Ducros was alluding here to the large original watercolours that he painted on commission for English, Swedish and Russian aristocrats, and in which he was able to create a personal style by developing the techniques that were embryonically present in the illuminated prints of his first years in Rome.

STYLISTIC MATURITY: ROME 1782–94

In the seventeenth century, but especially in the eighteenth, the upper classes of Europe looked on a time of study in Italy as an indispensable part of any *honnête homme,* gentleman or cavalier's education. They would travel across the Continent in order both to assimilate the classical cultural heritage and to increase their knowledge of the social and political practices of the various states they passed through. On their way, but above all when they reached Rome, the gentlemen who went on this Grand Tour,[8] this educational journey of initiation, also had an opportunity to acquire objects which, when they returned home, would serve as status symbols, embodying their cultural power. The medals, cameos, sculptures and archaeological vestiges (or copies sold as such) that graced their stately homes also helped to confirm their aristocratic credentials. The wealthiest visitors would have a fashionable portraitist (Pompeo Batoni, Angelika Kauffmann or Jacques Sablet, fig. 23) paint them with a famous monument in the background, or buy Italian landscapes which, once on the walls of their homes, would remind visitors that their host had enjoyed the privilege of travelling to the sources of the 'civilised' world. Most of Ducros's large watercolours were landscapes intended for these distinguished patrons on the Grand Tour, and some of them still grace the stately homes they were bought for in England (Stourhead, Dunham Massey, Coughton Court) (figs. 11, 50), Sweden (Drottningholm, Lövstad) and Russia (Pawlovsk).

The themes of Ducros's watercolours constitute a *vade mecum* to the sites most frequented by travellers. Foremost are the ancient Roman monuments that Ducros reprised from his prints, affording them now a more ample treatment. The Colosseum, for example, of which he and Volpato offered a general topographical view, is the subject of several very large-format watercolours representing the interior and exterior of the building with a wealth of effects aimed at producing an impression of grandeur (cat. 13, 22). Ducros chose low-angle viewpoints which heightened the monumental quality, usually underscoring this further with the inclusion of small figures (*macchiette*). He increased the size of his watercolours by sticking together several sheets of paper and then mounting these on canvas. Once framed and under glass, they could compete in scale with oil paintings. Finally, Ducros liked to isolate and collage certain architectural features in order, quite literally, to make them stand out. Ancient ruins had been a source of inspiration to painters from Panini to Hubert Robert,[9] and the archaeological developments of the eighteenth century stimulated new interest, all the more so since these ruins embodied the aesthetic categories now shaping the sensibilities of the 'Grand Tourists': the sublime (Edmund Burke) and the picturesque (William Gilpin, Uvedale Price). But Ducros did not limit himself to the monuments of the Eternal City. He also went out into the countryside, following in the footsteps of Horace or seeking out picturesque views. If we compare his two views of *the Temple of the Sibyl in Tivoli* (cat. 15, 17), painted within a few years of each other, we will observe his art's growing responsiveness to meteorological conditions, a developing interest in the variations wrought on the landscape by rain and fair weather, and in the resulting light. This sensitivity was evidently shared by a number of painters working in Rome at the time – Thomas Jones and Pierre-Henry de Valenciennes of course, but also John Robert Cozens (fig. 24) and John 'Warwick' Smith, who frequented the same dealers and collectors, and who, indeed, must certainly have played some part in this evolution in Ducros's watercolours. In 1787, the Swiss artist remarked to a fellow countryman that 'The sky is to the landscape what the face is to the human figure; it is the sky that, by its accidents of light and shade, suffuses the landscape with a tone that is sad or gay, sombre or serene, peaceful or agitated, in keeping with the character which one wishes to represent.'[10] Ducros was increasingly drawn to the spectacle of nature: 'O how I prefer to be in Tivoli under the waterfalls at sunrise, Newton would have broken down light there without a prism', he wrote to the Genevan naturalist Charles Bonnet in July 1783, adding: '[...] what a fine thing it is to study Nature, and who, Sir, is more familiar with these pleasures than your good self?'

Ducros would often leave Rome and explore the hinterland in search of subjects with a wild natural beauty, like that of the *Cascata delle Marmore* near Terni, which had once struck fear but now inspired visitors with a 'delightful horror' of the sublime. Ducros painted these falls where the waters of the Velino crash into the Nera on several occasions and, in the Lausanne version, pulled off the technical feat of rendering the spray of the water using simply the reserve of the white paper (cat. 19). Ducros thus acquired a solid reputation as a painter of waterfalls, as can be seen from the 1785 edition of the Roman publication *Memorie per le Belle Arti*. The British were particularly keen on his work and

Fig. 24 Robert Cozens, *The Colosseum seen from the north, 1780*, National Gallery of Scotland, Edinburgh

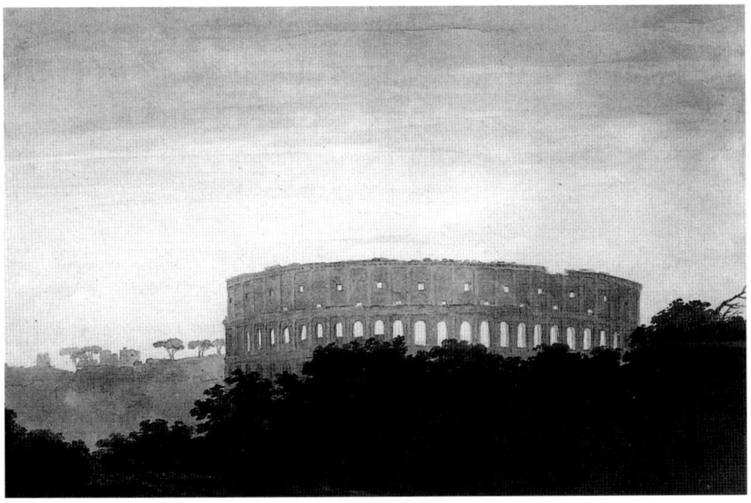

Fig. 25 Louis Ducros, *The Temple of Minerva Medica, Rome, 1785–1786*, watercolour on paper, 67.3 x 103 cm. Dunham Massey, Altrincham, Cheshire

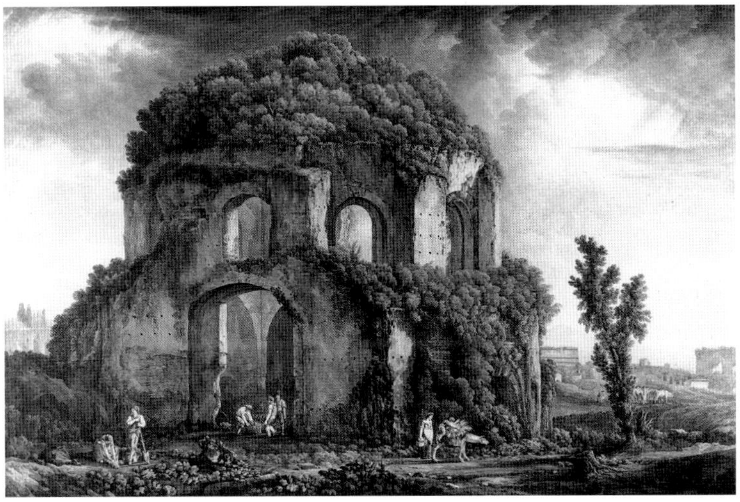

Lord Breadalbane bought two watercolours of the falls at Terni and Tivoli that same year, while Lord Grey of Wilton noted in his journal: 'We went to see the paintings of M. Ducros a landscape painter who seems to have a good deal of merit. His views of the fall of Terni are much admired.'[11]

However, it was his encounter with Sir Richard Colt Hoare that proved decisive (fig. 10).[12] Ducros met the owner of Stourhead (Wiltshire) and future patron of the young Turner when he was in Rome in 1786. Sir Richard, who also painted watercolours himself, would become a lifelong and fervent admirer, commissioning the Swiss painter on a number of occasions and thus building up the biggest collection of Ducros watercolours in Great Britain.[13] Storms, waterfalls and torrential rivers are the dominant themes in these views of Rome and its environs, of which only three represent the city's monuments (*Arch of Titus*, *Arch of Constantine* and *Interior of the Colosseum*, cat. 12, 14, 22), and then in an overgrown state. We are a long way here from the peaceful, picturesque prints of the 1780s. The true subject is not Antiquity but Nature, which takes possession of the monuments and ultimately engulfs them. This development corresponds to a shift in sensibilities, in aesthetic expectations and in the criteria for appreciating Beauty which had occurred among part of the cultivated public: from regularity, order and measure, the norms of the classical sensibility, tastes had gradually moved towards an appreciation of irregularity, chaotic grandeur and strangeness. The spectacle of waterfalls and gorges reflected this new fascination with the sublime and picturesque aspects of nature, in accordance with the aesthetic categories that were fashionable in England. The next phase therefore comes as no surprise: the painter's only subject now was Nature, devoid of references to history. Leaving the beaten track of the Grand Tour, in 1793–94 Ducros was in the Abruzzi, painting landscapes that no artists had ever studied before. The sites he represented obviously have neither the *aura* nor the iconographic tradition of the *loci classici* in Rome and Tivoli, but Ducros treats the waters of the Liri like the falls of the Aniene and the wild rocks of the Abruzzi like the stones of Roman ruins. That said, the accents are more dramatic, with dark tones, stormy skies and a growing taste for closed spaces that leave little room for distant vistas.

DRAMATIC INTENSITY: NAPLES AND MALTA 1794–1806

Once he had moved to Naples, Ducros became less and less a topographer and more and more a stager of scenes. Histories of landscape painting traditionally distinguish between supposedly 'objective' topographical views (*vedute*) and idealised views (or *capriccios*). Thanks to the erudite research of André Corboz, we now know that, although topographic views do offer extremely precise detail, they are not all objective in the sense in which we have understood that term since the invention of photography. There are numerous ways of meddling with reality, notably by changing the proportions of buildings, shifting the scene sideways, and including multiple viewpoints. But in some of his works Ducros goes further than mere optical correction: using precise, recognisable elements of the landscape he produces idealised views. This is the case, for example, in *the View of Posilippo* (cat. 30), on the back of which he wrote '*veduta del Posilippo*'. What we have here, in fact, is a real montage, and we can actually measure the degree of credence we need to accord the term *veduta*. The starting point is a very precise view of the banks of the Pausilippo in which we can even make out the mysterious Villa Emma, which belonged to the diplomat, geologist, volcanologist and antiquarian Sir William Hamilton. To this the painter has added a second tier of steep hills, with the whole being crowned by the distinctive form of the Castello Sant'Elmo. The Riviera di Chiaja, which should logically be in the background, is transformed here into a Vesuvius towering over Naples. In another landscape painted towards the end of his career, Ducros took this genre even further by creating a *capriccio* in which the Rocca Pia from Tivoli is placed on Rome's Isola Tiberina.

The Neapolitan period saw shadow become increasingly important in Ducros's work and the domination of plant elements is very marked in watercolours such as *The Temple of Mercury at Baia*, *The Grotto of Pausilippo* or *The Virgil's Tomb* (cat. 38, 34, 31). The surface of these compositions is filled with closely-packed planes and the sky is reduced to a mere oculus. The fascination of the pre-Romantic artists with caverns and grottoes is well known. The theme inspired Ducros's fellow countryman, Caspar Wolf,[14] to paint some of his finest works in the 1770s. The second half of the eighteenth century witnessed important progress in the study of the earth (geology, crystallography, etc.) and artists too played a role here by illustrating a good number of scientific publications. La Croix, Ducros's childhood friend, engraved plates for the *Oeuvres* of the Geneva naturalist Charles Bonnet. The diplomat William Hamilton, one of Ducros's main patrons in Naples,[15] was fascinated by the antique but also published one of the first scientific books about volcanoes (*Campi Phlegraei. Observations on the Volcanoes of the Two Sicilies*) (fig. 26). But the influence

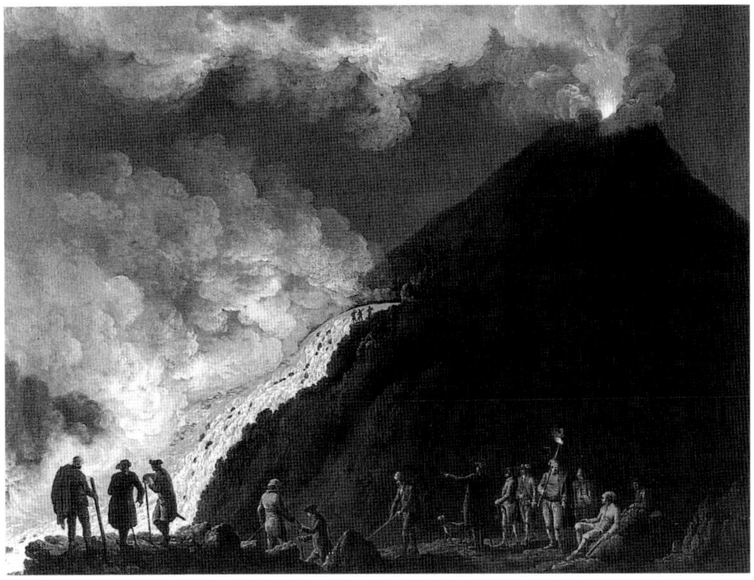

Fig. 26 Jakob Philipp Hackert, *Eruption of Vesuvius in 1774*, *c.1774–1775*. Staatliche Museen Kassel, Neue Galerie, Kassel

of science cannot explain everything. We must not lose sight of the fact that the majority of Ducros's admirers in Naples were English, men steeped in Edward Young's *Night Thoughts* and Ossian's melancholy poems and thus particularly receptive to the irrational and the fantastic. Looking at Ducros's *Night Storm at Cefalù* (cat. 39), indeed, it is hard not to think of Gothic novels such as Horace Walpole's *Castle of Otranto* and Ann Radcliffe's *Mysteries of Udolpho*, tales that were saturated with fantastic and mysterious elements designed to provoke anxiety in the reader. In this painting he creates an almost excessive compendium of natural wildness – storm, tempest, explosion – of the kind that might terrify the beholder. But the fascination with the extraordinary and the presentations of sublime spectacles found in certain works from the end of Ducros's Italian sojourn are not solely the result of these literary and scientific influences. These watercolours also express the painter's troubled temperament and the anxiety engendered by his exile, his financial setbacks and the upheavals of the revolutionary era.

Of course, Ducros's work did not develop in the linear way I have set forth here. This gradual shift, revealing the artist's disquiet, took place in successive leaps, with hesitations, backtracking and long spells of relative calm. At the same time as these tormented works, Ducros painted more transparent works such as *the Temple of Serapis at Pozzuoli* (cat. 32) or a series of marine paintings that also reveal his taste for picturesque scenes. Nevertheless, even in these watercolours we can detect a fantastic element which, as in *the Launch of the Archimedes*, sets his watercolours apart from the precise, smooth works of his great rival, the German painter, Jakob Philipp Hackert. We get the feeling that Ducros is issuing a challenge to landscape artists when, following Vernet, Volaire and Wright of Derby, he paints the erupting Vesuvius. With their work in mind, he was no doubt trying to show that, used in large formats, watercolour could achieve dramatic effects that were even more complex than those of oils. He would exploit the alternating opacity and transparency of the layers of paint, readily using gouache or oils for highlighting and varnish for the finish. His highly sophisticated technique poses all sorts of problems to restorers[16] – and historians.

Ducros did in effect retouch and add to his works, and sometimes did so several years after they were painted. This was because of the way he worked in the studio: taking the preliminary drawing, he would apply an underlayer, then a finishing layer and, finally, the retouching. These operations were often limited to certain portions of the surface while other pages were left white, notably those which would later be filled with groups of figures. The master had a fairly sophisticated way of dividing up the work, leaving his assistants to accomplish certain stages that he considered less important, or for which he felt less competent. This was the case for the groups of figures during his Neapolitan period, when he was working with the mysterious Mazzola, whose elegant style we can recognise in the watercolours of Naples and Malta. Between 1794 and 1801, some of these figures thus 'travelled' from one watercolour to another, from *the Temple of Serapis in Pozzuoli* to *the Fountain of Neptune at Valletta* (cat. 43). Ducros also worked with tracing paper,[17] which allowed him to select parts and combine them with others in the *capriccios*, or to respond quickly to a new commission, or again, to reprise a drawing executed several years before. This makes it particularly difficult to date his works.

The large watercolours of Malta that Ducros took back to Lausanne at the end of his life constitute a fairly homogeneous ensemble. They were no doubt painted in 1800 when the artist was in Valletta and may have been retouched in Lausanne seven or eight years later. Here Ducros demonstrates his power as an organiser of scenes and his mastery of composition, with multiple points of view, the manipulation of landscape elements by moving them laterally and the emphasis on monuments in order to obtain a grandiose effect. Following on from the Maltese works, Ducros still had time to paint a view of Lausanne, *The Cathedral and the Old Hospital*, in which, for the last time, he gave one last demonstration of the diversity of his ways of

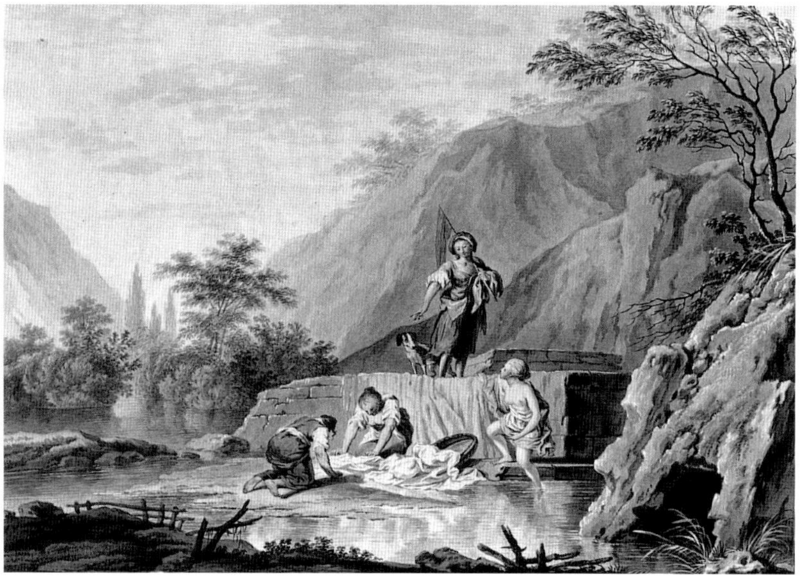

Fig. 28 Louis Ducros, *Washerwomen, c.1773–1776,* watercolour, 29.5 x 38.5 cm. Kunstmuseum, Bern

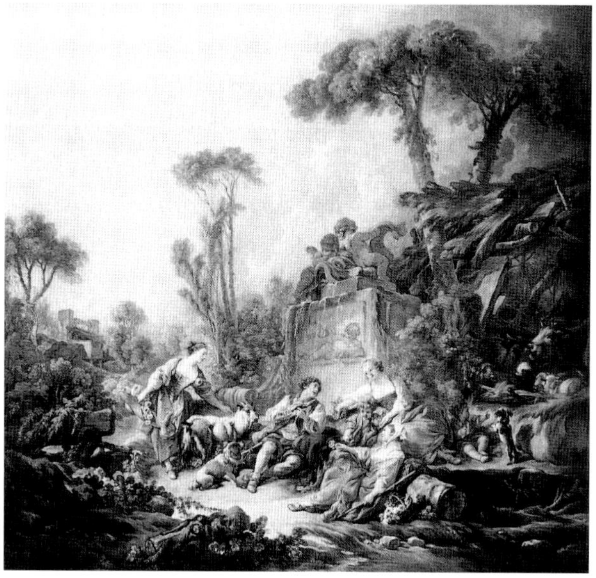

Fig. 29 François Boucher, *Shepherd's Idyll, 1768.* The Metropolitan Museum of Art, donated by Julia A. Berwind, New York

From what we know of his work prior to his encounter with Italy, we must recognise in Ducros a landscape artist whose style shows little individual character. He is said to have been quite interested in analysing natural phenomena beginning with his years as an apprentice painter in Switzerland. We also know, thanks once again to Pierre-Louis De la Rive, that he ranged far and wide over the countryside of Geneva and Savoy drawing from nature. The rare works from that period that have come down to us, for example the *Washerwomen* conserved in Bern's Museum of Fine Arts (fig. 28), are more in keeping with the spirit of pastoral landscape à la François Boucher (1703–1770) (fig. 29) and do not suggest the makings of a great topographical artist. We should note, however, that the essential elements were already in place: the play of transparency, the diversity of the composition's centres of interest organised around a principal motif, and the contrast between the rough earth, the smooth vegetation and the vaporous atmosphere. Ducros skilfully combines a fine sense of composition, picturesque anecdote with group scenes, and the idea of the embellished landscape. To that we can also add his ability to lay out a composition that already evinces a mastery of space through the play of overlapping diagonal lines. Yet the weakness he shows in drawing the human figure limited his ambitions. What future was there in carrying on the pastoral-landscape genre when Claude-Joseph Vernet (1714–1789) had been setting the standard from Rome with his style since the early 1740s? Finally, lest we forget, Ducros did not arrive in Italy with a career behind him. Born in Switzerland, as an artist he was to become thoroughly Italian and fundamentally Roman.

II

Luc Boissonnas has taken the first step in elucidating the questions surrounding Ducros's arrival in Rome,[3] along with the draughtsman and engraver Isaac Jacob Lacroix (1751?–c.1800). Boissonnas identifies in particular the role played by Anton Balthasar Dunker (1746–1807) – Lacroix and Ducros appear to have studied with Dunker in Bern around 1775 – as an intermediary with Jacob Philipp Hackert (1737–1807). Living in Rome since 1768, Hackert was one of the dominant personalities in landscape painting at the time, working in the tradition of Claude Lorrain (1600–1682) and Claude-Joseph Vernet. A great traveller throughout Italy, he knew the land well and translated his familiarity into a topography that shows strong draughtsmanship (fig. 30). Hackert was also a contemporary of Ducros and we cannot overlook the fact that the latter's strategy to make himself known, which he began to carry out from 1780, would place him in direct competition with Hackert. I shall come back to this. For now, upon closer inspection, we see that Lacroix's name alone appears in connection with Hackert as a collaborator when he executed an etching entitled *Veduta della Città di Cesena* (View of the City of Cesena) in 1777 after Hackert's original painting.[4]

During this same period, references to Ducros's name are far rarer and it is difficult to get a clear sense of his place in the

Roman milieu. The first known works date from 1778. In the spring of that year he was taken on as a draughtsman by Nicolaas Ten Hove, a Dutch traveller, to accompany him on a four-month voyage throughout the Kingdom of the Two Sicilies. How should we interpret this silence of nearly two years in a city that leaves no one indifferent? If we accept that Ducros arrived in Rome with the firm intention of remaining there and getting his work recognised – which subsequent events would confirm – we can reasonably conclude that he must have begun with a period of observation and adaptation.

Rome was, at the time, a cosmopolitan city boasting a population of around 160,000. Less populous than Naples, the city nevertheless welcomed each year its contingents of tourists from all over Europe, who increased the number of inhabitants by tens of thousands, especially during religious holidays. Travel had a very different dimension in that age and cannot be confused with the simple change of place it has become today. A trip demanded elaborate preparations and would last several months. For most people, it was something that would occur only once in their lifetime. These travellers therefore represented a clientele well worth cultivating, a group of people eager to keep the memory of their discoveries and emotions alive.

One could also count on the culture of these 'travellers from the North,' who were all prepared to experience Italy either through literary images or visual representations. Ducros, himself an artist from beyond the Alps, was no exception. We should bear in mind, too, the time he spent in the company of 'Italianising' artists of the North, that is, seventeenth-century Flemish and Dutch artists, copying their works in the years prior to his departure for Rome. Yet to weigh precisely each artist's familiarity with Italy when concretely encountering the peninsula is no easy task. On the one hand, it would seem that this familiarity owes quite a lot to a myth fashioned by literature and travel chronicles. On the other, we must also give the great seventeenth-century models their due: the paintings of Nicolas Poussin (1594–1665), Claude Lorrain (1600–1682), Gaspard Dughet (1615–1675) and Salvator Rosa (1615–1673). More specifically, it was the artists working in Rome from 1751 to 1775, that is, during the directorate of Charles-Joseph Natoire (1700–1777), who were especially instrumental in preparing their younger colleagues' way of seeing. The work of Giovanni Paolo Panini (1691–1765) was still quite fresh in the minds of the residents of the Académie de France, where he had taught perspective. Although he himself was rarely collected in Great Britain, the idea of a fantastic architecture associated with a precise rendering of detail was introduced there by Charles-Louis Clérisseau (1721–1820), who regularly exhibited in London (fig. 31). Without him Robert Adam (1728–1792),

Fig. 30 Jakob Philipp Hackert, *View of a spring of the river Licenza on the Lucretil mount, 1780*, Goethe Museum, Düsseldorf

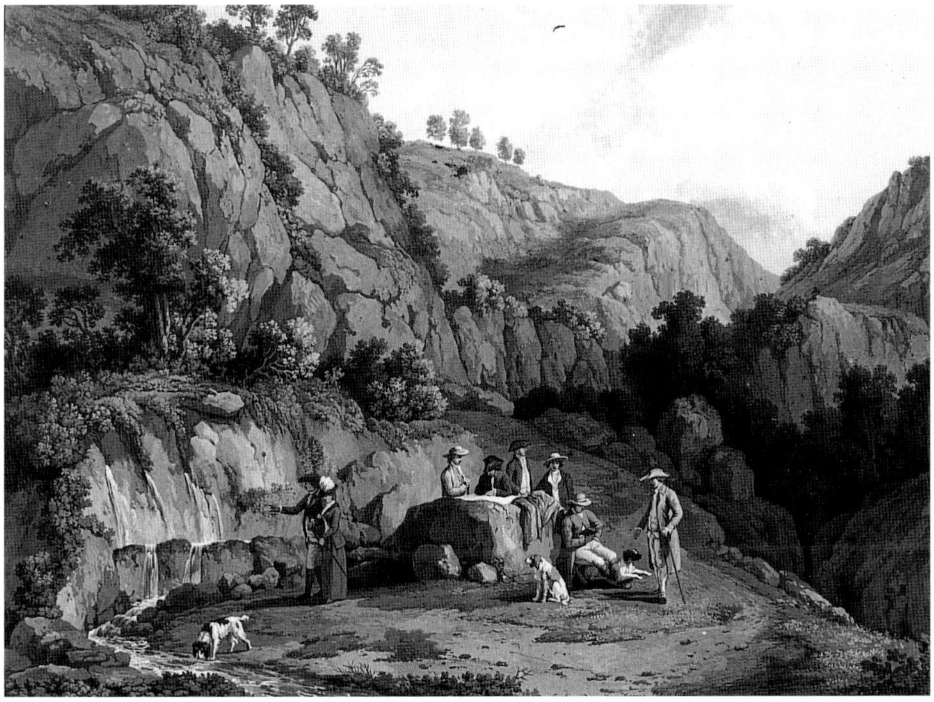

Fig. 31 Charles-Louis Clérisseau, *Architectural capriccio, 1781*, Hermitage Museum, St. Petersburg

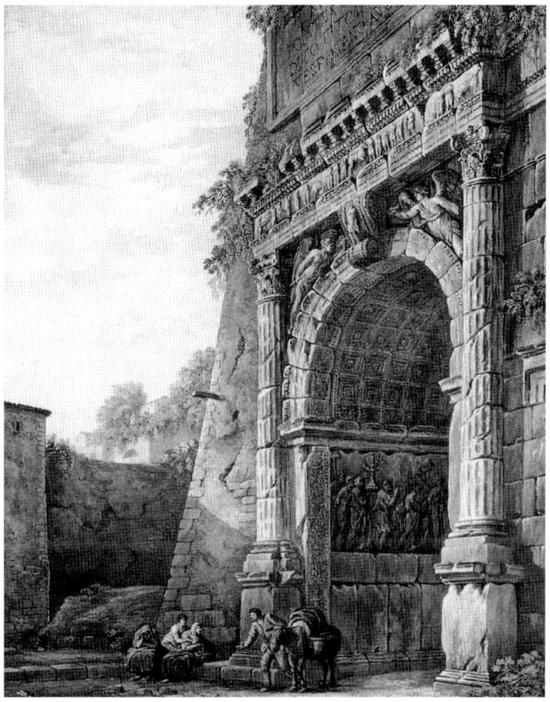

for instance, would never have produced the *Ruins of the Palace of the Emperor Diocletian at Spalato* (1764), which had a decisive influence on the advent of neoclassical architecture in Great Britain.[5] During the same period, Hubert Robert (1733–1808), who had returned to France in 1765, reinvented Panini's heritage there. The other great heritage was the art of Gaspard van Wittel (1653–1736); his tradition of the *veduta* was carried on throughout the first half of the century by figures as varied as Hendrik van Lint (1684–1763), Giovanni Battista Busiri (1698–1757) and Paolo Anesi (1697–1773).[6] From Rome, Giovanni Battista Piranesi (1720–1778), as an archaeologist, dominated art abroad. In 1760 he installed his studio and print shop along the Via Sistina, in the heart of the quarter where the clientele of visiting tourists – increasingly British over the years – usually put up.

Ducros surely took the time to master the language (did he speak it before arriving in Italy?) and to gather disparate threads into a skein of understanding in a city where such things are not immediately apparent to foreigners. At the same time, he probably realised that he had chosen the path of the topographical view.

III

Let us return to the spring of 1778, however, when Ducros was hired as a draughtsman to accompany Dutch travellers during their Grand Tour, from the south of Italy to Sicily and Malta. This engagement represented an exceptional chance for him. At the time, far more established artists often took advantage of such opportunities: Hackert, for example, had accompanied Richard Payne Knight (1751–1824) to the same places the year before. For Ducros, this was to be his means of scouting the land for the very first time. In 1778, Sicily remained a far-off island devoid of real existence in terms of its representation. The period's perception of this remote place, namely, a harsh barren land torn between the grandeur of a past that had to be sought out in ancient sites and the contemporary reality of the island's towns, was not always shared by actual travellers. By way of proof we have Nicolaas Ten Hove's rather spirited reaction in the journal that he kept during his trip: 'After all that we had seen [the group was in Catania and making its way to Syracuse], we were convinced of the shallowness of what Brydone says touching on the difficulties of the roads, the dangers and the cliffs… We set off from Catania on 1 June at 2 in the morning and arrived the next day in Syracuse… Although quite wretched, this city is not as squalid as Brydone lets on; there are several fine buildings and a few squares. It is true that the inhabitants there are incredibly impoverished: with nearly all of them suffering from scurvy, like most Sicilians, they give a striking idea of what a government can do for the welfare of a people who ought to be the richest of the earth given the nature of their land.'[7] Patrick Brydone had published in London in 1773 his *Tour through Sicily and Malta*, which proved highly successful amongst those who were keen to extend their voyage to the south, beyond the traditional stay in Naples. Couched in the form of letters addressed to William Beckford, Brydone's book offers a rather sombre view of the reality of the land, deeming Syracuse to be a city without comforts and reduced to a 'pile of rubble'.

Fig. 32 Louis Ducros, *An Inn at Barletta, 1778,* black chalk and grey wash, 20.8 x 27.5 cm. Rijksprentenkabinet, Rijksmuseum

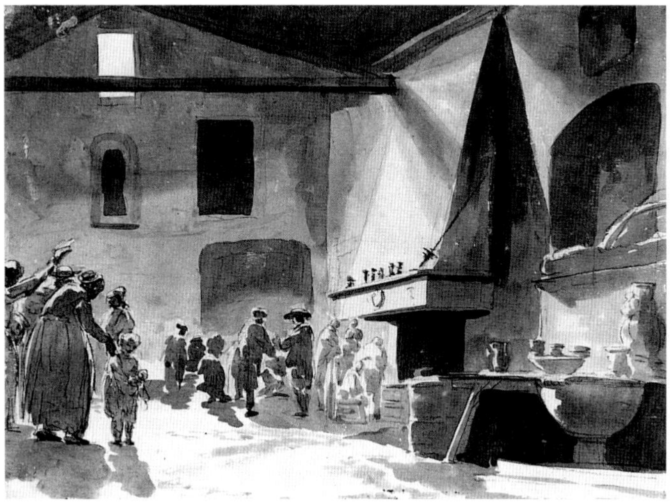

Fig. 33 Louis Ducros, *A Stop at San Vito, 1778,* watercolour, 32.5 x 52.2 cm. Rijksprentenkabinet, Rijksmuseum

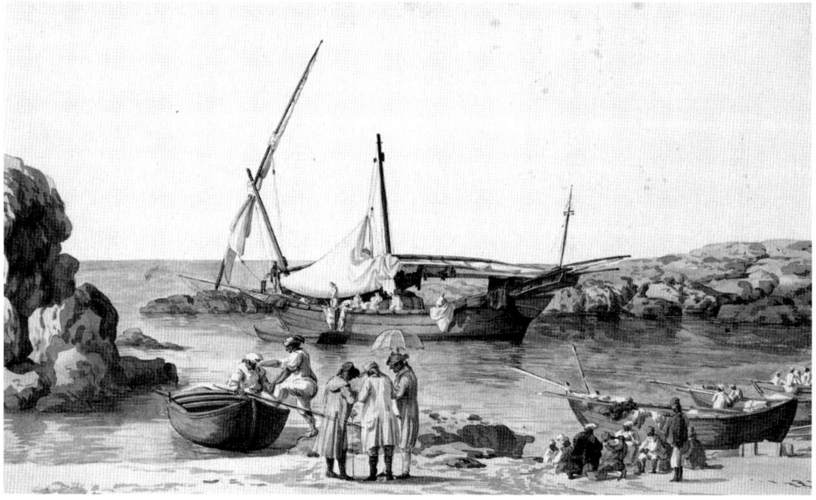

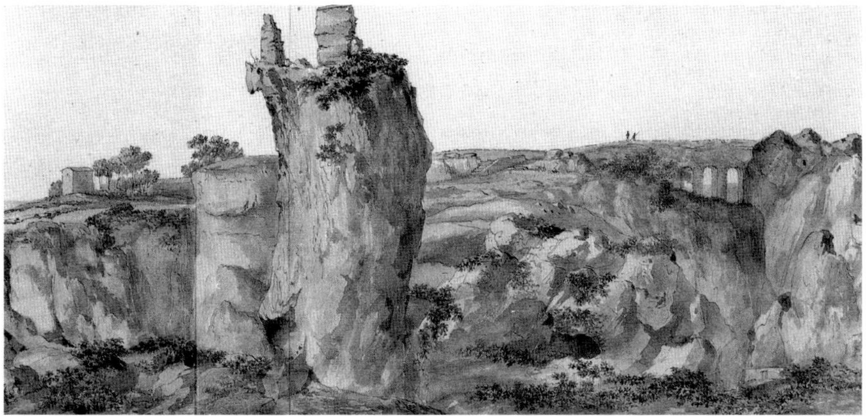

Fig. 34 Louis Ducros, *The Latomiae of Syracuse, 1778,* watercolour, 22.9 x 113.5 cm. Rijksprentenkabinet, Rijksmuseum

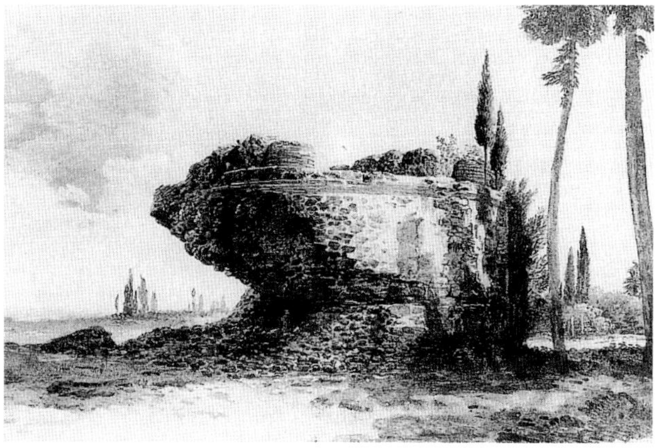

Fig. 35 Jean-Pierre-Laurent Hoüel, *Tomb in the convent of Santa Maria del Gesú, Catania, 1777.* Hermitage Museum, St. Petersburg

Ducros was thus confronted with a radically new reality. The results that we know of, however, confirm that he was far from being a novice draughtsman. He shows himself well in control of technique, both in quick sketches using *pierre noire* heightened with grey wash and larger-scale watercolours that were clearly reworked 'au logis', that is, back in his lodgings (fig. 32 and 33), as one artist residing in Sicily during the same period, Jean-Pierre-Laurent Hoüel (1735–1813), put it. Ducros also proves capable of adapting the old topography to the manner of the 1780s, a style joining accuracy in observation to a calm poetry infused with the picturesque. His *The Latomiae of Syracuse*, (fig. 34) shows an empirical approach that strives to depict the site according to its natural geology while placing it in its environment. Well before the great watercolours of 1793–94, Ducros treats the large isolated rock in the foreground as if it were an ancient ruin, likening this natural vestige, which is due to the collapse of the galleries carved in the rubble, to the remains of temples from antiquity.

As for Hoüel, the interests motivating his stay in Sicily were quite different from Ducros's. All of the difference between these two artists can be seen in this entry in his *Notebooks* that dates from 25 and 26 May 1777, during his sojourn in Catania: 'Today I was paid a visit by the English gentlemen and Mr. Ocre, a Prussian painter living in Rome, having just toured Sicily in a rather irregular and superficial way; they do sketches which they complete in their lodgings, as is the custom nowadays. The next day, 26 May, I called on them and saw drawings by Mr. Hackert, some of the Temple of Juno in Gigenti.'[8] Taking a close look at Hoüel's works, one understands implicitly that there exist two contrasting views of the landscape. Hoüel's manner puts inquiry at the heart of his interests (fig. 35). His way of perceiving things places great importance in the analytical eye, which on paper often translates into fragments, bits of nature or slices of life (daily chores or studies of local costumes). By inserting his own layouts, following the tradition of seventeenth-century Dutch art, he was already paving the way for Jean-Baptiste Camille Corot (1796–1875) and Richard Parkes Bonington (1802–1828).[9] Inversely, for Hackert and Ducros, the world is not made up of scattered units that form a vast catalogue of curiosities. Nature is an entirety, an 'all in one', and it is fitting to depict her in terms of composed landscapes. When Ducros draws a group of figures, he does so to make them better serve his small-scale pictures. He follows the sensibility of his day and age, which appreciates the art of composition.

IV

Ducros was back in Rome in August 1778. In two years, from 1779 to 1780, he would prove to be a skilful promoter of his art, eventually coming to dominate the scene after 1784. His taking up residence on the Strada della Croce in 1782, moreover, placed him at the heart of the affairs and the areas that travellers passing through the city would have known.

The international trade in prints was well established in Rome when Ducros chose to make a name for himself there. The trade had existed since the sixteenth century, developing in conjunction with an operating strategy that enabled the city to construct its image in time and space.[10] Gérard Labrot, building on the studies of Maurizio Calvesi, has also done a masterly job of grasping the role played by Piranesi, the first to expand Rome in such a dizzying way while revealing '...the image's secret fault: the overabundance of the past... [Rome] made history, but yesterday and the day before that, and its present is constantly

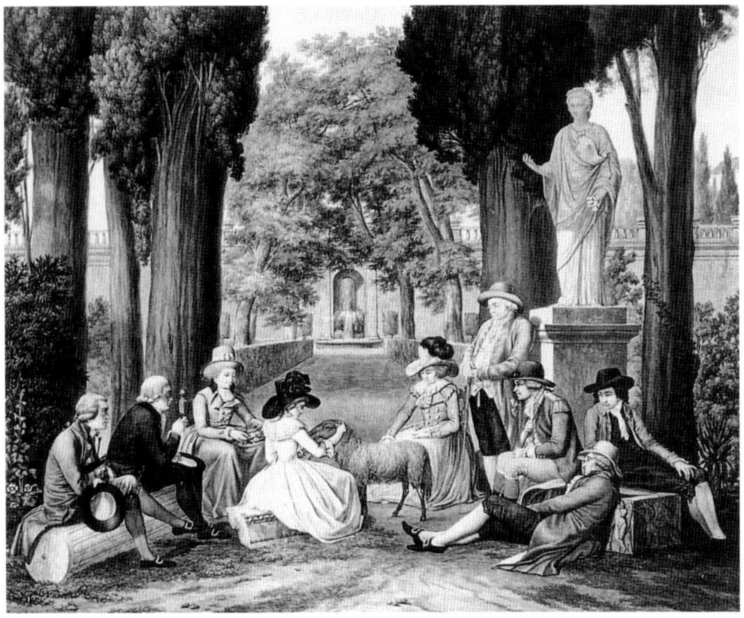

Fig. 36 Johann Georg Schütz, *The Duchess Anna Amalia von Weimar and her suite at the Villa d'Este at Tivoli, 1789*, pen and watercolour. Stiftung Weimarer Klassik-Museen, Weimar

crushed by the dazzling past.'[11] Implicitly, his oeuvre marks the dawn of an age of transition, when the slow initiation to a city, its culture and ideology was quietly crumbling away, to be replaced by a diffuse collection of slight, fleeting impressions. Ducros was a latecomer to this figurative strategy. Nevertheless, he was to play a part in it, especially in his way of translating reality in his pictures along with a concern for dazzling the viewer. In this way he prepared the shift of the image of Rome and Italy towards artifice.

From what the documents tell us, it is impossible to affirm whether Ducros's own strategy for spreading his work was the result of a reasoned or an intuitive choice. I am tempted to opt for the latter hypothesis, given the remarks of his contemporaries and because the strategy was only slowly put in place. Let us be frank, the man does not seem to have been liked much. Jealousy and resentment played their part; Ducros himself would deem those sentiments responsible for his being expelled from Rome in 1793. One can also guess, from a letter De la Rive addressed to his wife in November 1784, that Ducros did not make the task any easier for himself: 'The artists who wish to get on are obliged here [in Rome] to court Hackert, Reiffenstein, Angelica; beyond them, there are no recommendations with the foreigners, who all end up there. Ducros has set them all against him thanks to the care with which he has avoided playing up to them, and he's the worse for it.'[12] The circle that Angelica Kauffmann (1741–1807) brought together around her became one of the most important centres of interest for the art community, especially for German artists. The arrival of Johann Wolfgang Goethe (1749–1832) in October 1786, along with the admiration that he felt for the circle, added all the more to its influence. Johann Friedrich Reiffenstein (1719–1793), an *antiquario*, aesthete and close friend of Hackert's, was deemed the finest connoisseur in Rome and one of the personalities who were simply impossible to avoid at the start of one's Grand Tour.[13]

We can well understand then, comparing Ducros's works with those being promoted in this circle (fig. 36), that Kauffmann's group could hardly have overlooked them. Yet at the time of De la Rive's remark, the situation was noticeably changing thanks to a twofold combination of circumstances. Louis-Jean Desprez (1743–1804) left Rome for Stockholm in 1784 and Hackert set off for Naples in 1785. In the space of a few months, Ducros saw himself relieved of his two main competitors. It is from this moment on that we can date his very large format watercolours.

Ducros well understood by this time that the taste of his age went in for the art lover who, after purchasing his prints, no longer stored them away in portfolios only. They were now quite often found hanging in interiors, framed like paintings and protected by a sheet of glass. And along with this change in the status of the medium came a revolution in technique. In France they had been turning out colour prints since 1740 and the process was rapidly refined thanks to Jean-François Janinet (1752–1814) and later Philibert Louis Debucourt (1755–1832). Engravings imitating first pencil (around 1740), then wash drawings (1769), made originals accessible to a greater number of collectors, creating for the first time the illusion of the original other than by merely copying the same means of expression. Once that understanding had been well established, Ducros was to adjust its workings to a potential clientele who were eager to be a part of this new social model.

He now developed an extremely clever – albeit contradictory – system based on widely distributing his works in order to better establish their rarity. We are not yet in that age when the Impressionists could take advantage of the then completely new trilogy of the gallery, the art dealer and the critic in order to enter a trade structure that would get their works into circulation and create a demand for them abroad. Ducros joined forces with Giovanni Volpato (1732–1803), choosing engraving as his way of laying the foundation stone of his enterprise. Thanks to Volpato's reputation – his studio was held in real esteem in Rome – and the quality of the prints enhanced by Ducros, the Swiss artist would succeed in making a name for himself. Pierre Chessex has examined this question in detail, showing the difference that existed in buyers' various interests.[14] Everything depended in fact on the way a work was viewed, the process underlying the replication of images and the number of hands seamlessly involved in the course of producing them. For the lover of prints, these elements were crucial, all the more so since the assistants employed to touch up the engravings did not always achieve the same technical perfection. For the souvenir collector, the result held more importance than the process. If the completed work cancelled out altogether the engraved line that served as its support, creating the greatest degree of confusion with an original watercolour, the pleasure would be all the greater. We should take care not to hold this against the artist, especially since he attached only relative importance to this stage of his oeuvre. We must bear in mind above all that the art lovers who went on the Grand Tour were not all equally wealthy. Their interests and expectations differed. Although they shared the same cultural background, not all of them were discerning connoisseurs – far from it, indeed.

The divergence in the status of the reworked engravings and the medium-scale watercolours is quite real. Done on small sheets of paper measuring around 50 x 60 cm, the watercolours, as originals executed by the artist's hand, already possess the qualities seen in Ducros's large-scale works. It was these latter watercolours that truly made Ducros's reputation with well-heeled art lovers. Stretching over several sheets, they attain dimensions that were uncommon for the period, often exceeding 75 x 100 cm. The high prices that he asked for these pictures suggest, moreover, that they involved no small amount of exacting work. Yet all of this cannot be dissociated from the studio practices with which Ducros had already been familiar for quite some time. Regrettably, today we know little about this group work apart from the names of a few assistants that can be gleaned from the documents. Still more bothersome is the problem of the figures peopling Ducros's landscapes, an open question since Pierre Chessex made the first inroads there. We do know enough about the art-trade milieu in Rome, however, for it to serve as a tool to advance our understanding. On the one hand, Ducros innovates completely, isolating his creations from the flood of commonplace images that could have hindered their spread owing to the backlash that a necessary levelling of the subjects would generate. On the other, we should bear in mind that he did build a genuine system whose logic only gradually took shape, in order to put this system at the service of creating the exception. Once the 'souvenir factory' was firmly in place, Ducros provided himself with every available tool to excel.

Fig. 37 Louis Ducros and Giovanni Volpato, *Temple of Antonious and Faustine, c.1780,* etching and watercolour on paper, 51 x 73.8 cm. Musée cantonal des Beaux-Arts, Lausanne

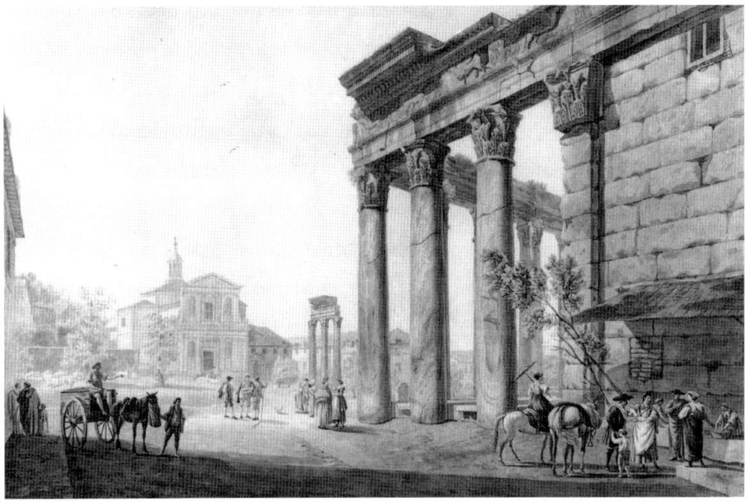

V

Ducros's achievement was to successfully produce a synthesis of the taste of his age and then to create works corresponding to it. His images are sketched out according to a delicate balance of geometry and sentiment. While the former is more on display in several engravings of the Volpato series (fig. 37), it never reaches the level of the architectural spirit that suffuses the works of Ch.-L. Clérisseau, for example. Thus, Ducros's sense of geometry never goes so far as to cancel out the figures that lend life to his compositions. Caprice, situated at the far end of verisimilitude, is only an occasional presence in the work. For Ducros, nature is fundamentally a spectacle that has to come to terms with the true. Whether arranged by man or captured as it is in the wild, the natural law governing nature cannot be conceived without the addition of an emotional force to man's imitation of her. Ducros's entire outlook is contained in this way of seeing. After his exile from Rome in 1793, this approach would make his depiction of unfamiliar places like the Abruzzi easier.

Ducros's art developed against a theoretical background whose starting point is found in Roger de Piles' *Cours de peinture par principes* (A Course in Painting by Principles), published in Paris in 1708: 'The essence and the definition of Painting is the imitation of visible objects by means of form and colour… The more Painting forcefully and faithfully imitates nature, the more it leads us quickly and directly to its end, which is to appeal like plays upon its waters so gaily its delectable harmonies fill the soul of every visitor with astonishment and awe.'[28]

From the earliest retouched etchings, made in collaboration with Volpato, Ducros would add villas and gardens to his repertory of subjects, emphasising especially their aspect of 'open-air drawing rooms'. The mix of groups of figures, occasionally pushed to the point of overloading the composition, underscores that atmosphere. The longitudinal vistas along the wooded avenues or the openings from a terrace are designed to show these channelled waters to advantage. The vistas of Villa Doria Pamphili punctuate the perspective that leads to the statuary overlooking the open-air theatre in the distance. Oddly enough, water adds life to the sculptured setting while depriving a half-drowned woman, who has just been pulled from the ornamental pool, of hers. The anecdote, meant to be picturesque, forces the line all the same. It brings to mind the many years the artist spent copying the Dutch and the Flemish.

The opulence of water can also show itself to be quieter, more subdued, as in *The Gardens of Villa Corsini* (cat. 10), where a line engraving is first given a grey wash before being reworked in watercolour and heightened here and there with gouache. The Palazzo Corsini in Trastevere was part of the Rome of Ducros's day. The palace had been sumptuously reconstructed between 1732 and 1736 by the Florentine architect Ferdinando Fuga (1699–1780). The gardens, which stretch over twelve hectares (about thirty acres) at the foot of the Janiculum, now make up Rome's Botanical Gardens. Ducros chose a raised point of view with a clearing to the right towards the palace. The central motif of the fountain, hemmed in on each side, stands out against a clump of trees. The layout is not new. In fact, Ducros deliberately placed his watercolour in a well-established tradition, which can be seen in one of the finest landscapes of Locatelli's youth, *Landscape of the Roman Countryside with Washerwomen near a Fountain*, dating from 1725.[29] By filtering his topographical view through the ideal landscape, Ducros vies here with painting. He also reveals to us one of the keys to his success, that is, his ability to transpose reality in terms of models capable of evoking the appropriate recollections amongst buyers of art.

The imagery of fountains is so prevalent, moreover, that it leads the artist to view open-air wash-houses in the same terms. The *Washerwomen in the Roman Campagna*, has a counterpart in a red-chalk drawing by Fragonard, executed in the summer of 1760. In his composition, Fragonard focuses on the exuberance of the vegetation and the light. Simply suggested by a line drawing, his figures do not attract the viewer's eye. Even if we know that Fragonard cared little for topography, the disparity between the two backgrounds comes nonetheless as quite a surprise. Closed by a few houses and a mountain in Fragonard's composition, in Ducros's the background opens onto the Roman countryside. For the latter, the need to narrow the view explains his turning to the old Flemish convention of dividing the composition in two with an abrupt diagonal line: closed towards the viewer and open towards the distance. His real discovery is to have brought the water right up to the edge of the page. Limpid, shimmering, clouded by the wash being soaked there and wrung out, the water here points to the symbolic power of fresh water and its purity. The water of the wash-house becomes the fountain of daily chores while the washerwomen act as intermediaries.

The motif of flowing water, rivers and cascades is found throughout Ducros's oeuvre and would warrant a whole study of its own. His contemporaries tell us of the degree of success he managed to achieve in his way of making waters seem to cascade down while lending a palpable reality to the wisps of thin, moist mist enveloping them. A large number of his compositions were constructed on a dual rhythm associating liquid and solid elements according to highly contrasting juxtapositions: cascade and dense vegetation, or river and rock revealing a strong geological structure. He would then superimpose his chance occurrences with a poetic realism that owes not a little to scientific theories: 'O how I prefer to be in Tivoli under the waterfalls at sunrise, Newton would have broken down light there without a prism...'[30] Examining the works, one is surely justified in wondering what exactly was Ducros's understanding of Newton's experiment with the scattering of light and the solar spectrum. He certainly shared the period's interest in observing light, but did not yet break it down into individualised colour lights. He indeed seems closer to the poetic approach that Goethe would later develop, especially in applying the idea that illuminated areas of half-light appear blue. It is true, however, that Ducros situated his work at the very heart of a scientific problem that was essential to the eighteenth century, that is, analysing the fleeting effects of nature and understanding the dualism of the palpable and the impalpable.[31]

VI

His travels in Sicily in the summer of 1778 had introduced the theme of the seaside into Ducros's oeuvre. It was only with his settling in Naples in 1793, however, that sea water would supplant fresh water as a motif. In the space of a few years, following the stay in Malta of 1800–1801, the idea of clarity that long governed his poetic descriptions was to gradually give way to a veritable maelstrom of elements. Shadow increasingly covers the landscapes and water now turns violent. The sea proved just the medium for translating these new passions. Ducros would manipulate the viewer's sensibilities in order to create a sublime malaise.

We must go back a few years earlier, however, to around 1785, when the artist drew *The Marmore Waterfall* (cat. 19). Although the piece clearly belongs to this period, it must also be seen as a true precursor of the sublime landscape. Tightly constricted by the vegetation, the falls run across the whole of the page's upper part. From there, Ducros was to brilliantly renew Hackert's reading of the scene (fig. 40), which dates from around 1779. The sublime aspect of the waterfalls results from the contradiction between the relationships of scale. The large tree to the left with its gnarled trunk belongs to the viewer's space, located beyond the picture. It allows us to remain outside the work while having direct access to the falls' visual effect at the top of the page. Then suddenly our eye drops to the bottom of the sheet, drawn by the scaled-down figures. The contradiction with the vegetation surrounding them is complete. And it is then that we experience, in unison with the painted figures, the effects of the tiered cascade, as if we had entered the picture's inner space. In its simplicity, *Cascata delle Marmore* is a masterpiece of spatial organisation formally demonstrating that 'the sublime is not: it arises'.[32]

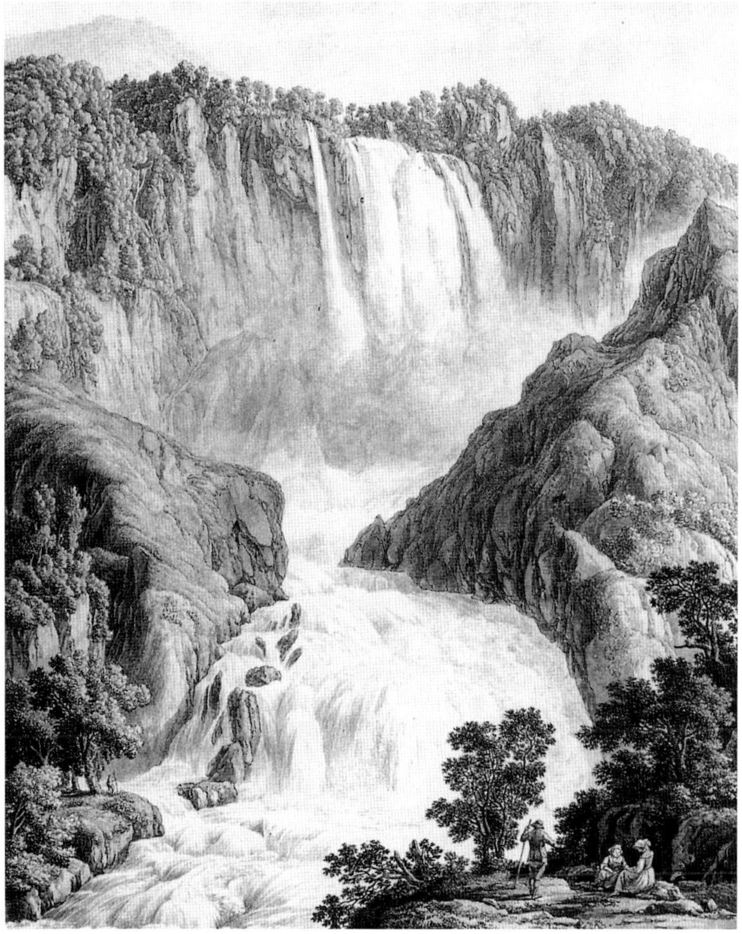

Fig. 40 Philipp Hackert, 1737–1807, *The Marmore Waterfall at Terni, c. 1779,* pen and black ink, brush and brown wash, with white gouache and graphite, 52.3 x 40 cm.
The Cleveland Museum of Art, Dudley P. Allen Fund, Cleveland

Elsewhere Ducros was to recapture the northern tradition of storms and shipwrecks, as in *The Squall behind the Customs House, Valletta*, (cat. 44). Albeit faithful to detail in its observation of the world, this picture is unreal in its framing of the image and its use of colour and light. Water has become foam and seems to make the fantastic buildings suddenly rise up from the ocean deep. At first glance, the figures huddled in the boat in the foreground give cause for alarm. Then, studying them more closely, the viewer discovers a group crowded around a table playing cards! That free-and-easy spirit, however, is thwarted by a landscape that seems weighted, oppressive. The brown shadows become more intense and the mannerism of the fine, watery spray no longer offers the illusion of reality.

The entire question comes down to where works like *Eruption of Vesuvius and Shipwreck* (cat. 36), and *Storm at Night, Cefalù* (cat. 39), lead us. The compositions, reversed, are similar and the two works could well make a pair. Even if the former remains in the space of the shipwreck à la Vernet (suggested by the life-saving rocks for the figures), the two landscapes belong to a new sensibility, one that owes a great deal to a belated reading of Edmund Burke's *A Philosophical Enquiry into our Ideas of the Sublime and Beautiful* (1757, French translation 1765), as Baldine Saint Girons has shown.[33] It would be rather imprudent then to limit the realisations of that sensibility to only the movements of the artist's biography. According to Burke, the ocean exalts the sublime.[34] Gloomy darkness, associated with the night, causes our vision to falter and enables us to recapture our original terror. To create confusion, Ducros went back to the elements that he had always been able to harmonise; water, earth and air. Previously, his storms on land, such as *Thunderstorm in the Valley of the Nera*, followed the lessons taught by the work of Gaspard Dughet and Nicolas Poussin. But from now on fire, too, plays its part in orchestrating violence and creating a real rift in nature. Was it truly as a visionary that Ducros invented these unreal

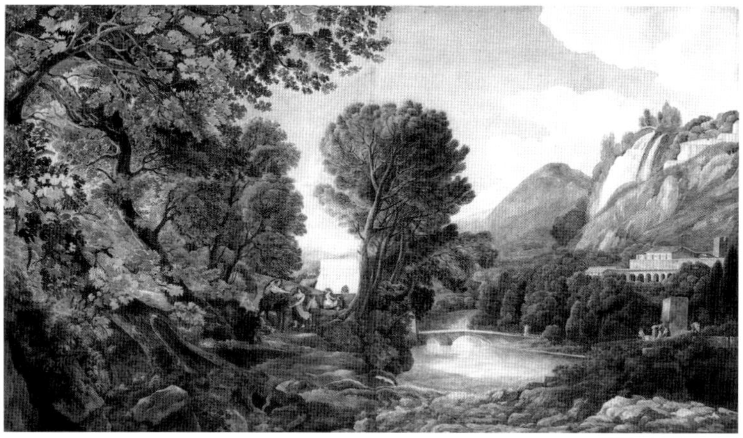

Fig. 43 Louis Ducros, *View near Licenza in Abruzzi*, watercolour on paper laid on canvas, 68 x 113.8 cm. Musée cantonal des Beaux-Arts, Lausanne

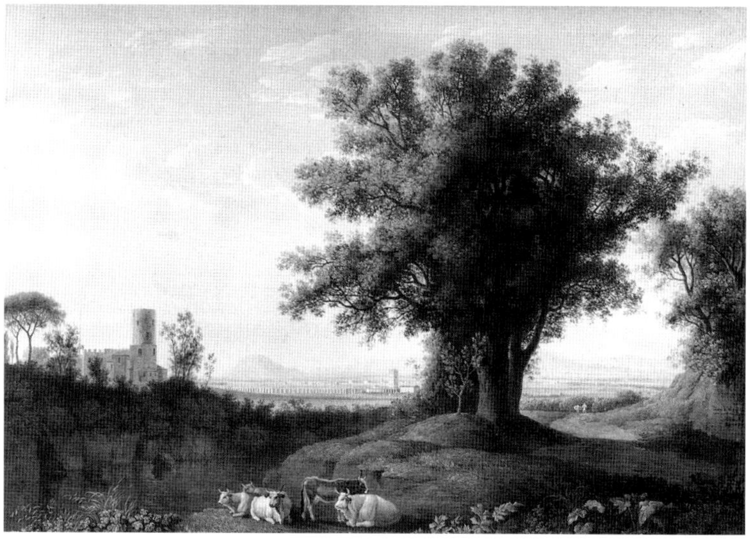

Fig. 44 Jakob Philipp Hackert, *Landscape near Rome, 1793*. Kunsthalle zu Kiel, Kiel

Fig. 45 Jakob Philipp Hackert, *Ruins of the Colosseum, 1774*. Kunsthalle zu Kiel, Kiel

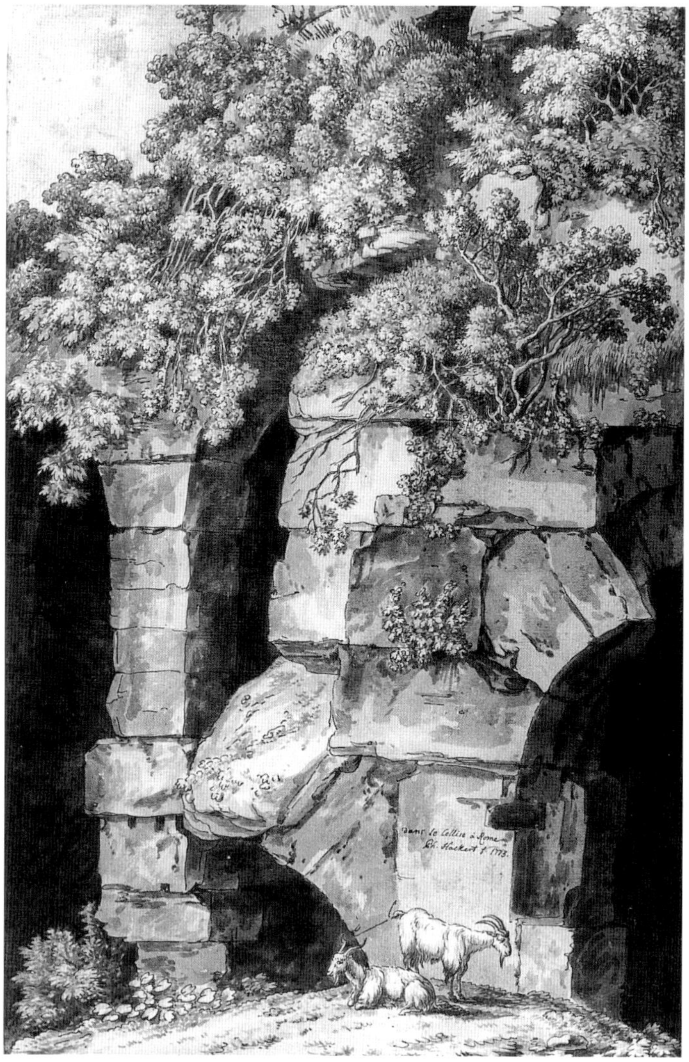

who also arrived in Rome for the first time in November 1776, were perhaps the most remarkable of the loosely affiliated group of British watercolourists whose finest works either record or recall this landscape, and offer some interesting parallels to Ducros's watercolours. Thomas Jones was born in 1742, the younger son of a Welsh landowning family, and had been intended for the church, but when a great-uncle who had paid for his education died intestate, Jones had to leave Oxford University before completing his studies, and in 1763, having decided to become a painter, apprenticed himself to his fellow-countryman Richard Wilson, whose own landscape style had been shaped by an extended visit to Italy in the 1750s and by his admiration for the work of Claude. It was not until 1776, at the age of thirty-four, that Jones was able to go to Italy, living first in Rome and then in Naples until 1783. His *Memoirs* (first published in 1951), based on the journal he kept in Italy, give a vivid picture of his daily life unmatched by any other eighteenth century artist, a minor masterpiece to set beside Goethe's *Italienische Reise*. While he hoped to make his reputation by securing commissions from Grand Tourists for large-scale oil landscapes in the classical style, he failed to secure the favour of the English dealers and *ciceroni* Thomas Jenkins and James Byres (the latter an important figure in Ducros's career), who dominated the Anglo-Roman art market, while another potentially important patron compared Jones's paintings unfavourably with those of Jakob-Philipp Hackert, undoubtedly the most successful and cosmopolitan foreign landscape painter then working in Italy. An encounter with Hackert in 1782 was described by Jones in rueful terms, and suggests something of the hostile undercurrents in the fiercely competitive art market. Hackert did not relish the prospect of rivalry and treated Jones to a patronising appraisal of his abilities. Jones, for his part, had no sympathy with Hackert's style, in particular '[his] minute finishing, which...was congenial to his own taste, who like most German Artists, study more the Minutiae than the grand principles of Art', and thoroughly disliked Hackert's haughty manner. 'I may here observe that there never was, perhaps, a man who was more endowed with the talent of making people believe that he was the greatest Genius that ever existed'.[3] Jones's failure to attract the patronage for which he longed did, however, mean that he was able to spend more time painting watercolours that record his surroundings in a completely straightforward, direct fashion, each location meticulously identified, and the date noted – a visual counterpart to his journal. Even more striking are his Italian oil sketches, mostly painted in Naples, and unknown until the 1950s, which date from 1782–83. Jones had first painted such studies from nature in Wales in the early 1770s, studies that are remarkable for his ability to set aside the compositional formulae he had learned from Wilson, and suggest that he arrived at the technique independently from French contemporaries, notably Pierre-Henri de Valenciennes (1750–1819), whose oil sketches of Rome, also painted c.1782–1784, are mostly concerned with capturing transient effects of light and atmosphere; Jones's Neapolitan studies are characterised by an almost geometric treatment of spatial relationships, beautifully calculated in the near abstract placing of the compositional elements, and analogous to a certain type of ultra-sophisticated contemporary architectural photography.

There is no evidence that Ducros ever sketched in oils in quite this way, although he must have observed his Flemish friend Simon Denis making such studies[4], and before he left Switzerland for Italy, Ducros is recorded as painting in watercolour from nature. Significantly, Ducros's friend and patron, the celebrated naturalist Charles Bonnet, recommended the close study of nature as the only means of discovering and conveying 'truth', while another close friend, Pierre-Louis De la Rive, later recalled 'the obsession inspired in me by Ducros of always doing wash watercolours on the spot'.[5] This practice of working from nature unites Ducros with the most avant garde landscapists then based in Italy. In many ways, the watercolours of John Robert Cozens (1752–1797) offer the most intriguing comparison with Ducros's landscapes, not least because of the suggestion first made by a British art historian, C.F. Bell, in 1917, and subsequently amplified in 1935[6], that it was under 'the robust and sympathetic influence of Ducros' that Cozens began to

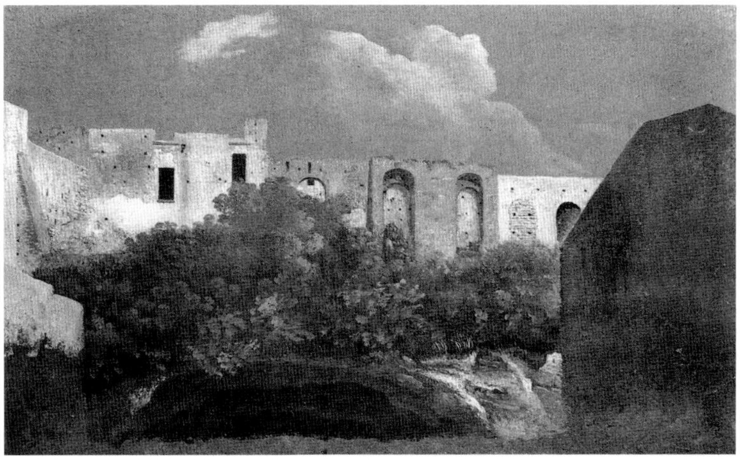

Fig. 46 Thomas Jones, *Buildings and Ruins, Naples, c.1782.*
Glynn Vivian Art Gallery, Swansea

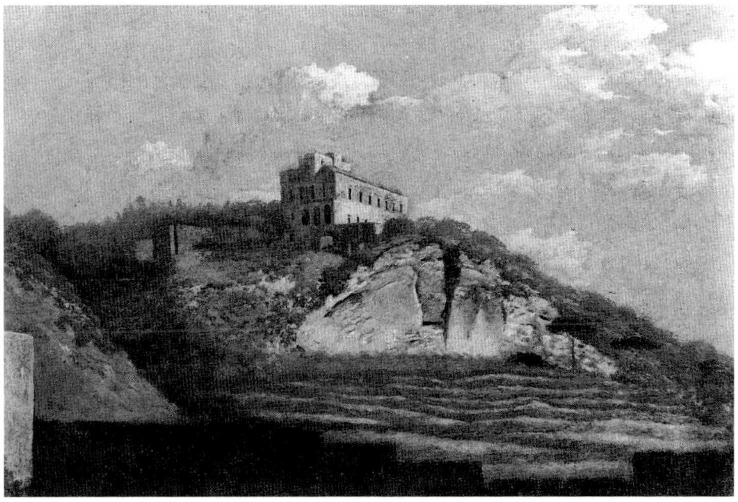

Fig. 47 Thomas Jones, *The Hill of S. Martino, Naples.*
Fitzwilliam Museum, Cambridge

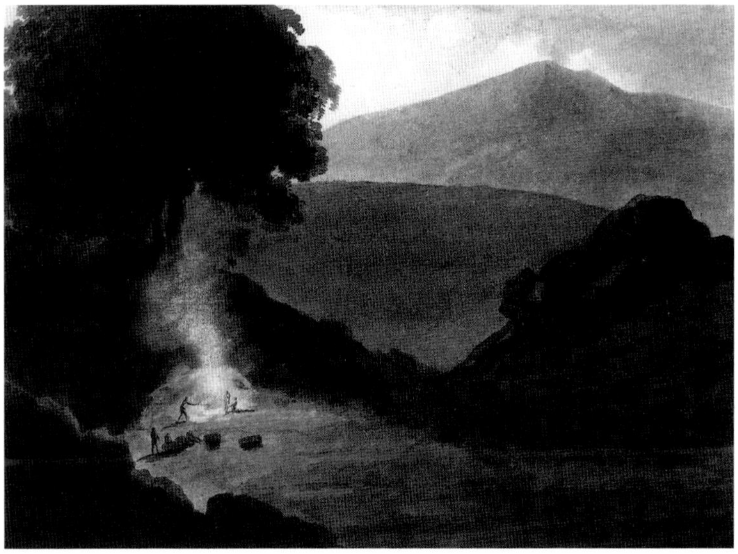

Fig. 48 Robert Cozens, *View of Etna from the Grotto of Capro.*
British Museum, London

experiment while in Rome between 1776 and 1779. But this hypothesis is less convincing in the light of our fuller knowledge of Ducros's life. Bell believed that Ducros had gone to Rome in around 1770, but it has subsequently been established that he did not arrive until the end of 1776, indeed probably within weeks of Cozens. The drawings made by Ducros during his expedition with Nicolaas Ten Hove to southern Italy and Sicily in 1778 are topographical studies of great freshness, comparable with similar examples by Houel, Desprez and Chatelet, but are very unlike Ducros's own mature work and provide no evidence that by 1779 he had developed a style that could have influenced Cozens. While it is true that the first twenty-four of Ducros and Volpato's large and impressive *Vues de Rome et ses environs* were published in 1780, it was not until 1783–84 – after Cozens's second and last visit to Italy in 1782–83 – that Ducros, encouraged by the success of his hand-coloured *Vues,* began to paint the large-scale watercolours that were to find such favour with British patrons in particular. It is perhaps of some significance that, while Hackert is mentioned on several occasions in Jones's *Memoirs*, and his influential status acknowledged, there is no reference to Ducros. This is partly because Jones lived in Naples from 1780 until his return to England in 1783 and was thus less aware of what was going on in Rome, describing instead the activities of friends who were also working in Naples – Francis Towne, William Pars, John 'Warwick' Smith, Pierre-Jacques Volaire, Michael Wutky and Giambattista Lusieri. Nevertheless, the absence of any reference to Ducros tends to confirm the probability that it was not until 1783–84 that his reputation became established both with his patrons and with his fellow artists, and casts further doubt on Bell's notion that his work was a formative influence on Cozens. Indeed, there could even be a case for reversing Bell's argument and suggesting that the reciprocal influence between Ducros and British artists in Rome may have been at least partly in the opposite direction. Could Ducros have seen any of Cozens's atmospheric watercolours of the Roman Campagna – a number of which he painted during his first visit to Italy, 1776–1779 – or known John 'Warwick' Smith's monumental watercolours of Rome, painted between 1776 and 1781? Such discussions of influences are apt to be too categorical; it would be safer simply to observe that the artistic milieu of Rome in the 1770s and 1780s was one in which aspiring artists were quick to seize on new ideas.

Cozens's watercolours are among the most haunting interpretations of the Italian landscape ever painted. Based on drawings made on the spot during sketching expeditions described by his friend Thomas Jones, some of the finished watercolours were painted in the course of Cozens's two visits to Italy, while others were commissioned by various patrons after his return to England. Up to ten or twelve versions exist of his most popular subjects, each subtly different, sometimes more intense and brooding, sometimes lighter toned and more decorative in mood. The influence of Claude is particularly apparent, both in composition and atmosphere: the origins of the uniquely melancholy beauty of Cozens's art may be found in the elegiac mood of many of Claude's paintings. His achievement lay in the transformation of such classical prototypes into genuinely Romantic works, and in imparting the highest imaginative significance to a subject by subduing its topographical content and enhancing its pictorial and emotional elements. Past and present, art and nature are united to haunting effect: 'all poetry', as one of the greatest landscape painters of the nineteenth century, John Constable, described Cozens's watercolours.

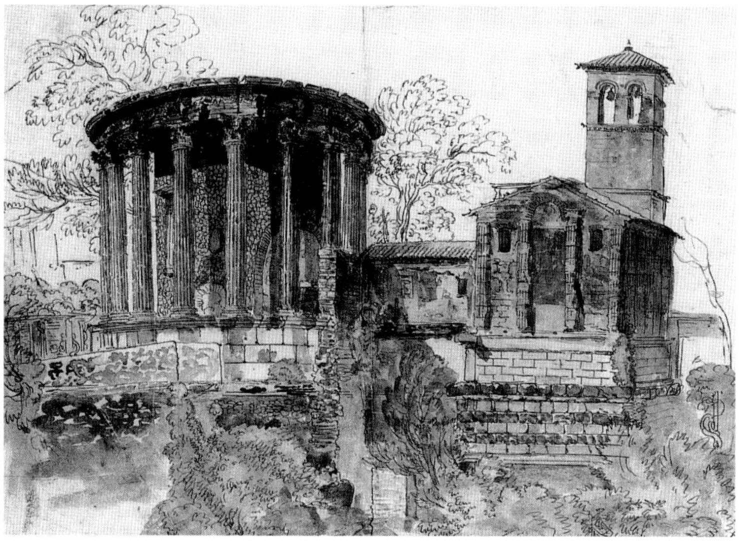

Fig. 49 Louis-Jean Desprez, *Temple of Vesta and the Temple of the Sibyl at Tivoli*. Nationalmuseum, Stockholm

Ducros's watercolours eschew the subtleties of Cozens's vision. His clients' taste was for depictions of easily recognisable places on an impressively large scale, enlivened with dramatic atmospheric effects. This emphasis on the sublime and the monumental was later to stimulate the development of J.M.W. Turner, who must have been deeply impressed by Richard Colt Hoare's collection of Ducros's work at Stourhead, as well as by his extensive representation of Piranesi's prints, Italian views by 'Warwick' Smith and by Colt Hoare's passionate enthusiasm for classical history and topography[7]. Ducros's

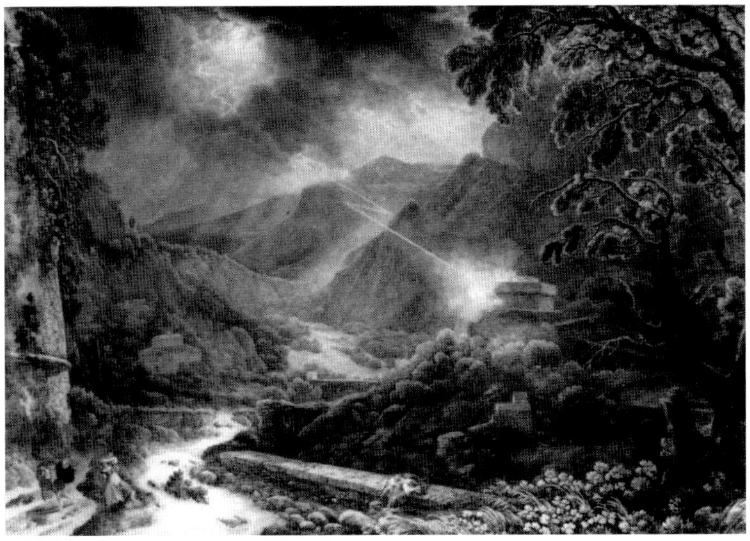

Fig. 50 Louis Ducros, *Storm in the Nera Valley*, watercolour, 77 x 113 cm. Stourhead, Wiltshire

technical mastery of watercolour was unmatched until Turner; contemporary critics noted his skill at capturing the most transient effects of light and atmosphere, while conveying the grandeur of nature in his views of the waterfalls at Terni and Tivoli. While Ducros's work has sometimes been dismissed as souvenir painting for Grand Tourists – his Swiss contemporary Philip Secretan described his disappointment at finding him 'a cold producer of landscapes engaged in selling gouaches to the English'[8] – we can now recognise his achievement in taking watercolour beyond its hitherto traditional limits. What distinguished him from his fellow artists in Italy working in the same medium was his sheer professionalism in developing an essentially intimate activity into a highly desirable, publicly acclaimed art form.

1 Bridel 1790
2 'The Memoirs of Thomas Jones' published by A.P. Oppé, *The Walpole Society,* vol. XXXII, 1951, p.60
3 *ibid.,* p.118
4 'Simon Denis (1755–1813) settled in Rome in around 1784 (see the letter from Pierre De La Rive to his wife dated 22 November 1784, ms. fr 2397, BPU, Geneva) and befriended several Swiss artists already established in the town, including Jean-Pierre Saint-Ours, Jacques Sablet and Ducros. His open-air oil studies were similar in character to those of Pierre-Henri de Valenciennes; some of them are reproduced in *In the Light of Italy: Corot and Early Open-Air Painting*, exh.cat. Washington, 1996, pp. 145–49.'
5 De la Rive 1832, p.11
6 'J.R. Cozens: Drawings and Sketches', *The Walpole Society,* vol. XXIII, 1935, pp.12–14
7 Lindsay Stainton, exh. cat. London 1985, pp.26–30
8 Philippe Secretan, *Journal de Voyage,* 3 January 1787, BCU , Fonds Pellis IS 4350, fol.32

1. STUDY FOR THREE FIGURES, 1778

Pen and ink, watercolour on paper,
27.5 x 37.8 cm
Lausanne, Musée cantonal des Beaux-Arts
Inv. 773

Literature: exh. cat. Lausanne 1995, p. 5;
exh. cat. Lausanne 1999, n. 40

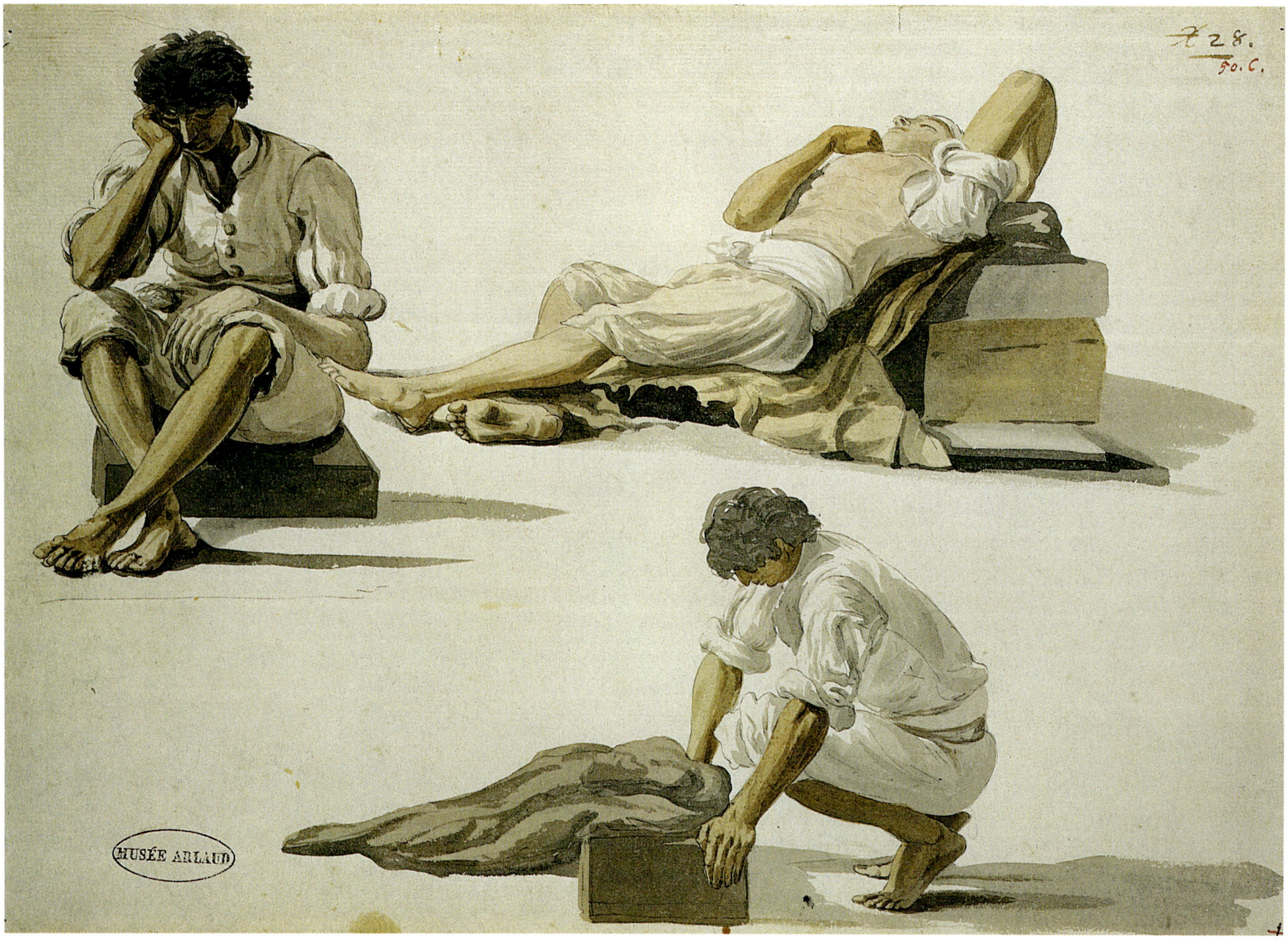

2. GENERAL VIEW OF THE CAMPO VACCINO, c.1778

Pen and grey wash, watercolour,
J Honig & Zoonen paper, 53.1 x 73.7 cm
Lausanne, Musée cantonal des Beaux-Arts
Inv. 888

Literature: Agassiz 1927, p. 36; Agassiz 1928, ill. 10; exh. cat. Lausanne 1953, n. 19; exh. cat. Rome 1954, n. 18; Haskell, Chessex 1985, n. 15; exh. cat. London 1985, n. 8; exh. cat. Lausanne 1986, n. 13; exh. cat. Rome 1987, n. 10; exh. cat. Lausanne 1998b, p. 57

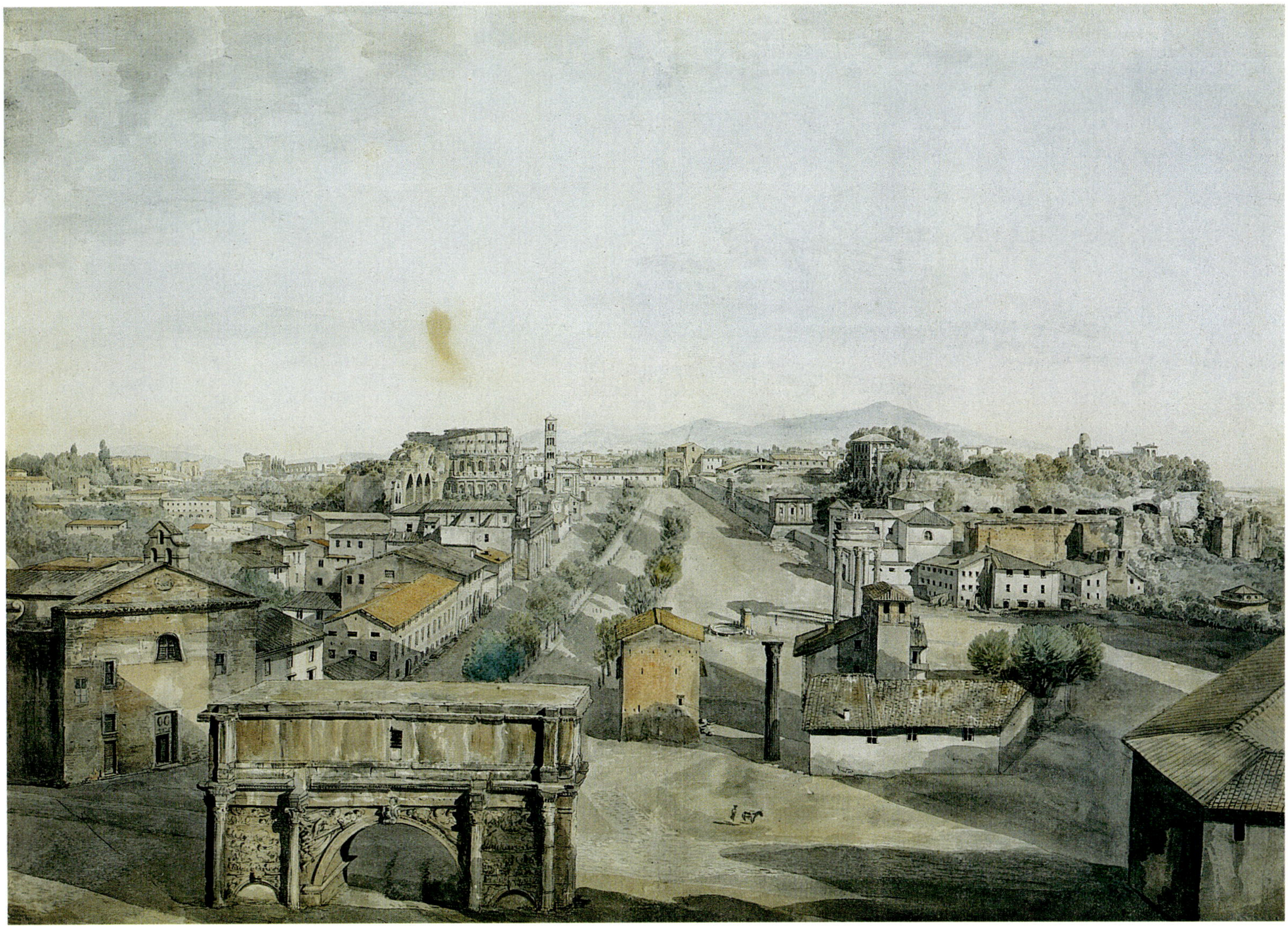

3. THE ARCH OF SEPTIMIUS SEVERUS, c.1780

Pen and black ink, grey wash and watercolour, J Honig & Zoonen paper, 52.5 x 74 cm
Lausanne, Musée cantonal des Beaux-Arts
Inv. 873

Literature: Agassiz 1927, p. 36; exh. cat. Lausanne 1953, n. 8; exh. cat. Rome 1954, n. 7; Chessex 1984 (1), p. 431; exh. cat. London 1985, n. 7; exh. cat. Lausanne 1986, n. 14; exh. cat. Rome 1987, n. 11; exh. cat. Bassano 1988, n. 233; exh. cat. Lausanne 1995, p. 5; exh. cat. Lausanne 1998b, p. 58

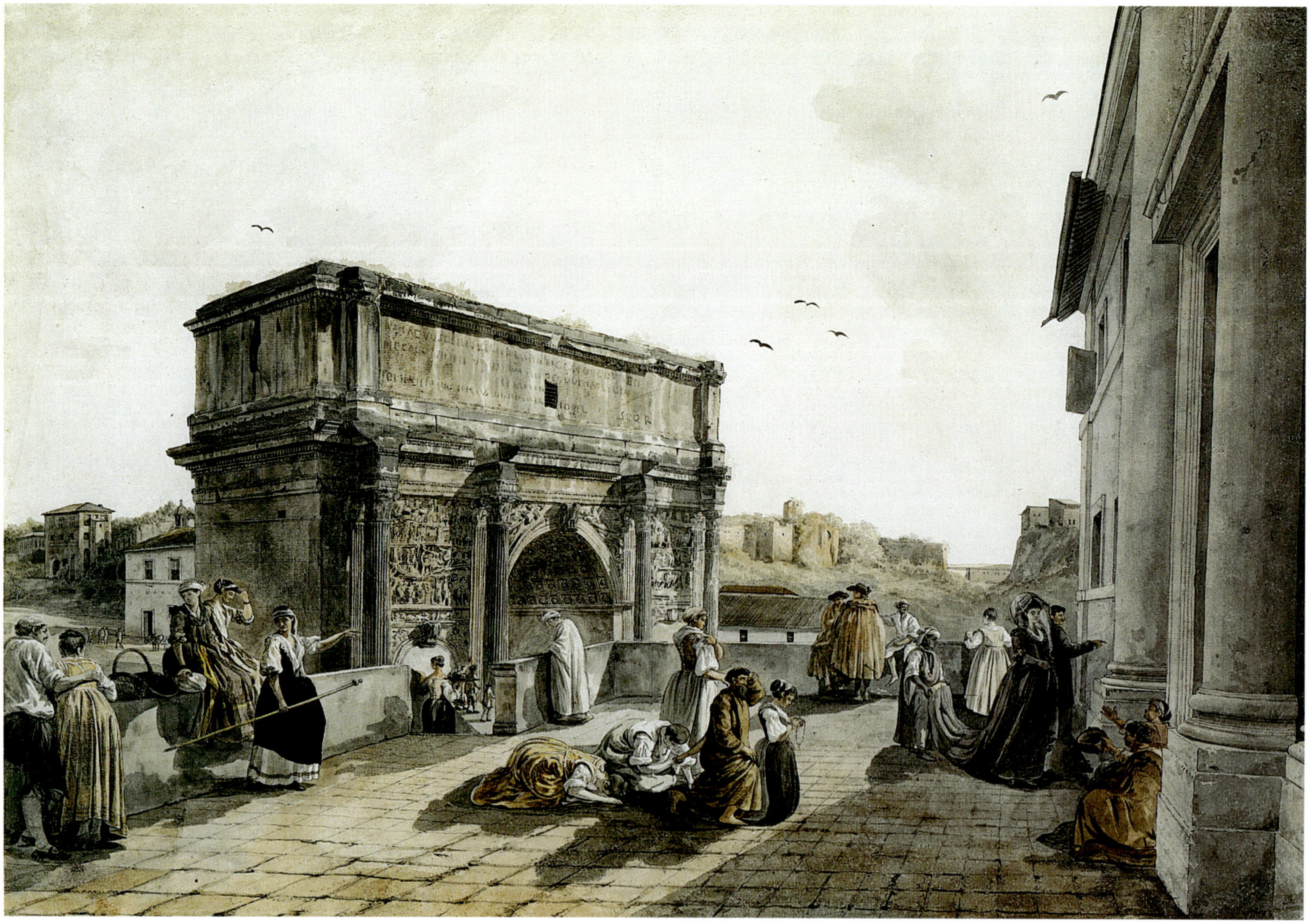

4. THE TEMPLE OF MINERVA MEDICA

Sepia wash over pen and pencil drawing
on paper, 53.7 x 75 cm
Lausanne, Musée cantonal des Beaux-Arts
Inv. 909

Literature: Haskell, Chessex 1985, n. 16;
exh. cat. Bassano 1988, n. 242

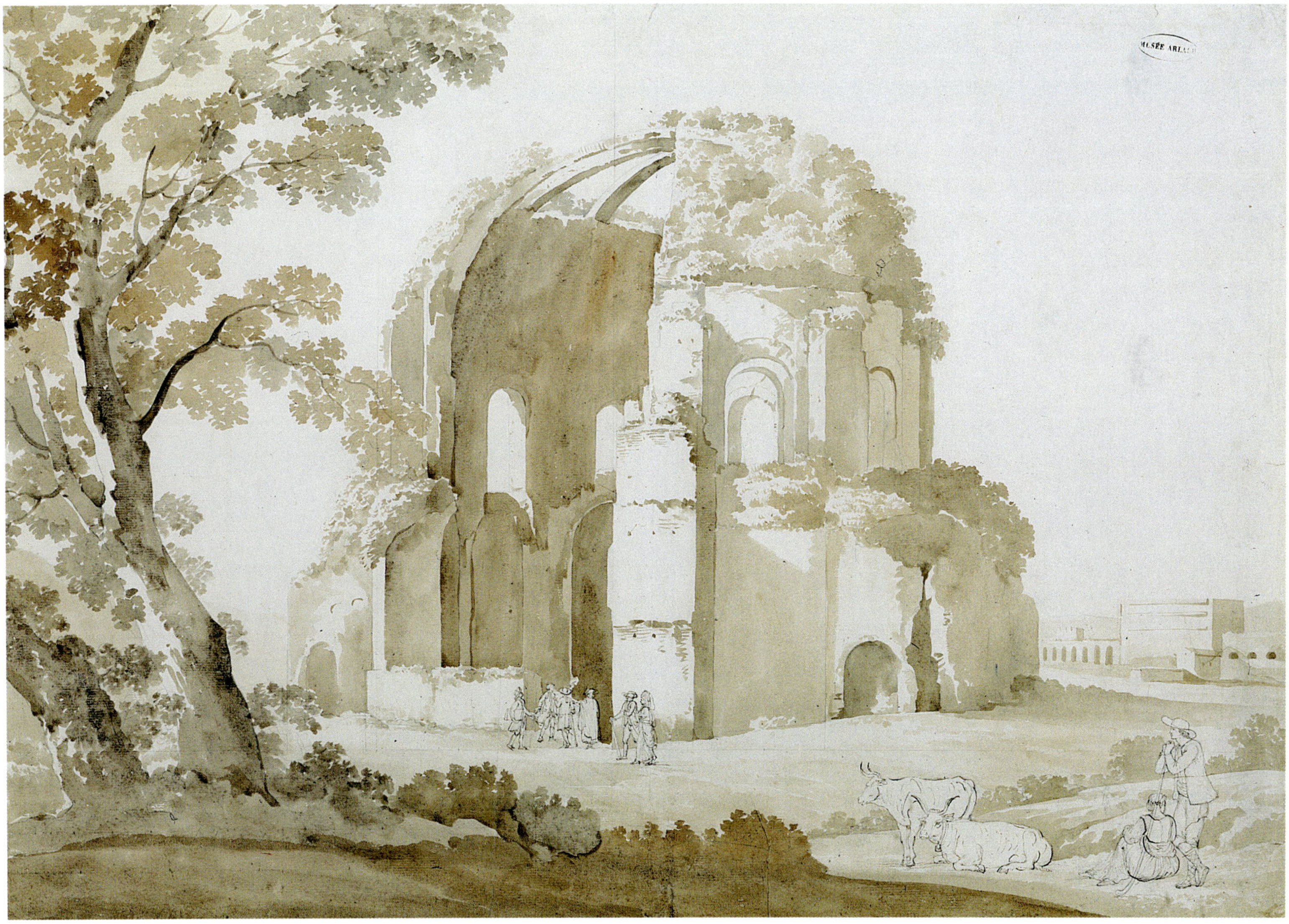

5. VIEW WITHIN THE CAPITOL, c.1780

Outline etching, pen and black ink, watercolour, C & I Honig paper, 51.8 x 74.5 cm (sheet size) ; 51.2 x 74 cm (image size)
Lausanne, Musée cantonal des Beaux-Arts
Inv. 879

Literature: exh. cat. Lausanne 1953, n. 12; exh. cat. Rome 1954, n. 11; exh. cat. London 1985, n. 9; exh. cat. Lausanne 1986, n. 22; exh. cat. Bassano 1988, n. 236b (as 'Piazza del Campidoglio'); exh. cat. Lausanne 1998b, p. 62

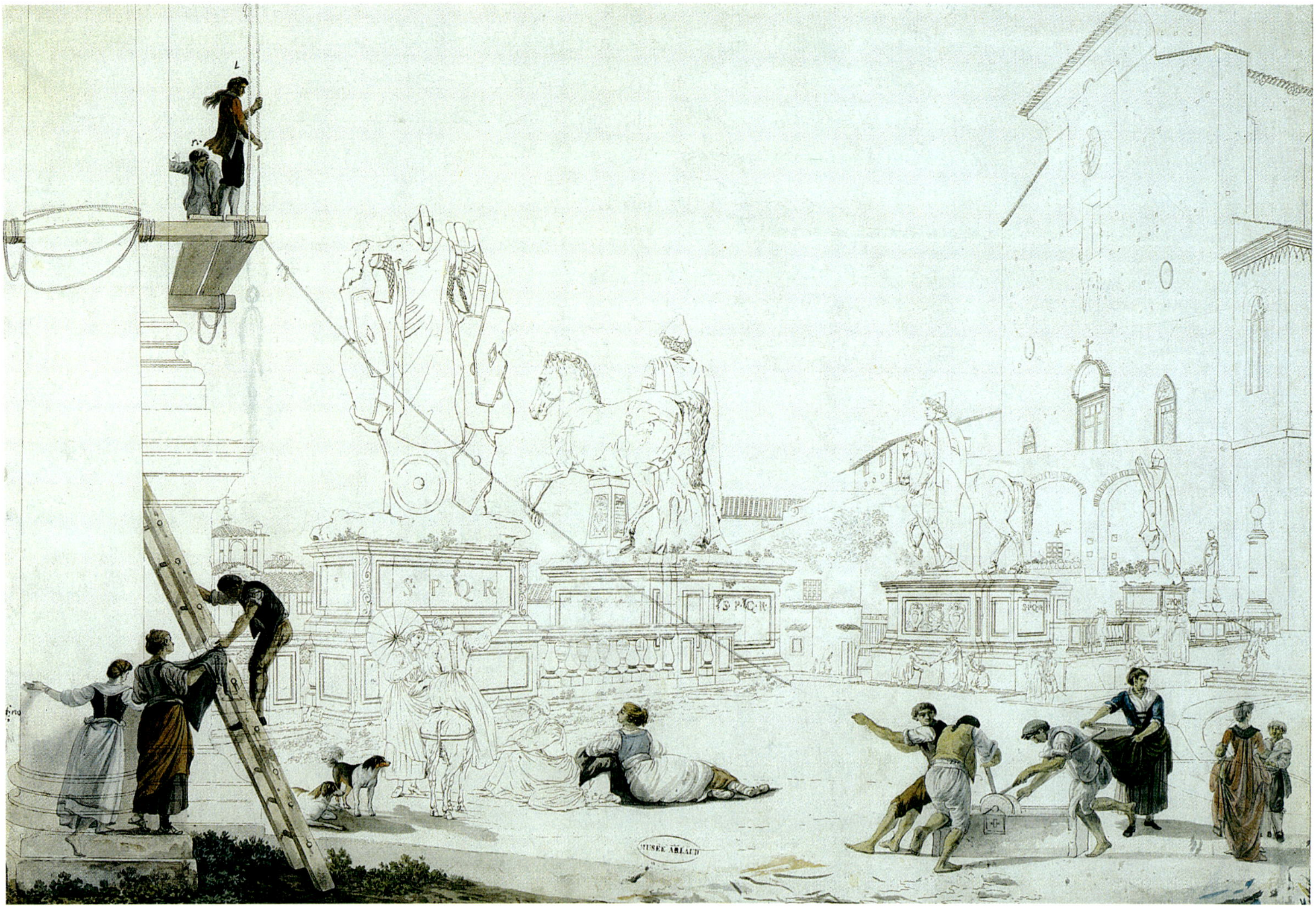

6. VIEW WITHIN THE CAPITOL, c.1780

Pen and wash of India ink and sepia on paper, 52.8 x 73.7 cm
Lausanne, Musée cantonal des Beaux-Arts
Inv. 874

Literature: Agassiz 1927, p. 37; exh. cat. Lausanne 1953, n. 9; exh. cat. Rome 1954, n. 8; exh. cat. Lausanne 1986, n. 21; exh. cat. Bassano 1988, n. 236a (as 'Piazza del Campidoglio'); exh. cat. Lausanne 1995, p. 3 et 5; exh. cat. Lausanne 1998b, p. 63

There have been many artistic renderings of the Piazza del Campidoglio, but the angle chosen by Ducros is unusual. By leaving out the palazzos built to Michelangelo's plans and the famous equestrian statue of Marcus Aurelius, he instead gives us a view from behind of the statues of Castor and Pollux and the Trophies of Marius, which stand out against the sky, as well as the brick facade of Santa Maria d'Aracoeli (on the right).

Although Ducros does not show the monumental steps, their presence is cleverly suggested by the figures seen emerging onto the square between the Twins.

The backlighting effect, the elegance of the figures and the finesse of the details – everything comes together here to give this view a mysterious charm, due to its mixture of spontaneity and clever presentation.

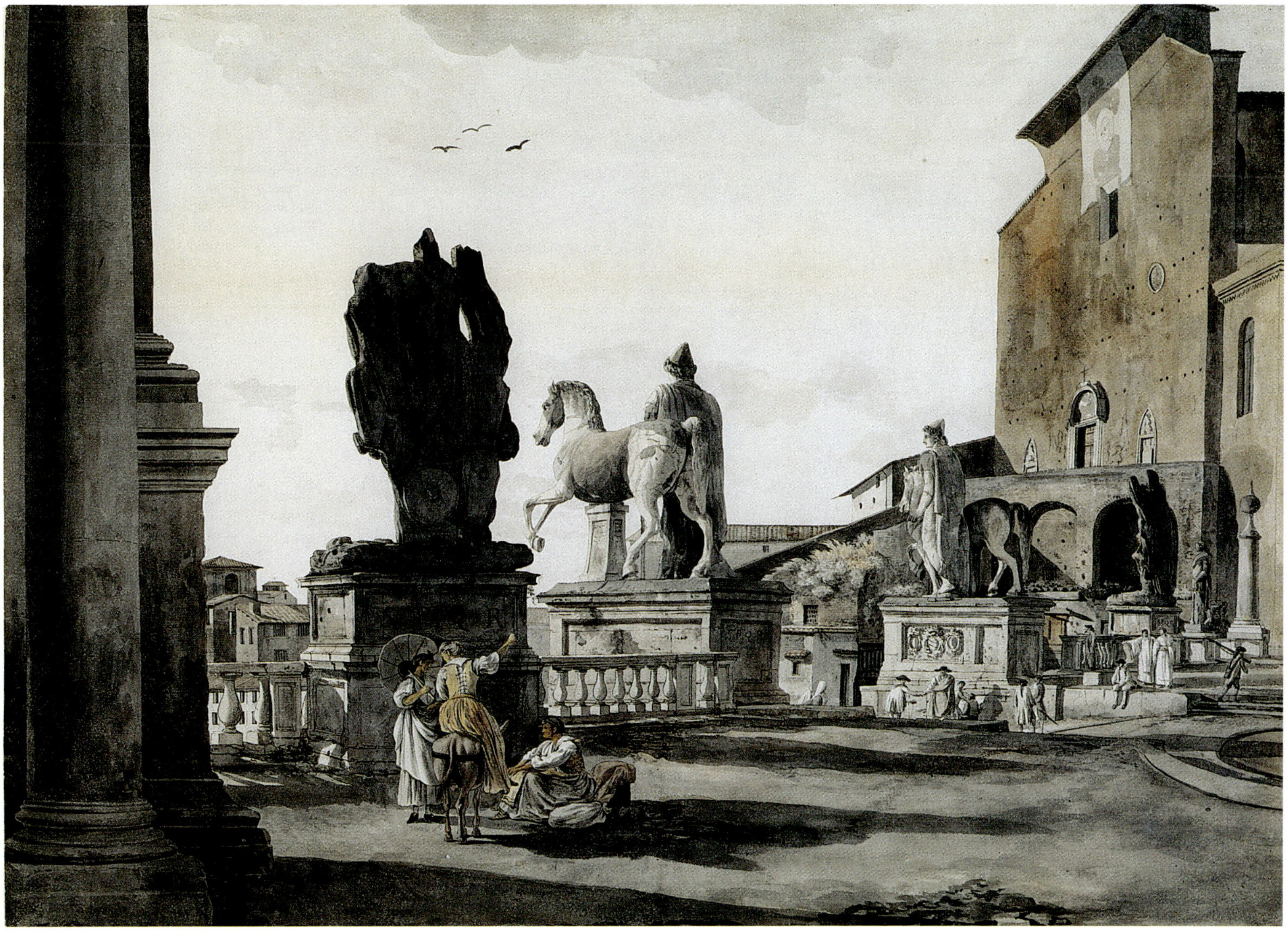

7. THE TEMPLE OF SATURN, c.1780

Pen and black ink, watercolour on paper,
53 x 74 cm
Lausanne, Musée cantonal des Beaux-Arts
Inv. 869

Literature: Agassiz 1927, p. 36; exh. cat. Lausanne 1953, n. 4 (as 'Temple of Concorde'); exh. cat. Rome 1954, n. 3; Chessex 1984 (1), p. 432 et note 19; Haskell, Chessex 1985, n. 21; exh. cat. Lausanne 1986, n. 16; exh. cat. Rome 1987, n.12; exh. cat. Bassano 1988, n. 234; exh. cat. Lausanne 1998b, p. 59

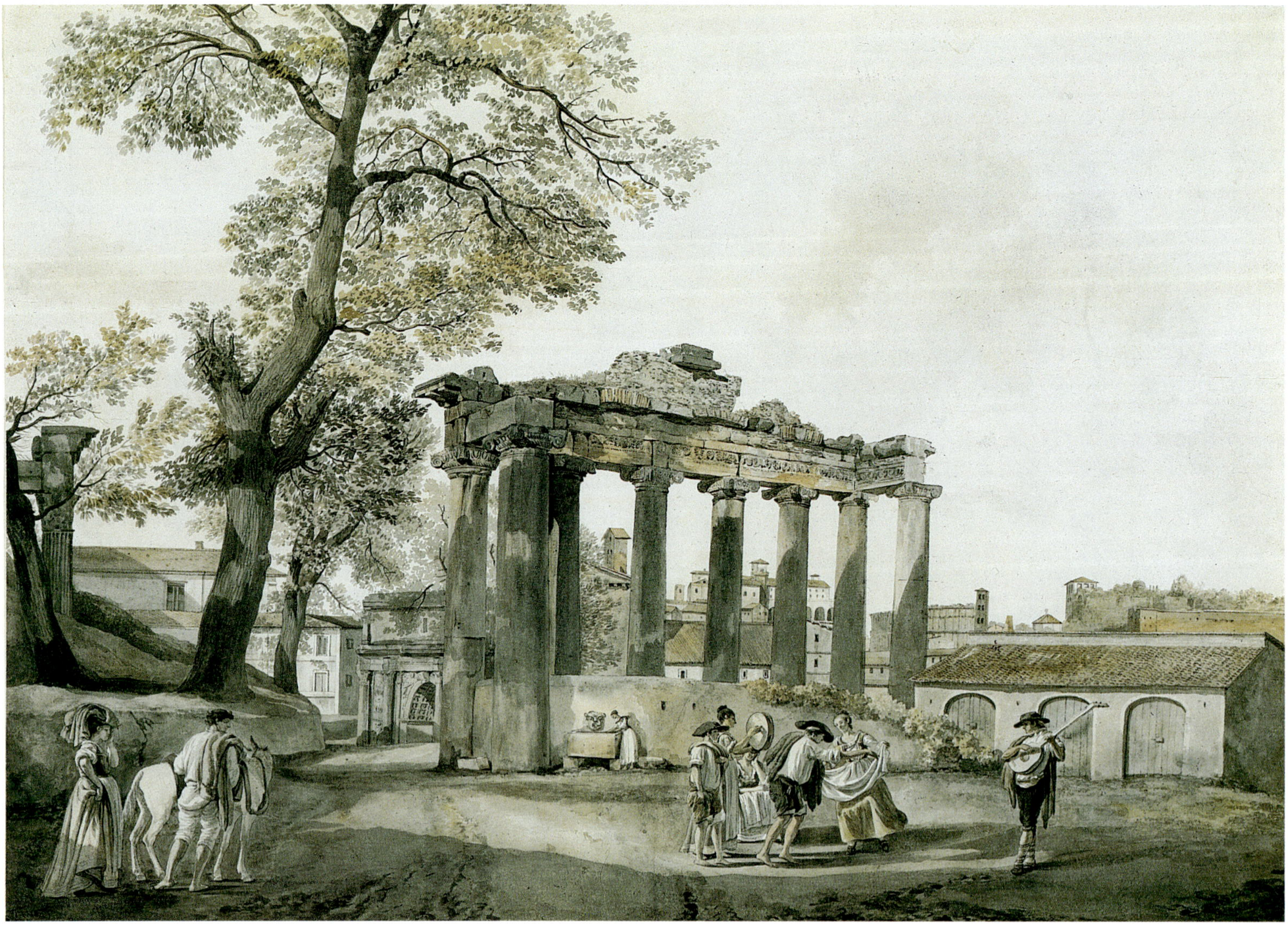

8. THE GARDENS OF THE VILLA FARNESE, c.1782

Pen and India ink wash, watercolour on J Honig & Zoonen paper, 74 x 53 cm
Lausanne, Musée cantonal des Beaux-Arts
Inv. 871

Literature: Agassiz 1927, p. 35; exh. cat. Lausanne 1953, n. 6; exh. cat. Rome 1954, n. 5; Haskell, Chessex 1985, n. 34; exh. cat. Lausanne 1986, n. 31; exh. cat. Rome 1987, n. 23; exh. cat. Bassano 1988, n. 252; exh. cat. Lausanne 1998b, p. 65

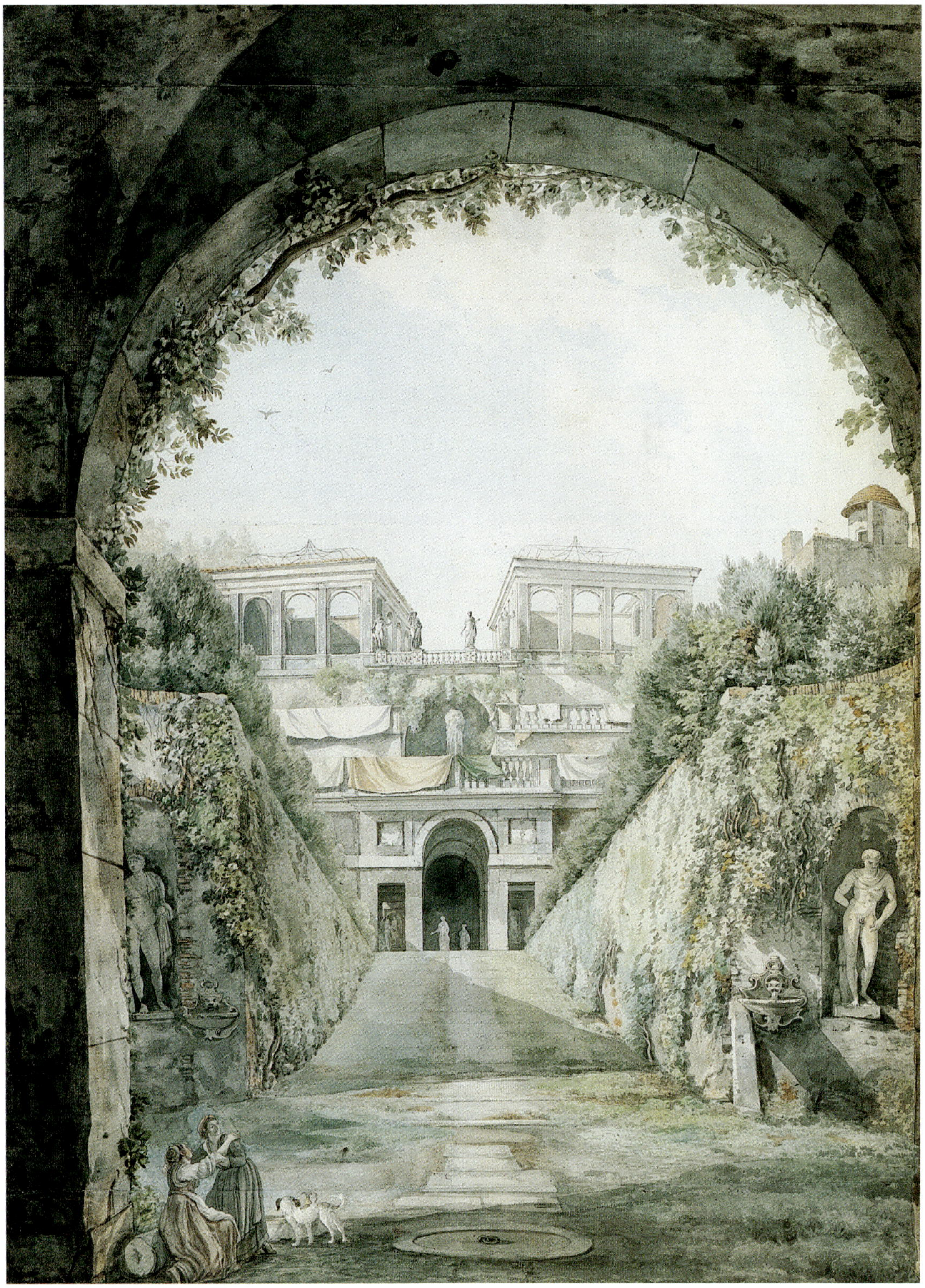

9. PALAZZINA BORGHESE, c.1782

Pen and India ink wash, watercolour,
J Honig & Zoonen paper, 53.2 x 73.8 cm
Lausanne, Musée cantonal des Beaux-Arts
Inv. 881

Literature: Agassiz 1927, p. 35; Agassiz 1928, ill. 5; exh. cat. Lausanne 1953, n. 14; exh. cat. Rome 1954, n. 13; Chessex 1982, p. 56 et ill. 3 (who erroneously talks of an 'engraving with watercolour'); Haskell, Chessex 1985, n. 29; exh. cat. London 1985, n. 14; exh. cat. Lausanne 1986, n. 36; exh. cat. Rome 1987, n. 28; exh. cat. Bassano 1988, n. 257; exh. cat. Lausanne 1998b, p. 67

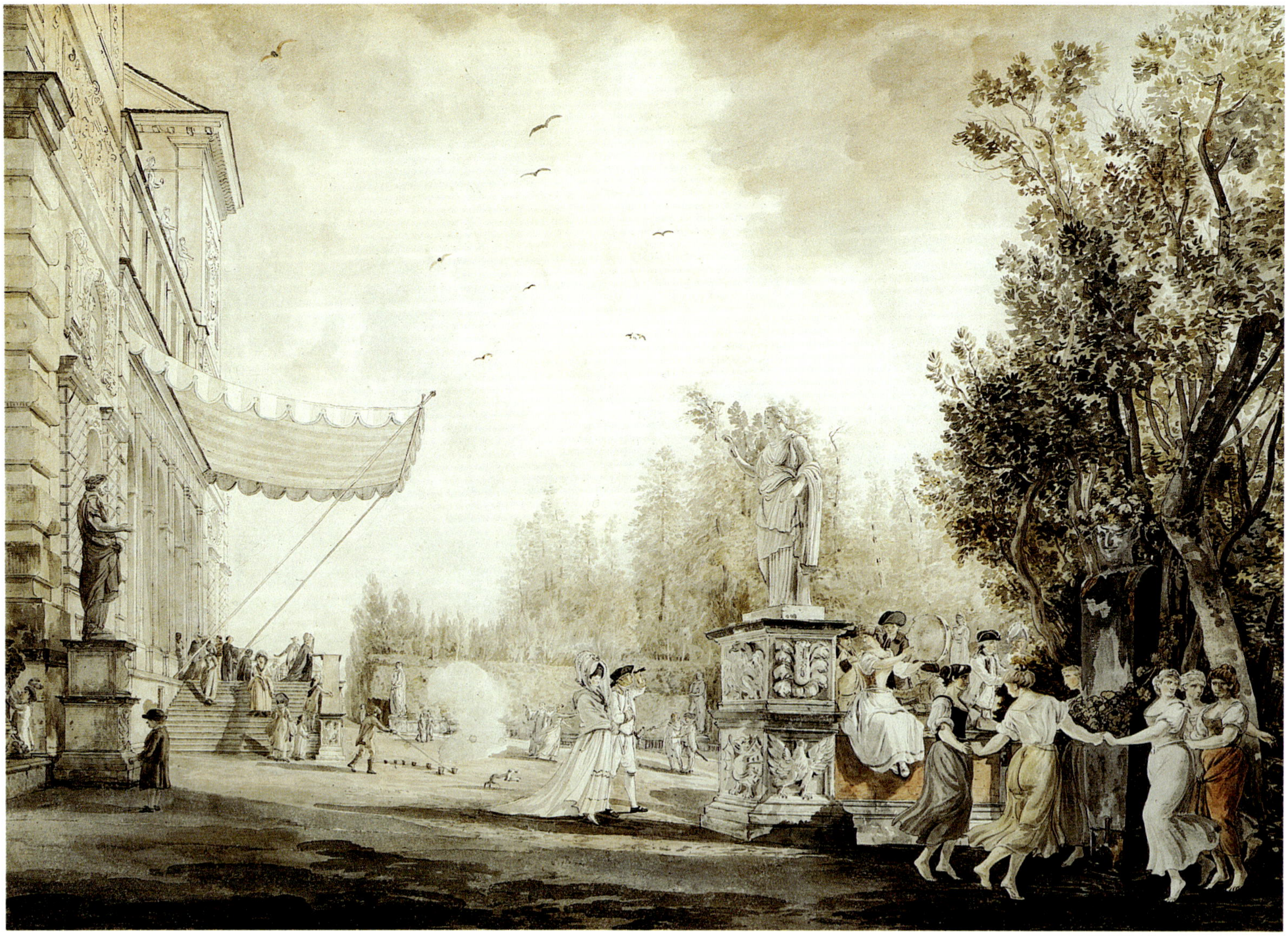

10. THE GARDENS OF THE VILLA CORSINI, c.1780

Louis Ducros with the assistance of Giovanni Volpato

Outline etching, grey wash, watercolour, heightened with gouache, J Honig & Zoonen paper, 52.9 x 74.3 cm (sheet size); 51.8 x 74.2 cm (image size)
Lausanne, Musée cantonal des Beaux-Arts
Inv. 880

Literature: exh. cat. Lausanne 1953, n. 13 (as 'The Vatican viewed from a Garden'); exh. cat. Rome 1954, n. 12 (*ibid.*) ; Haskell, Chessex 1985, n. II ; exh. cat. London 1985, n. 13 ; exh. cat. Lausanne 1986, n. 38 ; exh. cat. Rome 1987, n. 30 ; exh. cat. Bassano 1988, n. 259

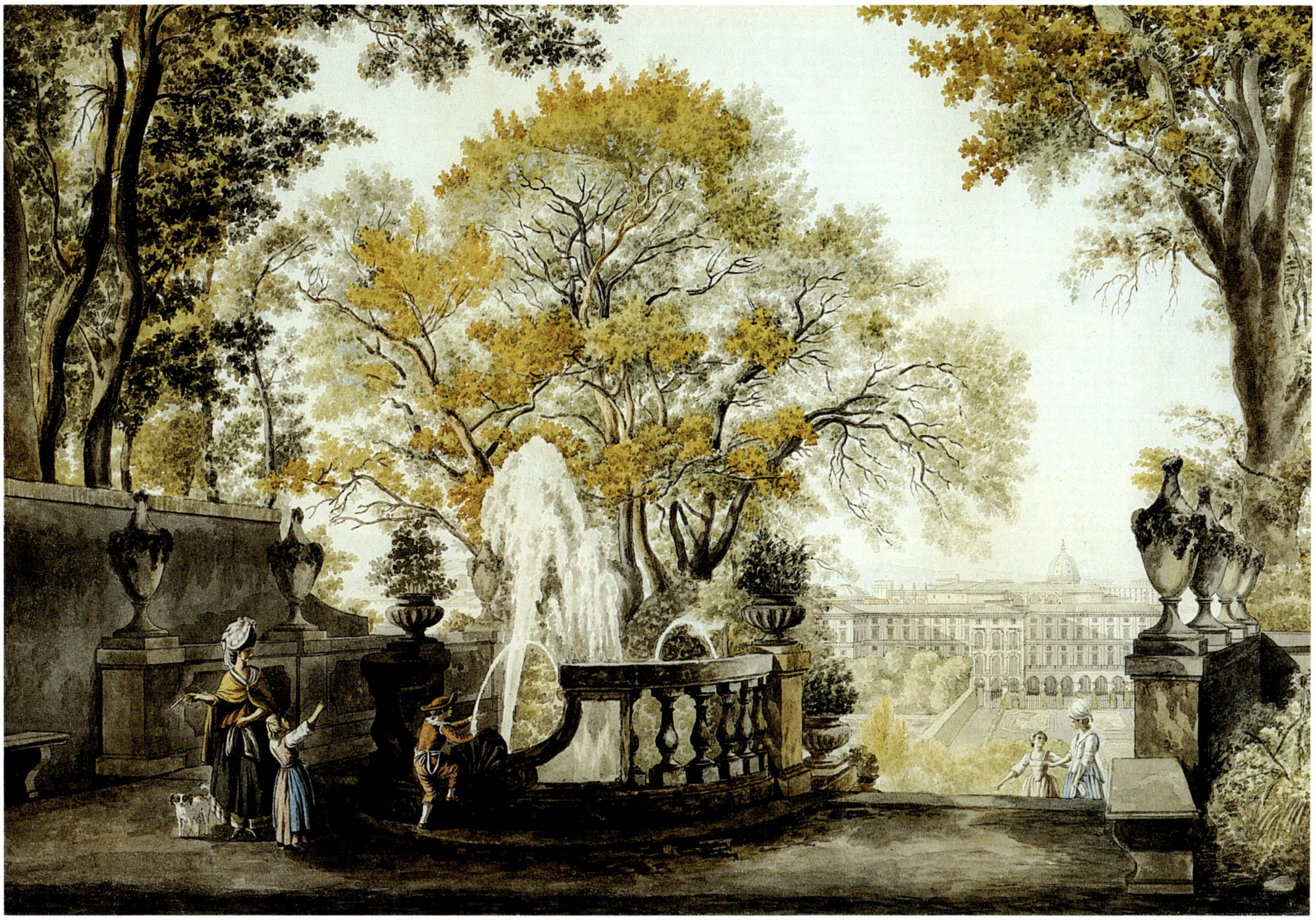

11. THE BASILICA OF MAXENTIUS, c.1780

Pen and brown ink, watercolour, heighted with gouache, D & C Blauw papers laid down on canvas, 80 x 112 cm
Lausanne, Musée cantonal des Beaux-Arts
Inv. 846

Literature: Agassiz 1927, p. 40; Chessex 1984 (2), p. 72; Haskell, Chessex 1985, n. 4; exh. cat. London 1985, n. 5; exh. cat. Lausanne 1986, n. 8; exh. cat. Rome 1987, n. 7; exh. cat. Bassano 1988, n. 231; exh. cat. Lausanne 1998b, p. 55

The Basilica of Saint Maxentius was one of the most greatly admired and oft-painted monuments in the Imperial Forum. For his view of what, since the fifteenth century (and until the archaeological work done by Fea and Nibby in the early nineteenth century), had been called the Temple of Peace, Ducros followed Piranesi's example and took a broad, diagonal perspective. In the background of the composition, we can make out the top of the Colosseum. In Ducros's day, the lower part of the basilica had yet to be revealed and the Forum was used by shepherds with their flocks. Indeed, this contrast between the past splendours evoked by the ruins and the presence of the peasants is a recurrent theme, almost a leitmotiv, in the accounts of eighteenth-century travellers.

By the clever use of broad shadows in the vaults of the basilica and undersized figures, Ducros achieves an effect of monumentality and magnitude that is heightened by the painting's imposing size. In 1780 Ducros and Volpato made a smaller-scale engraving of this work, a common practice of theirs in order to make the work more widely available to travellers in Rome.

The composition of the engraving is identical to that of the larger, more ample watercolour. The style of the unfinished figures suggests that this was a drawing from the 1780s that Ducros reworked at a much later date.

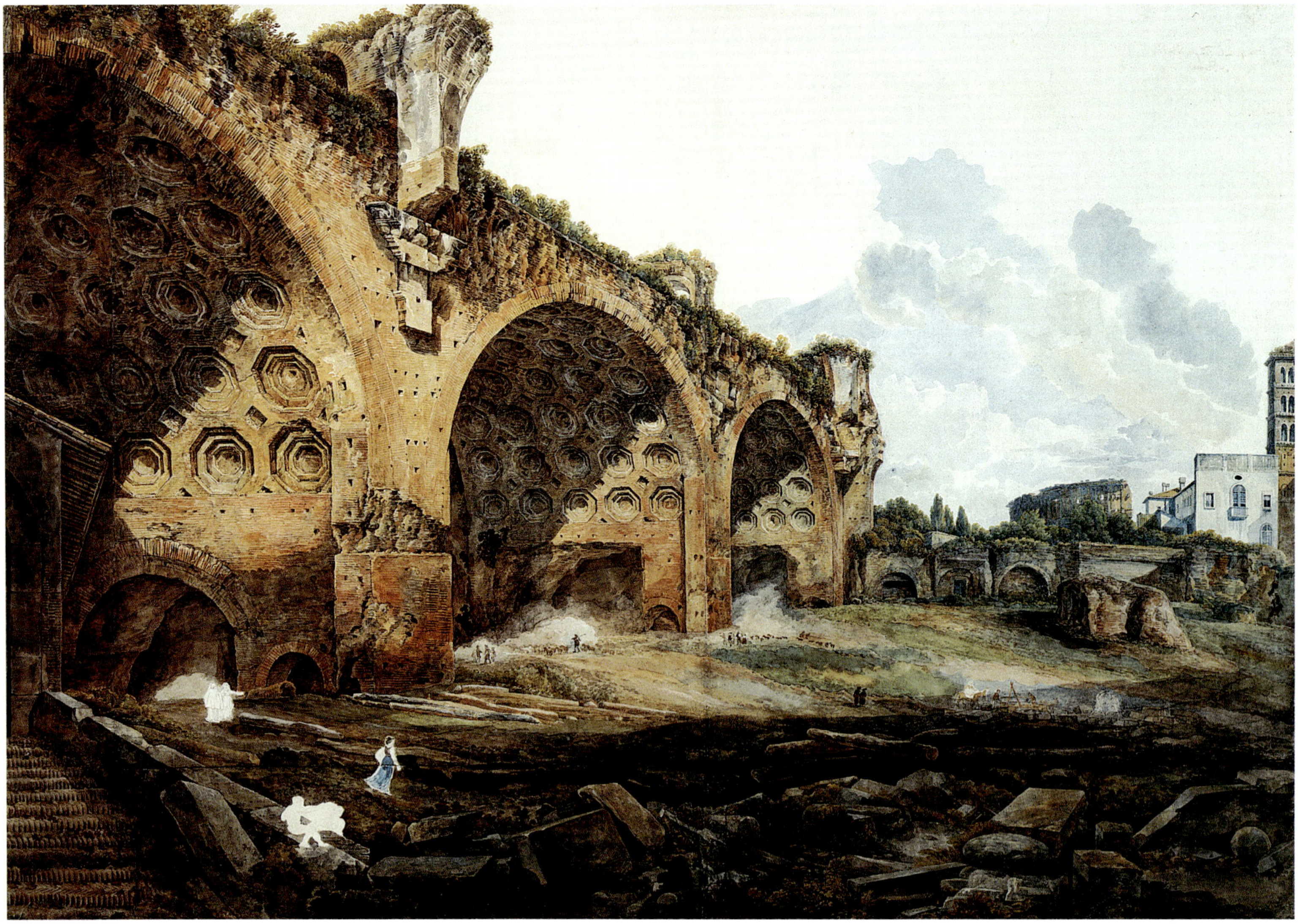

12. THE ARCH OF TITUS, 1782–1787

Pen and India ink, watercolour, heightened with gouache, D & C Blauw papers laid down on canvas, 103 x 67 cm
Lausanne, Musée cantonal des Beaux-Arts
Inv. 816

Literature: Chessex 1984 (2), p. 74; Haskell, Chessex 1985, n. 6; exh. cat. London 1985, n. 1; exh. cat. Lausanne 1986, n. 1; exh. cat. Rome 1987, n. 1; Cusatelli 1987, p. 239; exh. cat. Lausanne 1994, p. 11; exh. cat. Lausanne 1998a, p. 36; exh. cat. Lausanne 1998b, p. 49

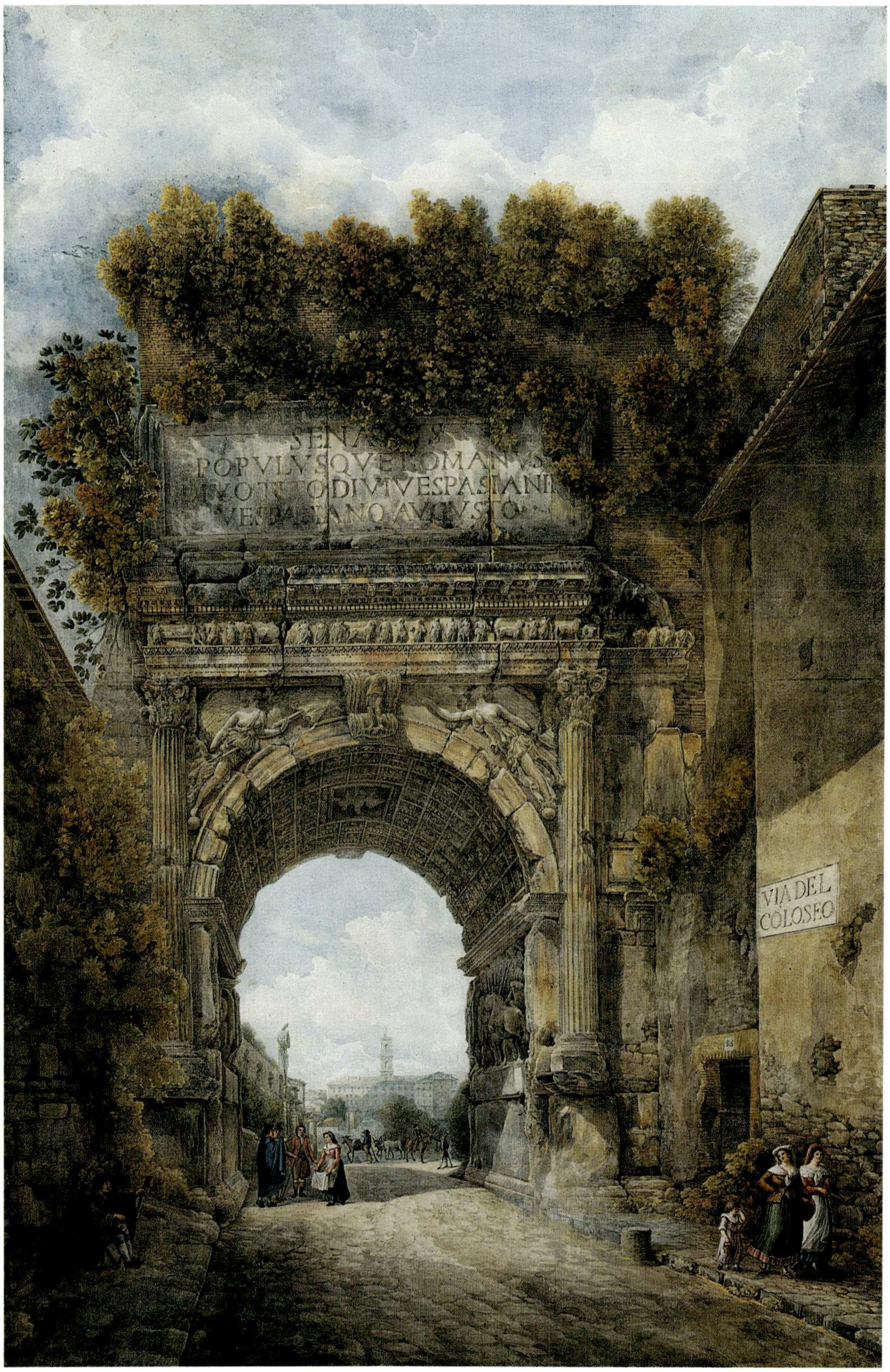

13. VIEW OF THE COLOSSEUM, c.1785

Pen and brown ink, watercolour, heightened with gouache, papers laid down on canvas, 78.7 x 116.7 cm
Lausanne, Musée cantonal des Beaux-Arts
Inv. 823

Literature: exh. cat. Lausanne 1953, n. 3; exh. cat. Rome 1954, n. 2; Chessex 1984 (1), p. 434; Haskell, Chessex 1985, n. 2; exh. cat. London 1985, n. 3; exh. cat. Lausanne 1986, n. 3; exh. cat. Rome 1987, n. 3; exh. cat. Lausanne 1998b, p. 51

Known since the Middle Ages as the Colosseum, the Amphitheatre of Flavius has been admired by travellers for centuries. A symbol of Roman grandeur surviving the ravages of history (from the Barbarians to the Roman builders who plundered its marble for their public edifices), it was also associated with the early days of Christianity because of the many martyrs who died there.

Following in the tradition of Giovanni Battista Piranesi and the French artists working in Rome in the mid-eighteenth century, Ducros sought to convey this grandeur by choosing a very low, wide-angled perspective on the site. Its monumentality is further heightened by the inclusion of below-scale figures, who are dwarfed by the antique ruins. Using the same technique, the artist also scales down the vestiges of the Domus Aurea in the background to the left, echoing the way Piranesi placed a tiny Arch of Constantine to the right of a huge Coliseum in his *Vedute di Roma*.

Executed in the 1780s, this work was painted on several separate sheets of paper which were stuck together to produce an unusually large format for watercolour. The papers were then backed with canvas, itself mounted on a stretcher and framed and glazed. Ducros used this process for all his large watercolours so that they could compete with works in oils. These were some of the first experiments with this method, which Turner and other English artists began to use systematically in around 1800.

This monumental view of the northern side of the Coliseum is also interesting as a document, for it shows the tricks used by Ducros to accentuate the perspective. He thus heightened the effect of grandeur due to his viewpoint by adding the left part of the structure, which he carefully cut out and stuck onto the sheet. Greenery is used to camouflage the joins of the sheets of paper. This collage technique is by no means uncommon in Ducros's work; he used it to give certain features of his landscapes an almost literal relief. To the same end, he often used to cover the dark areas in the foreground of his compositions with a varnish in order to contrast them with the cold, matt tones of the background.

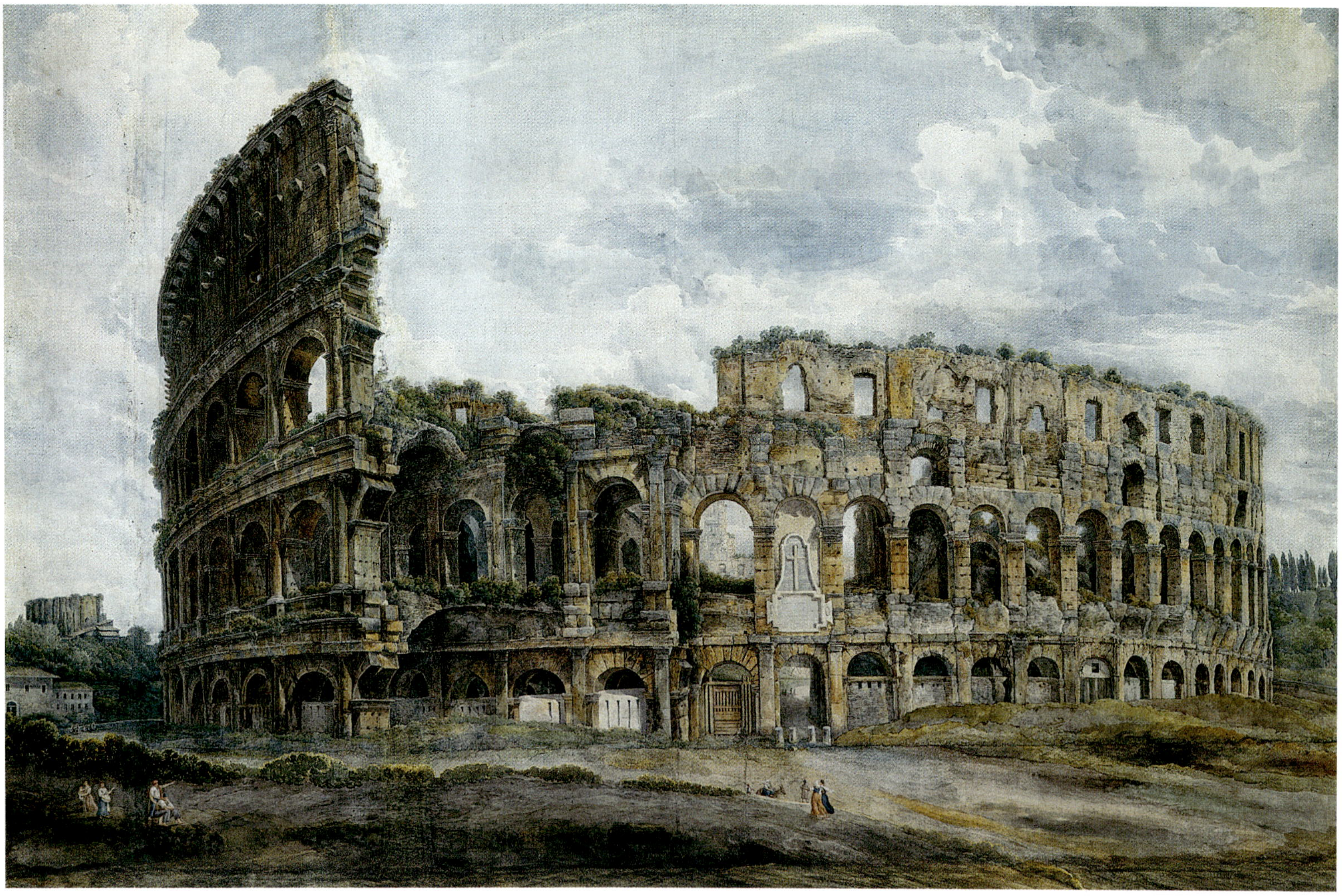

14. THE ARCH OF CONSTANTINE, 1785–1793

Pen and India ink, watercolour, heightened with gouache and oil, D & C Blauw paper laid down on canvas, 74.8 x 107.5 cm
Lausanne, Musée cantonal des Beaux-Arts
Inv. 817

Literature: S. Wagner, 'Kunstausstellung' in *Neus Allerley über Kunst...*, 14. Stück, Bern 1810, p. 53; exh. cat. Berne 1810, n. 37; Agassiz 1927, p. 37; exh. cat. Lausanne 1953, n. 2; Haskell, Chessex 1985, n. 5; exh. cat. London 1985, n. 2; exh. cat. Lausanne 1986, n. 2; exh. cat. Rome 1987, n. 2; Cusatelli 1987, p. 240; exh. cat. Lausanne 1998b, p. 50

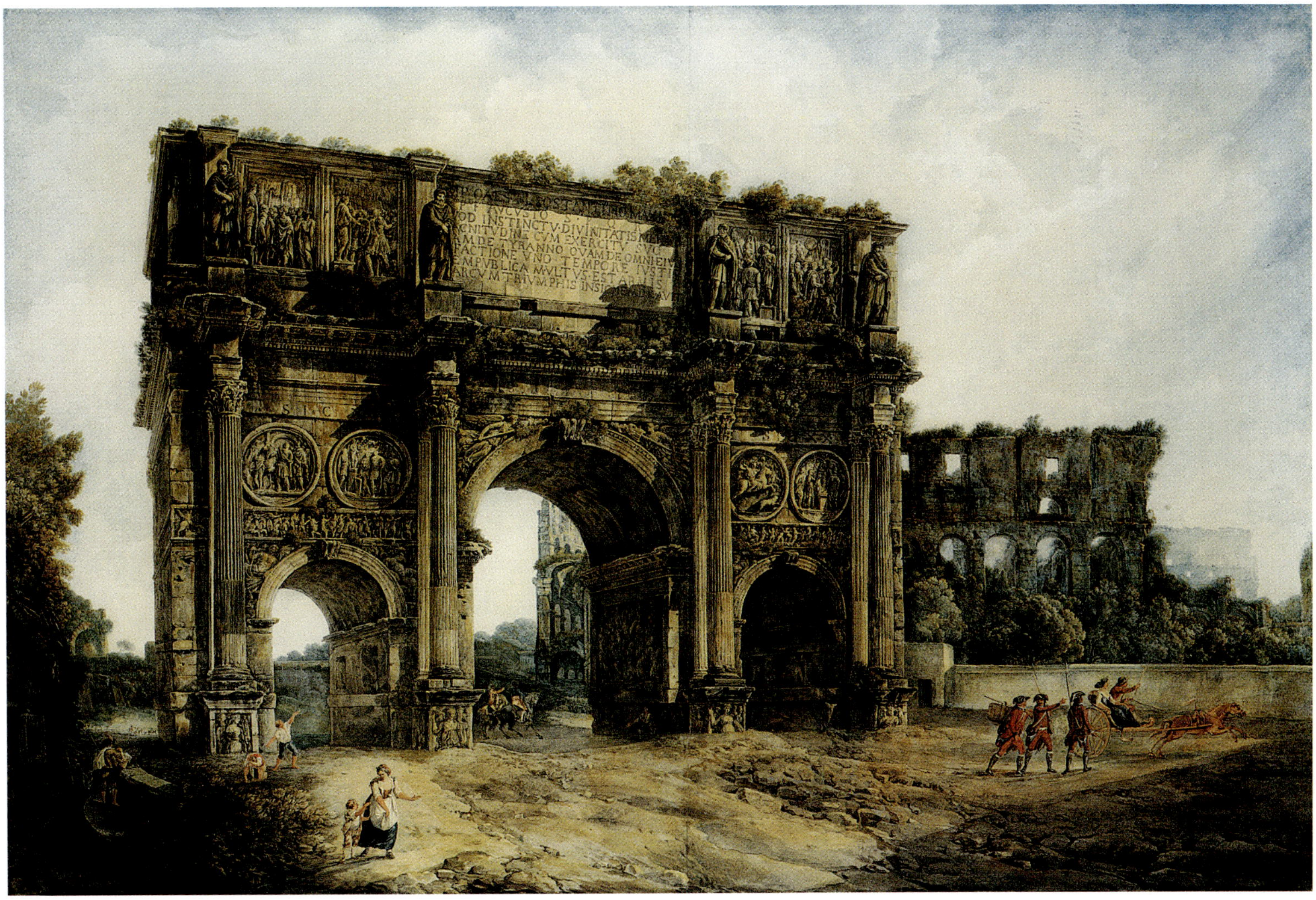

15. THE TEMPLE OF THE SIBYL, TIVOLI, c.1783

Pen and India ink, watercolour, D & C Blauw papers laid down on canvas, 75 x 111 cm
Lausanne, Musée cantonal des Beaux-Arts
Inv. 794

Literature: Agassiz 1927, p. 37; exh. cat. Lausanne 1953, n. 24; exh. cat. Rome 1954, n. 24; Haskell, Chessex 1985, n. 11; exh. cat. Lausanne 1986, n. 46; exh. cat. Rome 1987, n. 39; exh. cat. Lausanne 1998b, p. 71

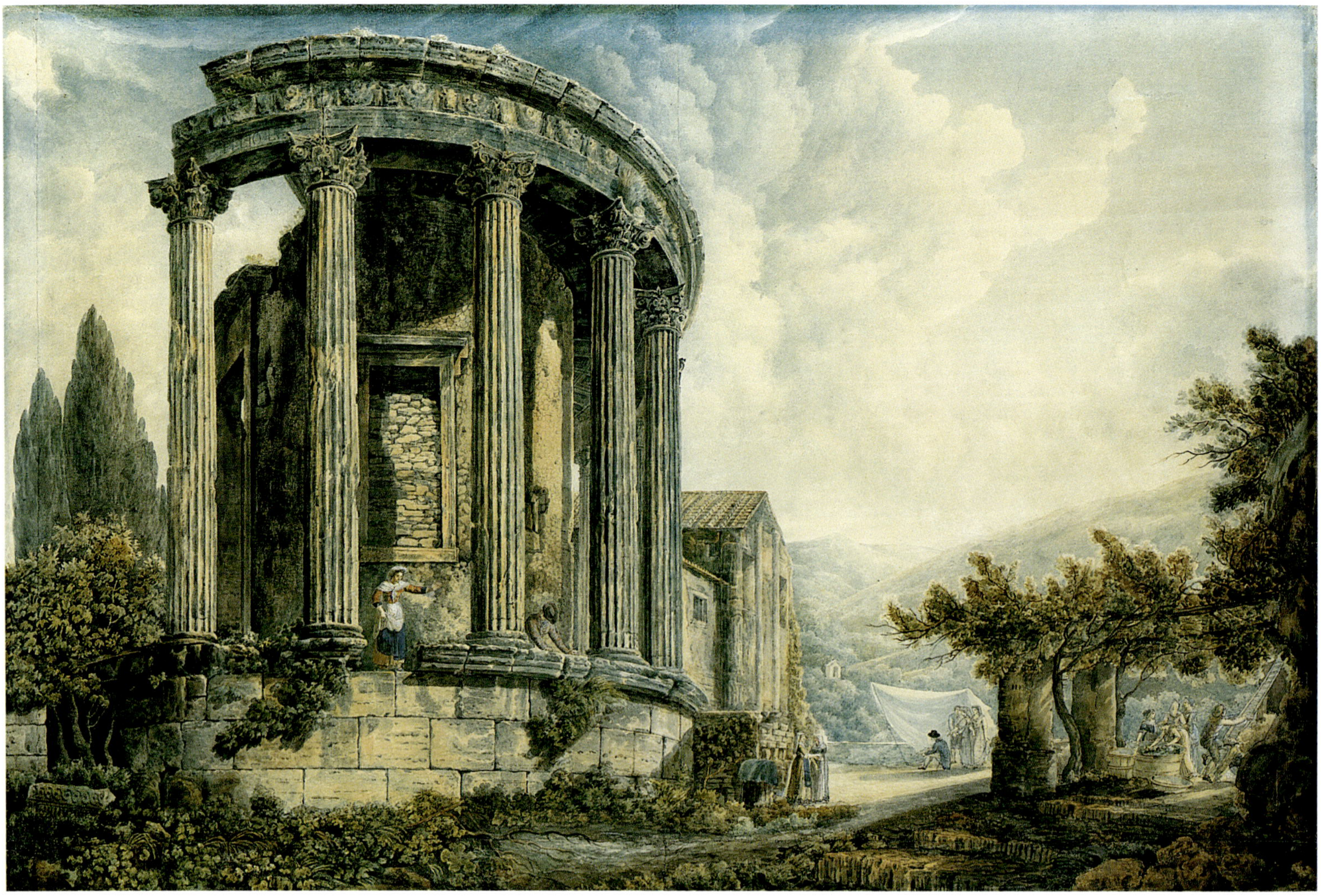

16. MONSIEUR DUCROS LOSES HIS HAT, 1784–1788

Giuseppe Mazzola (1748–1838)

Pen and India ink, watercolour on paper, 24.3 x 53.3 cm
Lausanne, Musée cantonal des Beaux-Arts
Inv. 894

Literature: exh. cat. Lausanne 1986, p. 121; exh. cat. Lausanne 2001, pp. 54–55

Like many other painters in Rome in the eighteenth century Ducros used assistants to draw figures in his landscapes and from 1784, there is evidence that Giuseppe Mazzola da Valduggia began to collaborate with him for this purpose.

Here, Mazzola is the author of a vivid scene, certainly an episode witnessed by him, in which Ducros is the innocent victim of a sudden change of weather.

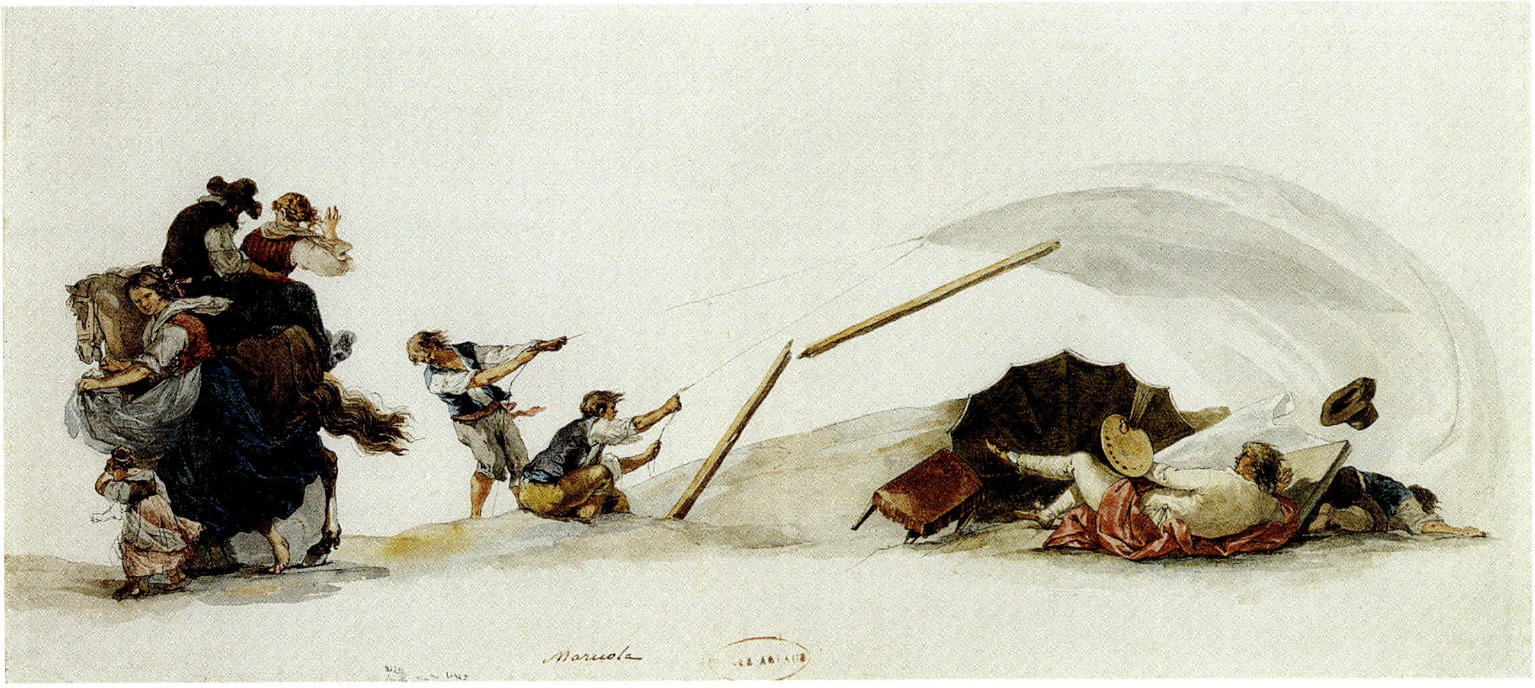

17. VIEW OF TIVOLI WITH THE TEMPLE OF THE SIBYL, c.1785

Watercolour, heightened with gouache and oil, D & C Blauw papers laid down on canvas, 66.7 x 102 cm
Lausanne, Musée cantonal des Beaux-Arts
Inv. 798

Literature exh. cat. Lausanne 1953, n. 25; Chessex 1984 (1), p. 435; Haskell, Chessex 1985, n. 10; exh. cat. London 1985, n. 18; exh. cat. Lausanne 1986, n. 48; exh. cat. Rome 1987, n. 41; Cusatelli 1987, p. 240; Chessex, exh. cat. Lausanne 1989, pp. 48–49; exh. cat. Lausanne 1998b, p. 73

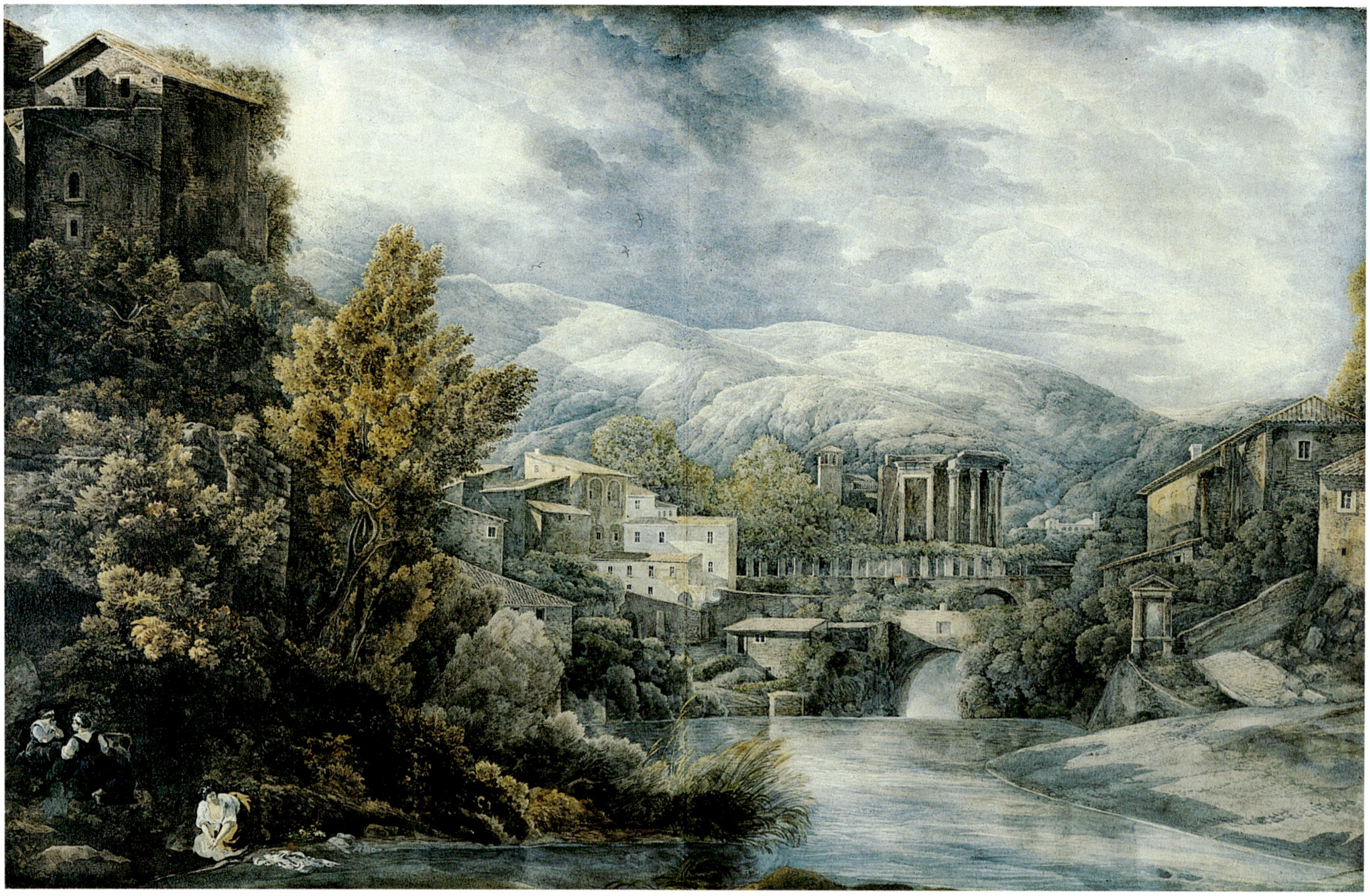

16. MONSIEUR DUCROS LOSES HIS HAT, 1784–1788

Giuseppe Mazzola (1748–1838)

Pen and India ink, watercolour on paper, 24.3 x 53.3 cm
Lausanne, Musée cantonal des Beaux-Arts
Inv. 894

Literature: exh. cat. Lausanne 1986, p. 121; exh. cat. Lausanne 2001, pp. 54–55

Like many other painters in Rome in the eighteenth century Ducros used assistants to draw figures in his landscapes and from 1784, there is evidence that Giuseppe Mazzola da Valduggia began to collaborate with him for this purpose.

Here, Mazzola is the author of a vivid scene, certainly an episode witnessed by him, in which Ducros is the innocent victim of a sudden change of weather.

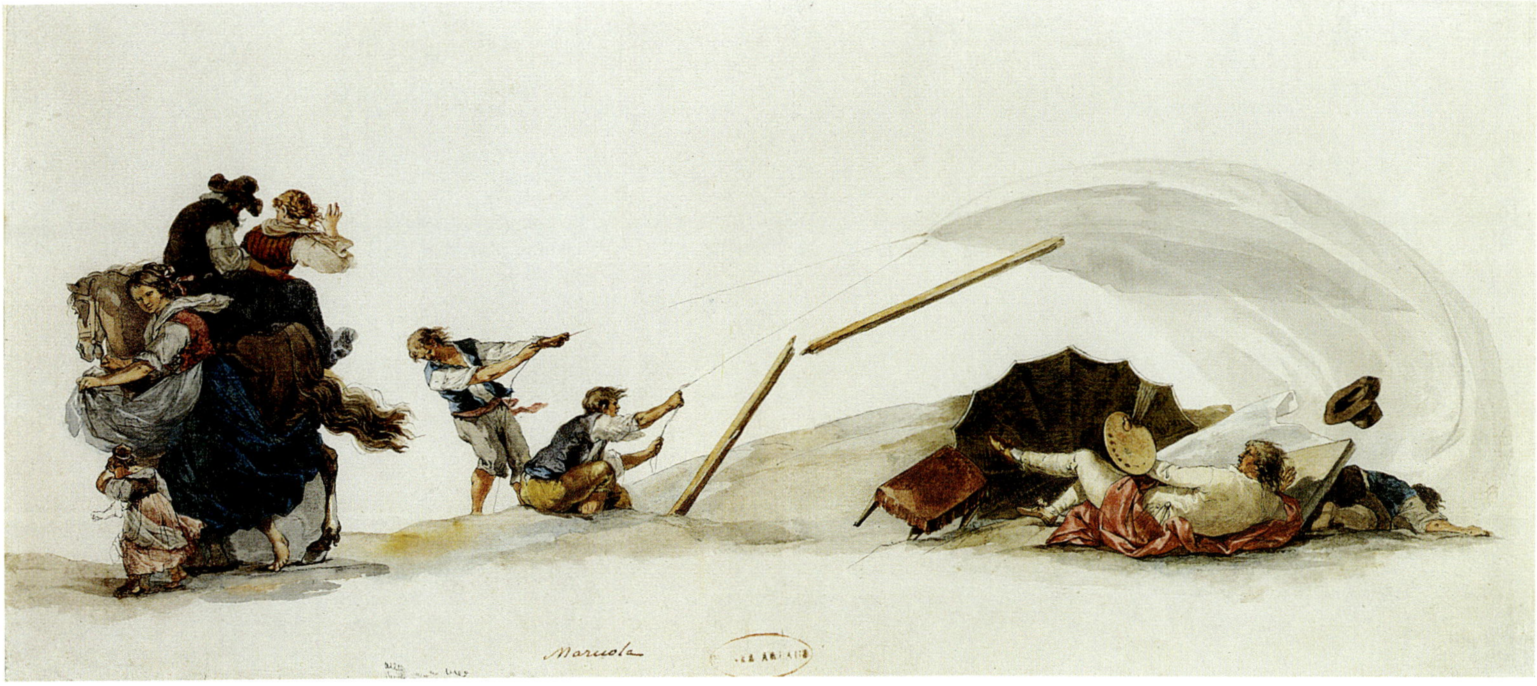

17. VIEW OF TIVOLI WITH THE TEMPLE OF THE SIBYL, c.1785

Watercolour, heightened with gouache and oil,
D & C Blauw papers laid down on canvas,
66.7 x 102 cm
Lausanne, Musée cantonal des Beaux-Arts
Inv. 798

Literature exh. cat. Lausanne 1953, n. 25; Chessex 1984 (1), p. 435; Haskell, Chessex 1985, n. 10; exh. cat. London 1985, n. 18; exh. cat. Lausanne 1986, n. 48; exh. cat. Rome 1987, n. 41; Cusatelli 1987, p. 240; Chessex, exh. cat. Lausanne 1989, pp. 48–49; exh. cat. Lausanne 1998b, p. 73

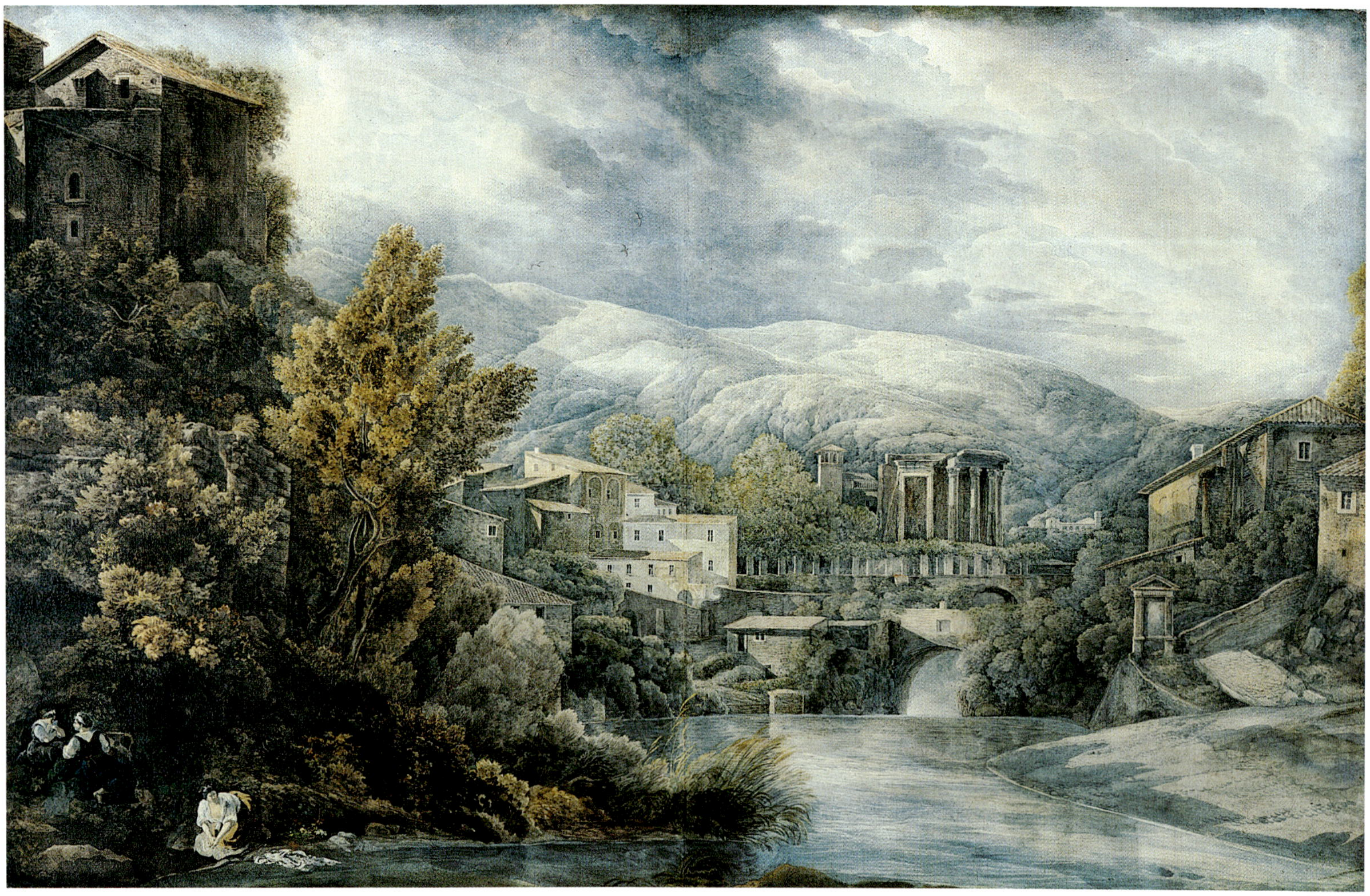

18. THE INTERIOR OF THE VILLA OF MAECENAS, TIVOLI, c.1785

Pen and India ink, watercolour, remains of varnish, D & C Blauw paper, 53.8 x 74.4 cm
Lausanne, Musée cantonal des Beaux-Arts
Inv. 907

Literature: Chessex 1984 (2), p. 75; Haskell, Chessex 1985, n. 23; exh. cat. London 1985, n. 21; exh. cat. Lausanne 1986, n. 51; exh. cat. Rome 1987, n. 44; Cusatelli 1987, p. 75

The ruins of the Santuario di Ercole Vincitore (1st century BC) were for many years thought to be vestiges of Maecenas's Villa, a monumental complex in Tivoli through which ran the ancient Via Tiburtina. Not much later than 1786, Ducros executed a large watercolour of Maecenas's Villa for Sir Richard Colt Hoare, which the latter described as an "underground view". As was his practice, Ducros kept a large tracing of the work and used it to make a smaller version, probably to make a print for colouring. Certainly, a view of this site appears in the list of *vedute* that he sold from his studio on the Strada della Croce, although no proof has ever been found.

Inspired by the *veduta* of the same site engraved by Piranesi a few years earlier, Ducros here makes his first attempt at painting grottoes, a theme that would become one of his specialities after 1793. Without adding white gouache, simply by using the reserve, he manages to light the interior of the monument by playing on the light flowing in laterally from outside and the inner light of the waterfall flowing through the ruin. The sweeping diagonal perspective and the contrasts of light and shadow give his watercolour a power and sublime quality that are exceptional for the period and look forward to the masterpieces of Turner.

Also noteworthy are the antique-style figures used to give life to the composition. These are very unusual in Ducros's work. Is this a profane version of Susanna at the bath, or a fantasy involving three mysterious characters? There is no evidence to help us decide, especially since the scene is so unusual for Ducros.

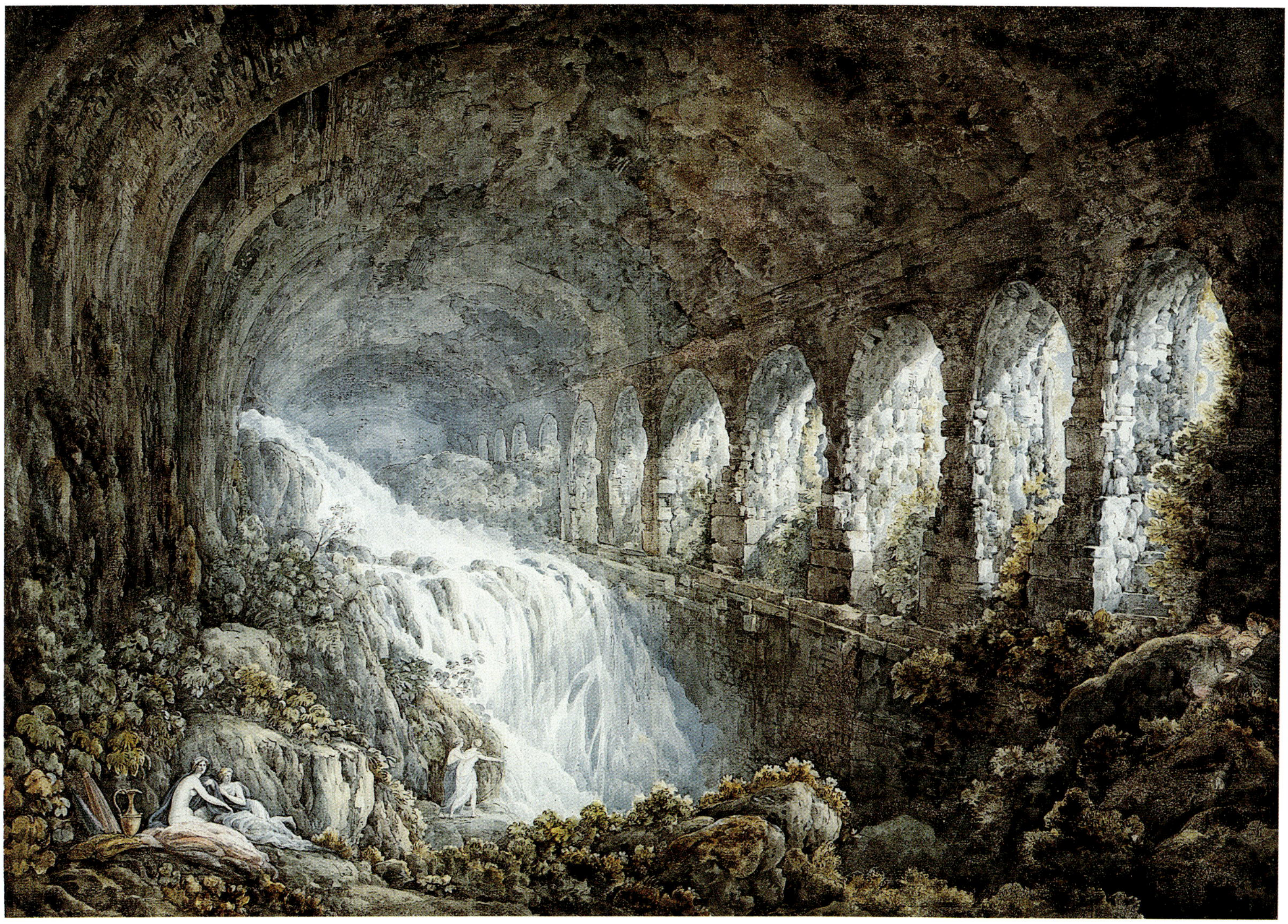

19. THE MARMORE WATERFALL, TERNI, c.1785

Pen and black ink, watercolour, heightened with gouache and oil, D & C Blauw papers laid down on canvas, 96.8 x 73.7 cm
Lausanne, Musée cantonal des Beaux-Arts
Inv. 814

Literature: Chessex 1982, p. 57; Chessex 1984 (1), p. 432; Haskell, Chessex 1985, n. 13; exh. cat. London 1985, n. 25; exh. cat. Lausanne 1986, n. 43; exh. cat. Rome 1987, n. 36; Brilli 1987, p. 288; Cusatelli 1987, p. 245; exh. cat. Lausanne 1998b, p. 81

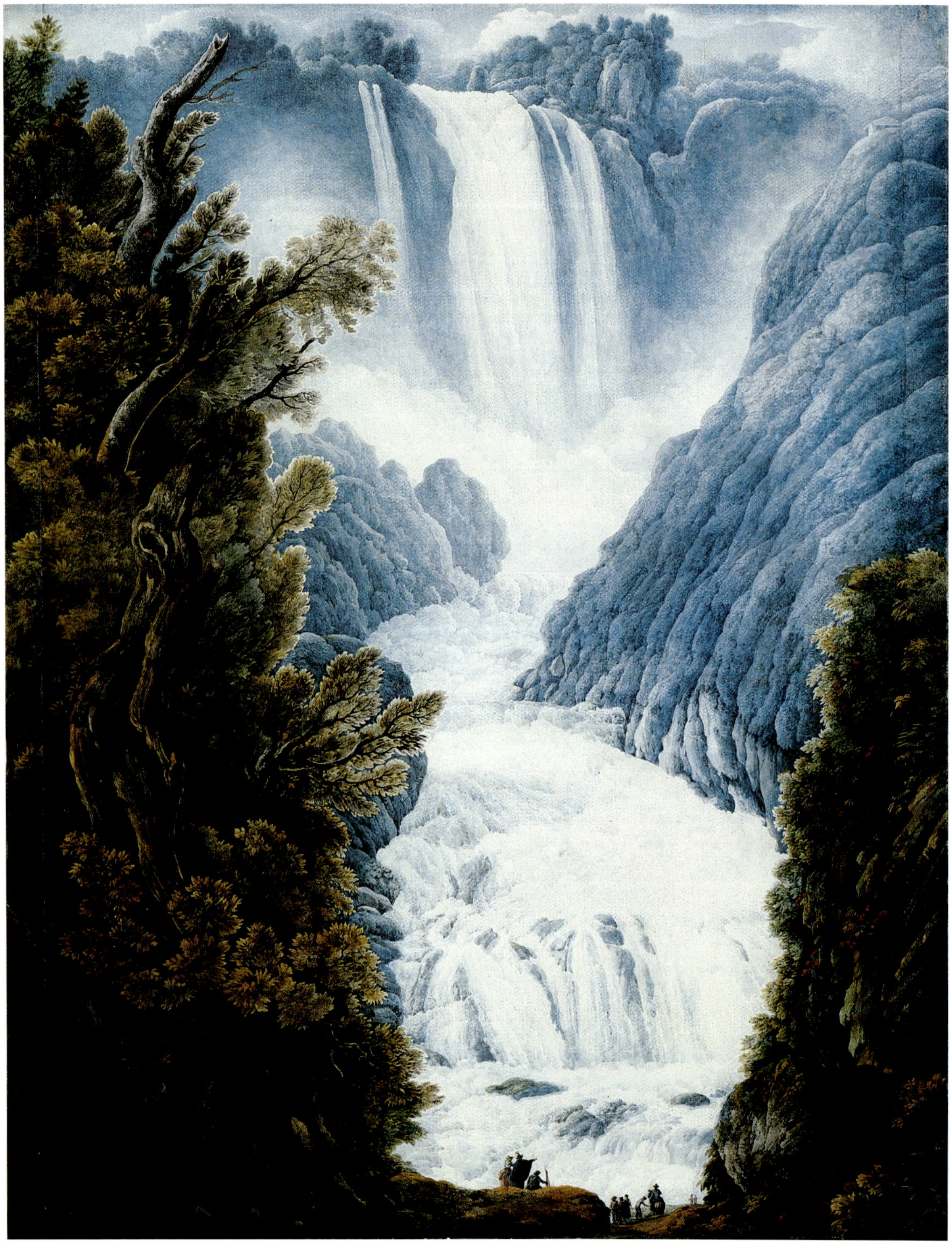

20. THE TEMPLE OF HERCULES, TIVOLI, c.1785

Watercolour, the figures heightened in gouache, J Whatman papers laid down on canvas, 76.5 x 111.5 cm
Lausanne, Musée cantonal des Beaux-Arts
Inv. 838

Literature: Agassiz 1927, p. 40; exh. cat. Lausanne 1953, n. 28; Chessex 1982, p. 40; Haskell, Chessex 1985, n. 9; exh. cat. London 1985, n. 22; exh. cat. Lausanne 1986, n. 50; exh. cat. Rome 1987, n. 43; exh. cat. Lausanne 1998b, p. 74

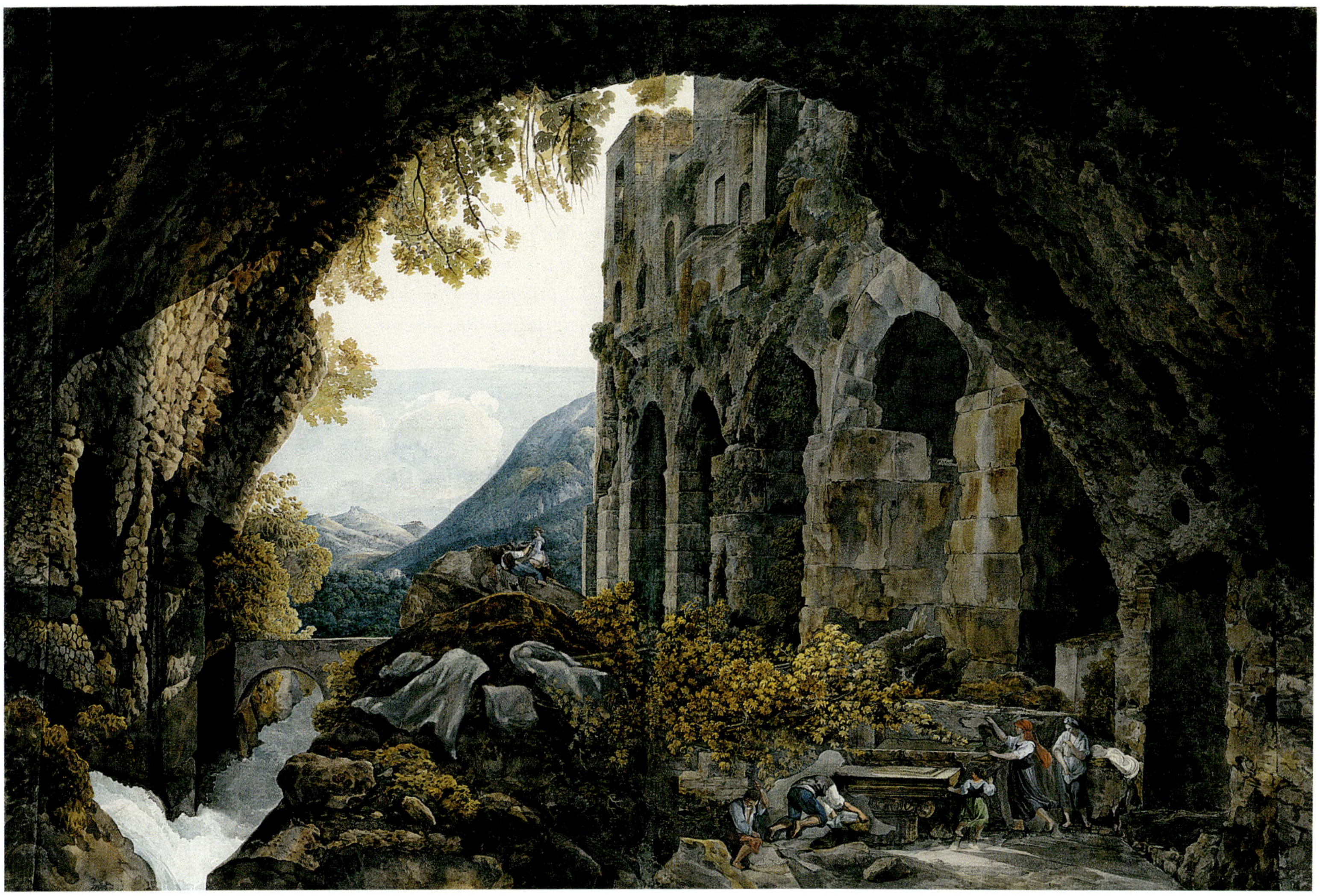

21. GROUP OF TREES, undated

Pen and ink, watercolour, paper laid down
on canvas, 66.6 x 103 cm
Lausanne, Musée cantonal des Beaux-Arts
Inv. 867

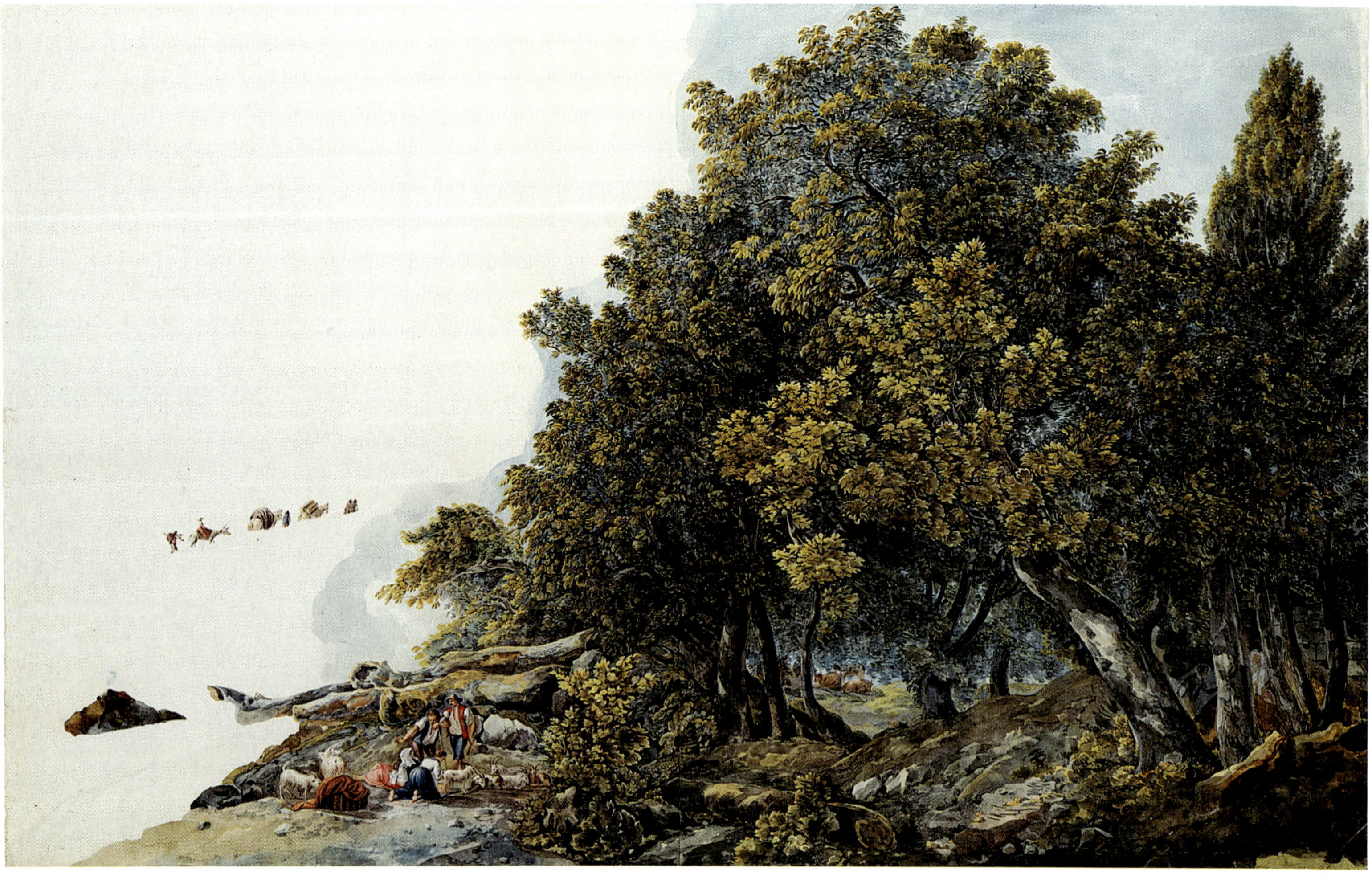

22. THE INTERIOR OF THE COLOSSEUM, c.1790

Pen and India ink, watercolour, heightened with gouache, D & C Blauw paper laid down on canvas, 75.7 x 114 cm
Lausanne, Musée cantonal des Beaux-Arts
Inv. 865

Literature: Agassiz 1927, p. 40; Agassiz 1928, ill. 8; Chessex 1984 (2), p. 73; Haskell, Chessex 1985, n. 3; exh. cat. London 1985, n. 4; exh. cat. Lausanne 1986, n. 4; exh. cat. Rome 1987, n. 4; Chessex, exh. cat. Lausanne 1989, pp. 46–47; Chessex 1992, p. 147; exh. cat. Lausanne 1998b, p. 53

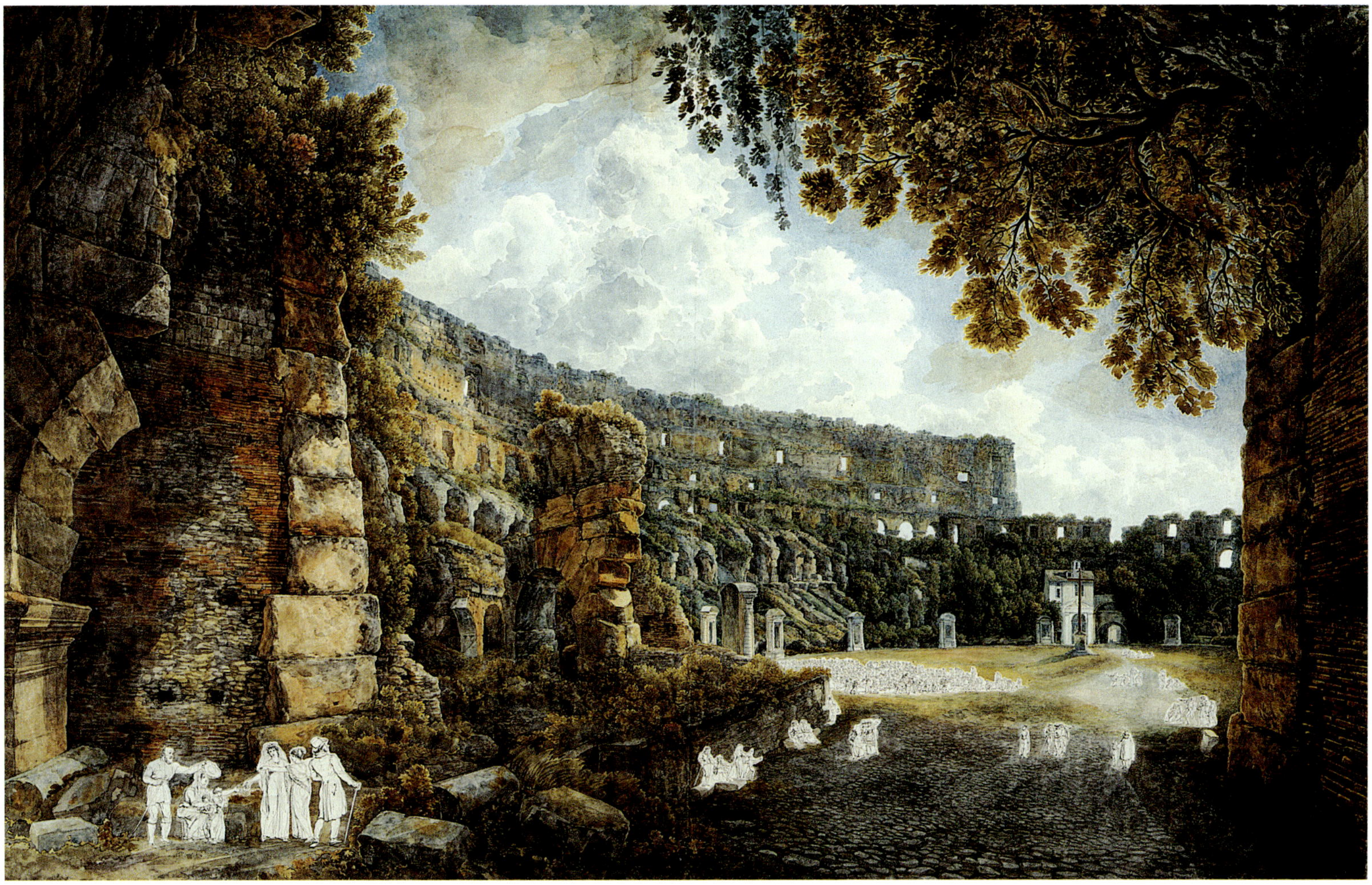

23. VIEW OF THE PONTE LUCANO AND OF THE PLAUTIAN FAMILY TOMB, c.1789

Watercolour, heightened with gouache, remains of varnish, D & C Blauw paper laid down on canvas, 65 x 100 cm
Lausanne, Musée cantonal des Beaux-Arts
Inv. 818

Literature: Agassiz 1927, p. 37; Haskell, Chessex 1985, n. 7; exh. cat. London 1985; exh. cat. Lausanne 1998b, p. 77

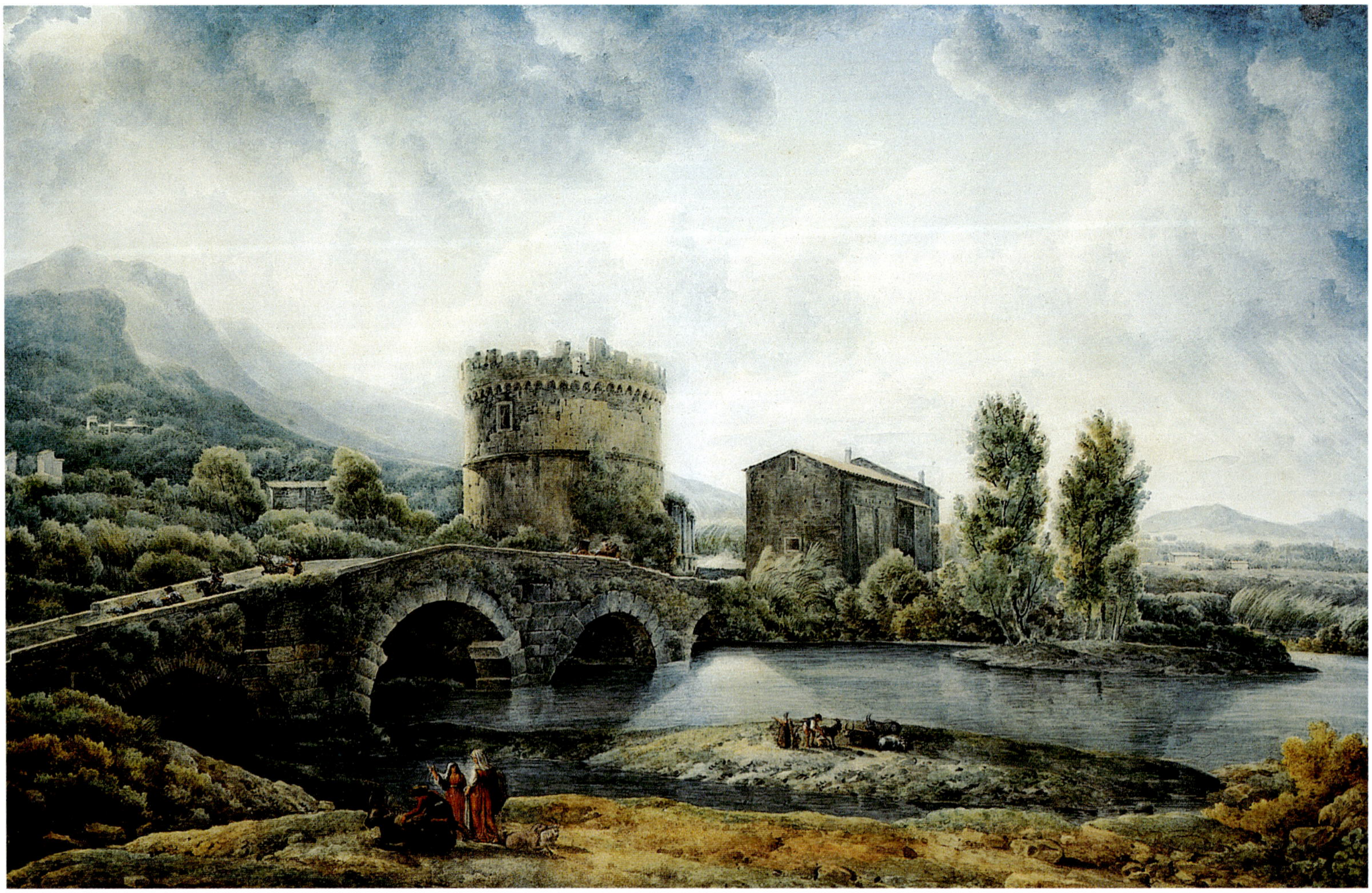

24. VIEW OF THE CORTILE OF BELVEDERE WITH THE LAOCOON IN THE MUSEO PIO CLEMENTINO, ROME, c.1789

Etching, watercoloured on paper,
52.9 x 74.3 cm
Lausanne, Musée cantonal des Beaux-Arts
Inv. 1999–009

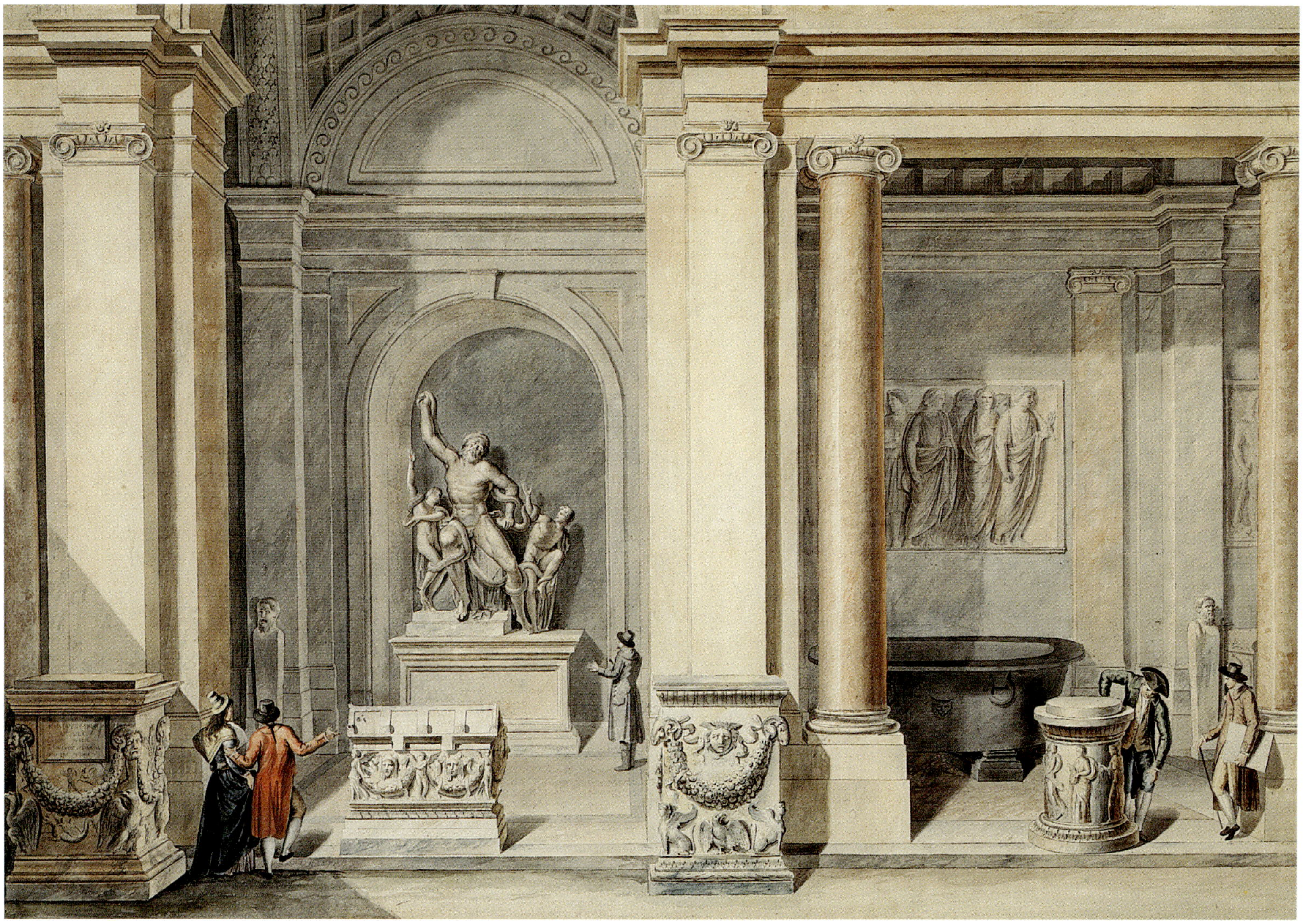

25. VIEW OF THE TEMPLES OF PAESTUM, c.1786–1788

Watercolour and grey wash, heightened with gouache and oil (the figures with pen and brown ink), D & C Blauw papers laid down on canvas, 76 x 112 cm
Lausanne, Musée cantonal des Beaux-Arts
Inv. 796

Literature: Agassiz 1927, p. 38; *Gazette des Beaux-Arts*, April 1982, fig. in *Chronique des arts*, p. 22; exh. cat. Lausanne 1953, n. 39; exh. cat. Rome 1954, n. 31; exh. cat. London 1985, n. 40

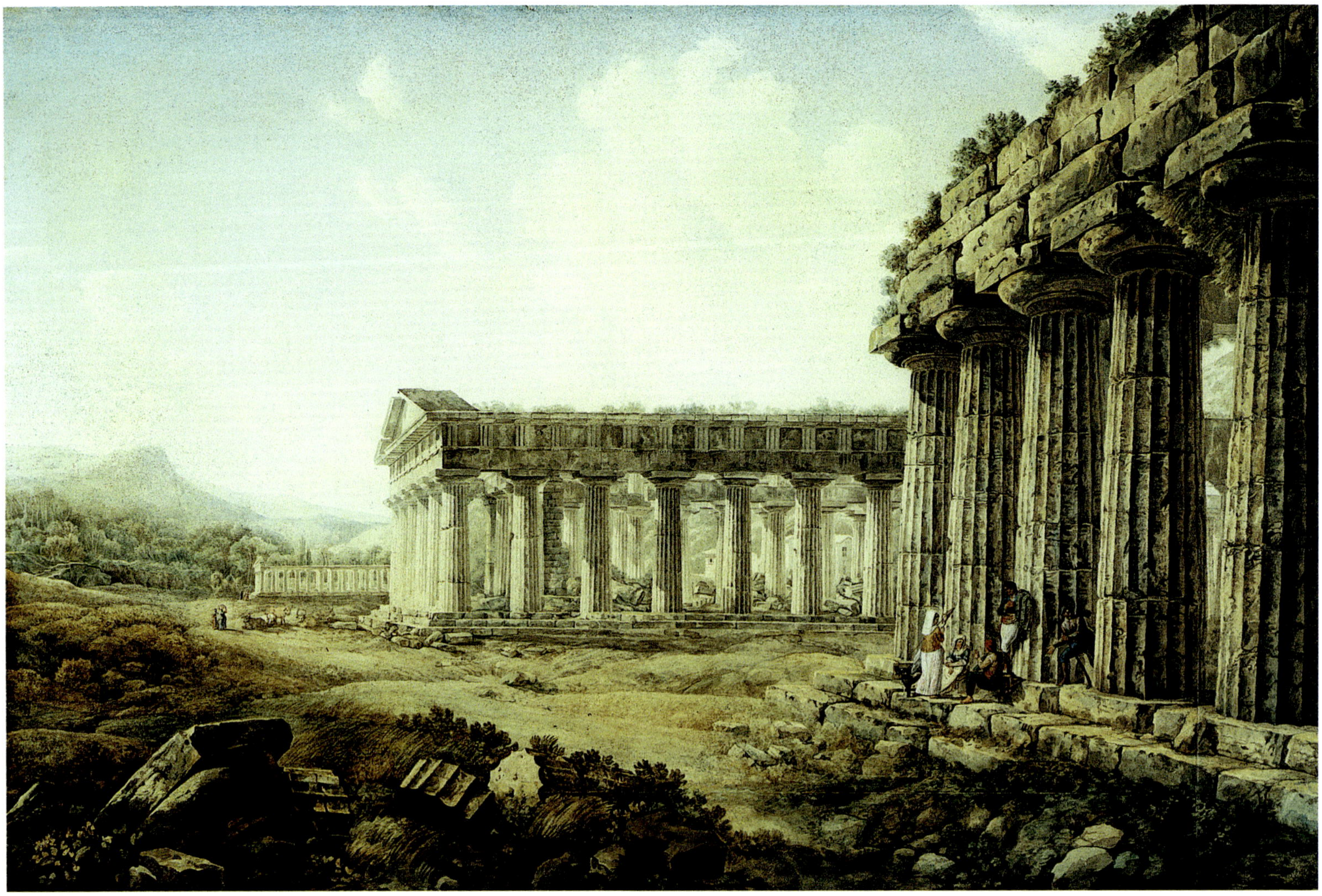

26. THE PORT OF CHERIELLA AT CASTELLAMMARE, C.1794

Pen and India ink, crayon, watercolour, heightened with gouache on paper laid down on canvas, 73 x 110.5 cm
Lausanne, Musée cantonal des Beaux-Arts
Inv. 809

Literature: Agassiz 1927, p. 44; exh. cat. Lausanne 1953, n. 41; Naples 1962 (ex catalogue); exh. cat. Lausanne 1986, n. 79; exh. cat. Rome 1987, n. 71; exh. cat. Lausanne 1998b, p. 100

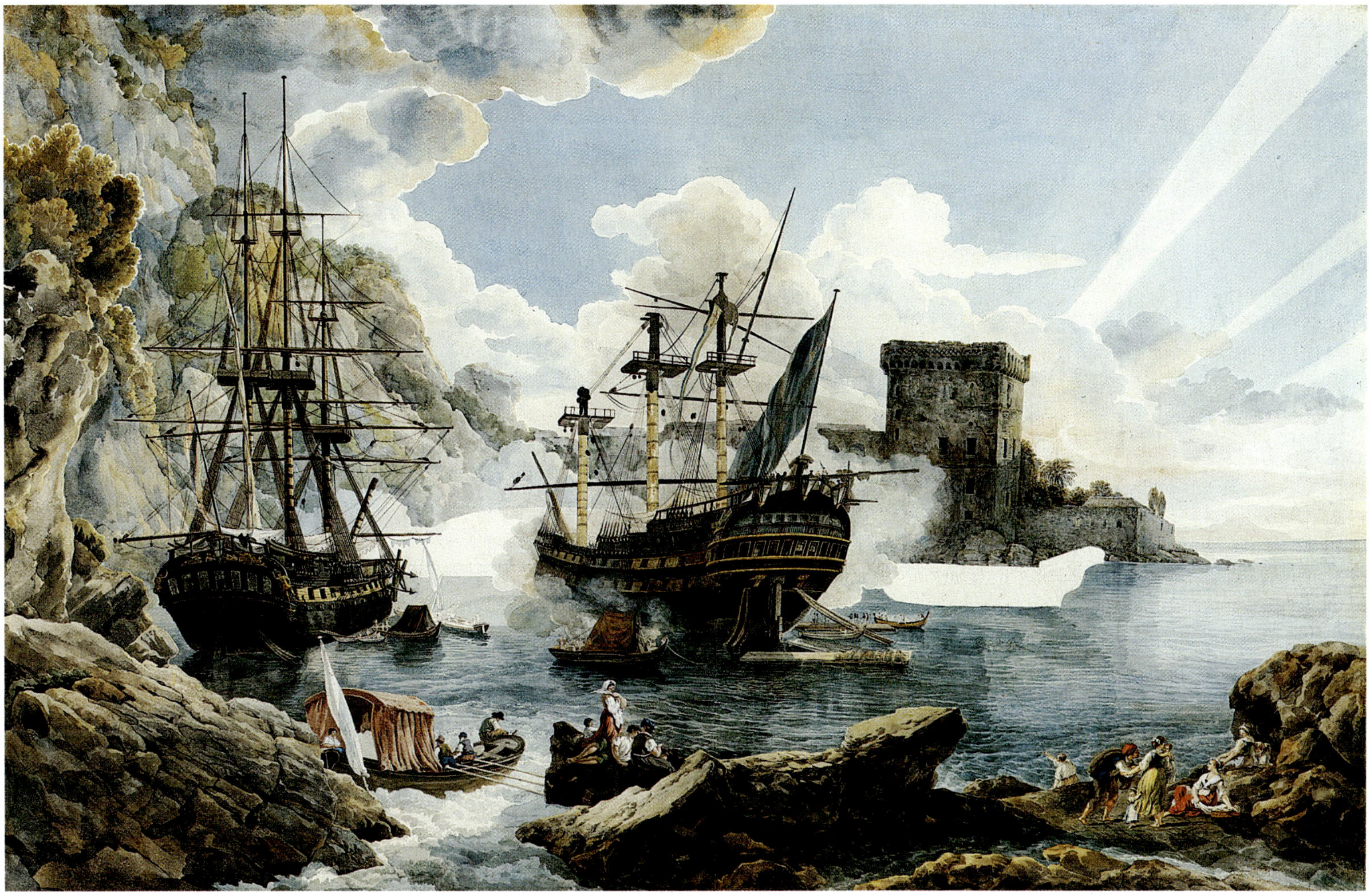

29. THE TEMPLE OF FORTUNE, MARECHIARO, NAPLES, 1794–1800

Pen and brown ink, pencil, watercolour, the figures heightened in gouache, D & C Blauw paper laid down on canvas, 76.5 x 113.4 cm
Lausanne, Musée cantonal des Beaux-Arts
Inv. 849

Literature: Agassiz 1927, p. 43; exh. cat. Lausanne 1953, n. 45; exh. cat. Rome 1954, n. 35; exh. cat. Naples 1962, n. 30 et pl. X; exh. cat. Lausanne 1974, n. 145; exh. cat. London 1985, n. 43; exh. cat. Lausanne 1986, n. 70; cat exp. Naples 1990

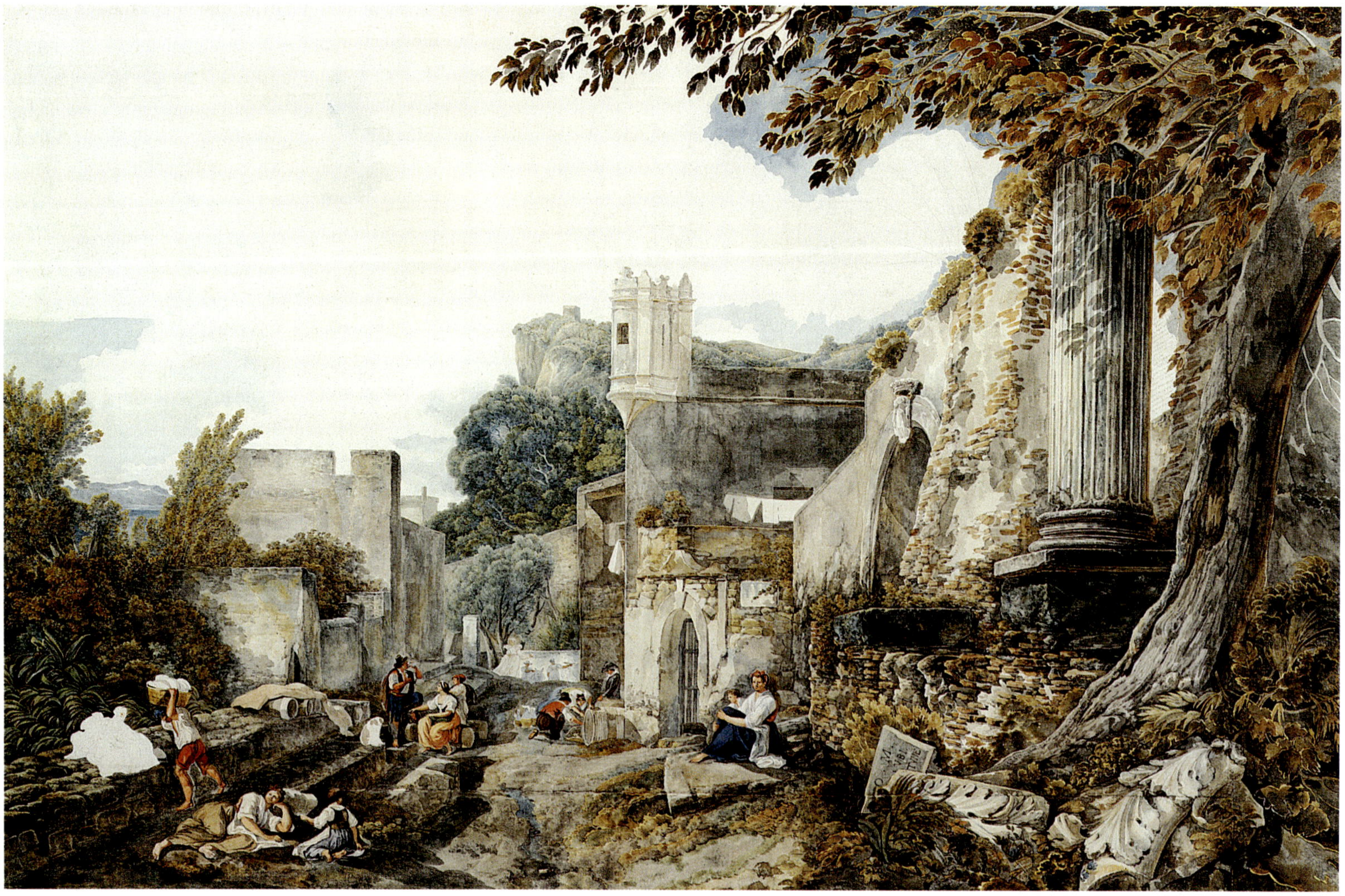

30. AN IDEALISED VIEW OF POSILLIPO, 1794–1800

Pen and black ink, watercolour, the figures heightened in gouache, D & C Blauw paper laid down on canvas, 75 x 115 cm
Lausanne, Musée cantonal des Beaux-Arts
Inv. 810

Literature: Agassiz 1927, p. 42; exh. cat. Lausanne 1953, n. 42; exh. cat. Rome n. 33; R.-Ch. Logoz, 'Un tableau de Ducros dans l'ancienne collection royale de Caserta' in *Gazette de Lausanne*, 1–2 September 1956, p. 7; exh. cat. London 1985, n. 36; exh. cat. Lausanne 1986, n. 76; exh. cat. Rome 1987, n. 69; exh. cat. Lausanne 1998b, p. 97

We know that, for all the precision of their details, Ducros's views are not at all objective (as we have come to understand that idea since the invention of photography). The artist had many possible ways of modifying reality and he used them all (changing the proportions of buildings, expanding the space, multiple viewpoints, etc.). In this watercolour he takes the proces even further. On the back of the canvas he has written "veduta del Posillipo" (View of Posillipo): the work itself shows us just how cautiously we need to interpret his words.

What we have here is a real montage. The starting point was the view of Posillipo from a specific location, under the arches of the Palazzo Donn'Anna. Here, however, Ducros has replaced the dark mass of the arches with a group of imaginary trees whose branches form a partial vault, and he has added a second tier of steep hills above the banks of Posillipo, crowing the ensemble with the distinctive mass of the Castel Sant'Elmo. Instead of the Riviera di Chiaja in the background, we have Naples surmounted by Vesuvius. This, then, is a landscape made up of real elements but arranged in accordance with the painter's imagination.

This landscape is precious because of it depicts the banks between Mergellina and the Palazzo Donn'Anna with great precision, affording a clear view of the mysterious villa of Emma and Sir William Hamilton with its distinctive semicircular terrace. A watercolour by William Pars, now lost, was one of the only other images showing the configuration of the Hamilton Villa at Posillipo, although it did so from the other side, with the Palazzo Donn'Anna in the background.

This painting evokes the years (1794–1795) when so many distinguished figures came to visit Sir William at the famous Casino on Posillipo.

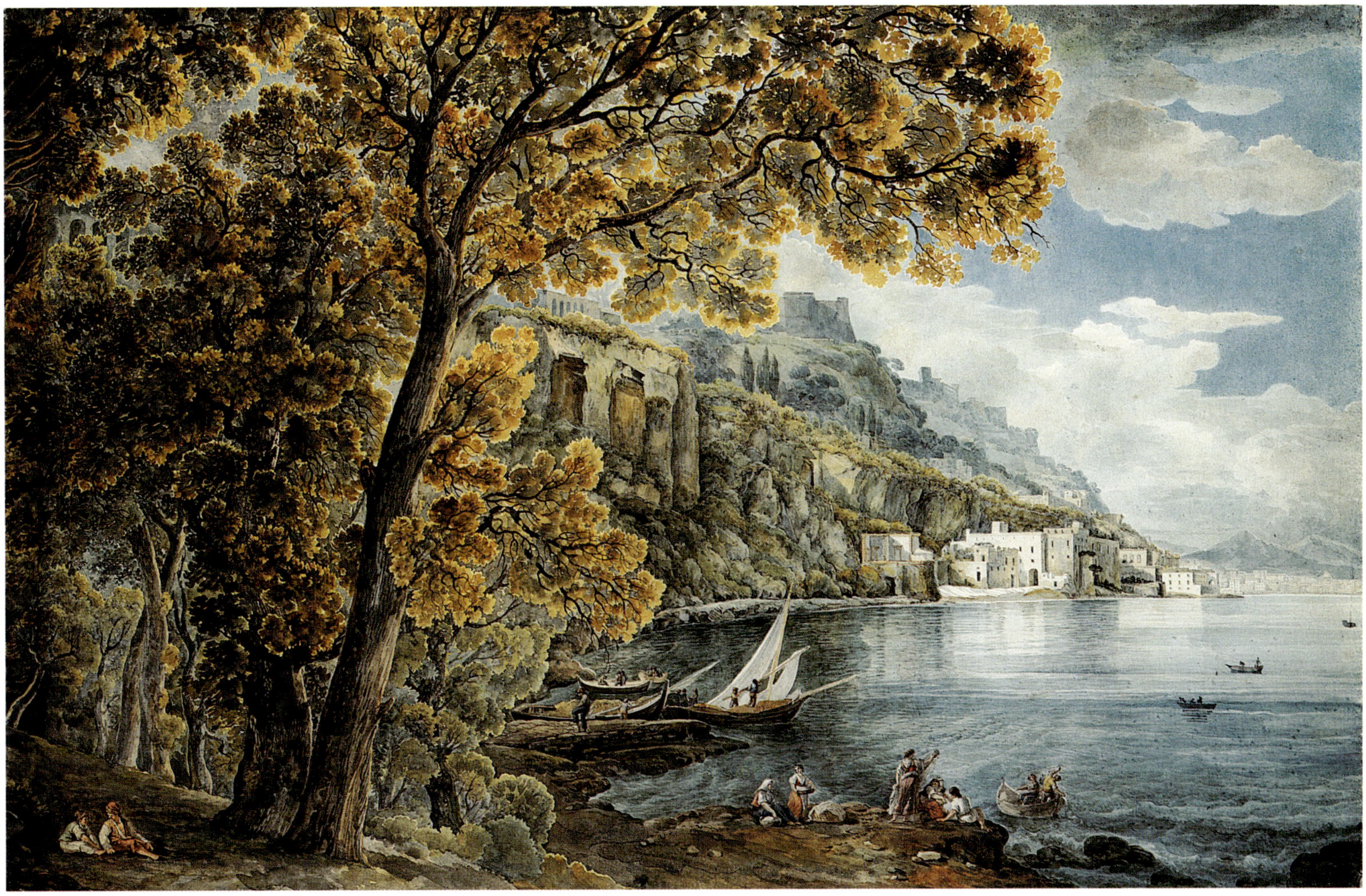

31. THE TOMB OF VIRGIL, POSILLIPO, 1794–1800

Watercolour, J Whatman papers laid down on canvas, 134 x 98 cm
Lausanne, Musée cantonal des Beaux-Arts
Inv. 847

Literature: Agassiz 1927, p. 43; exh. cat. Lausanne 1986, n. 75; exh. cat. Rome 1987, n. 68; exh. cat. Lausanne 1998b, p. 93

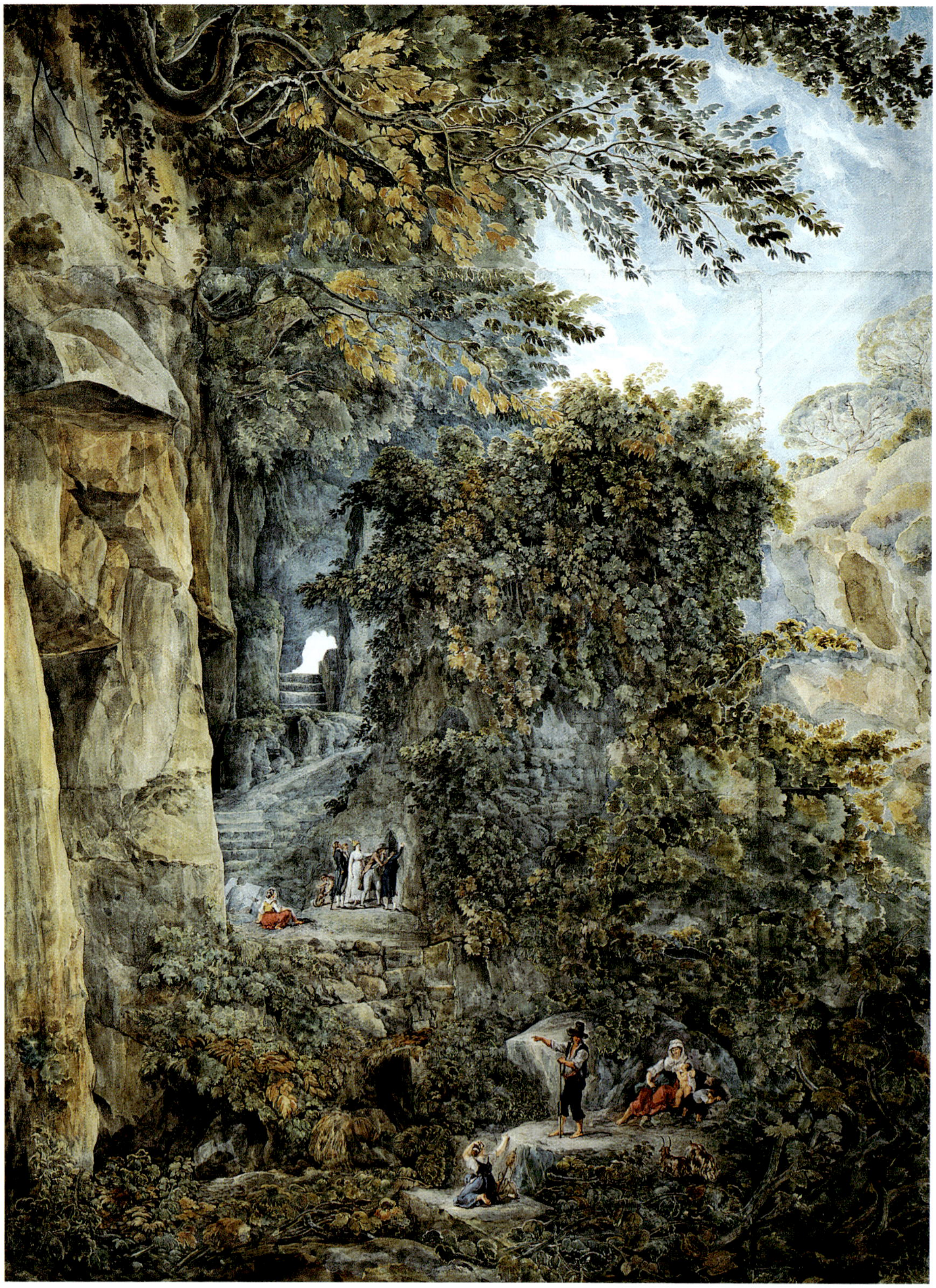

32. THE TEMPLE OF JUPITER SERAPIS, POZZUOLI, 1794–1800

Pen and India ink, watercolour heightened with gouache, James Whatman Turkey Mill Kent 1781 paper laid down on canvas, 77 x 115.5 cm
Lausanne, Musée cantonal des Beaux-Arts
Inv. 803

Literature: Agassiz 1927, p. 43; exh. cat. Lausanne 1953, n. 40; exh. cat. Rome 1954, n. 32; exh. cat. Lausanne 1986, n. 65

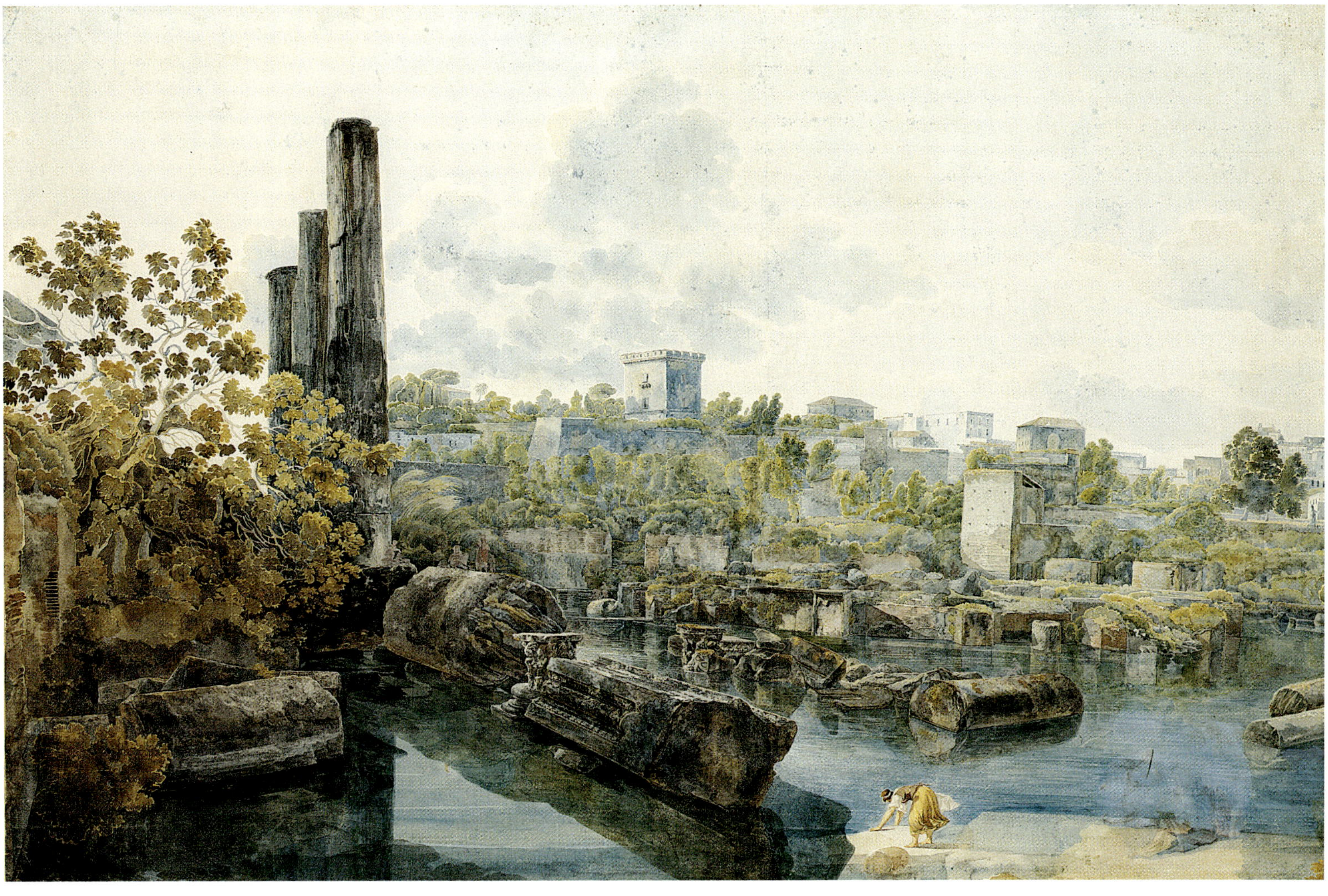

33. THE TEMPLE OF JUPITER SERAPIS, POZZUOLI, 1794–1800

Watercolour, D & C BLAUWpapers laid down on canvas, 73 x 107 cm
Lausanne, Musée cantonal des Beaux-Arts
Inv. 840

Literature: Agassiz 1927, p. 43; exh. cat. Lausanne 1953, n. 44; exh. cat. Rome 1954, n. 34; Chessex 1984 (1), p. 436; exh. cat. Lausanne 1986, n. 64; exh. cat. Rome 1987, n. 58; exh. cat. Lausanne 1998b, p. 99

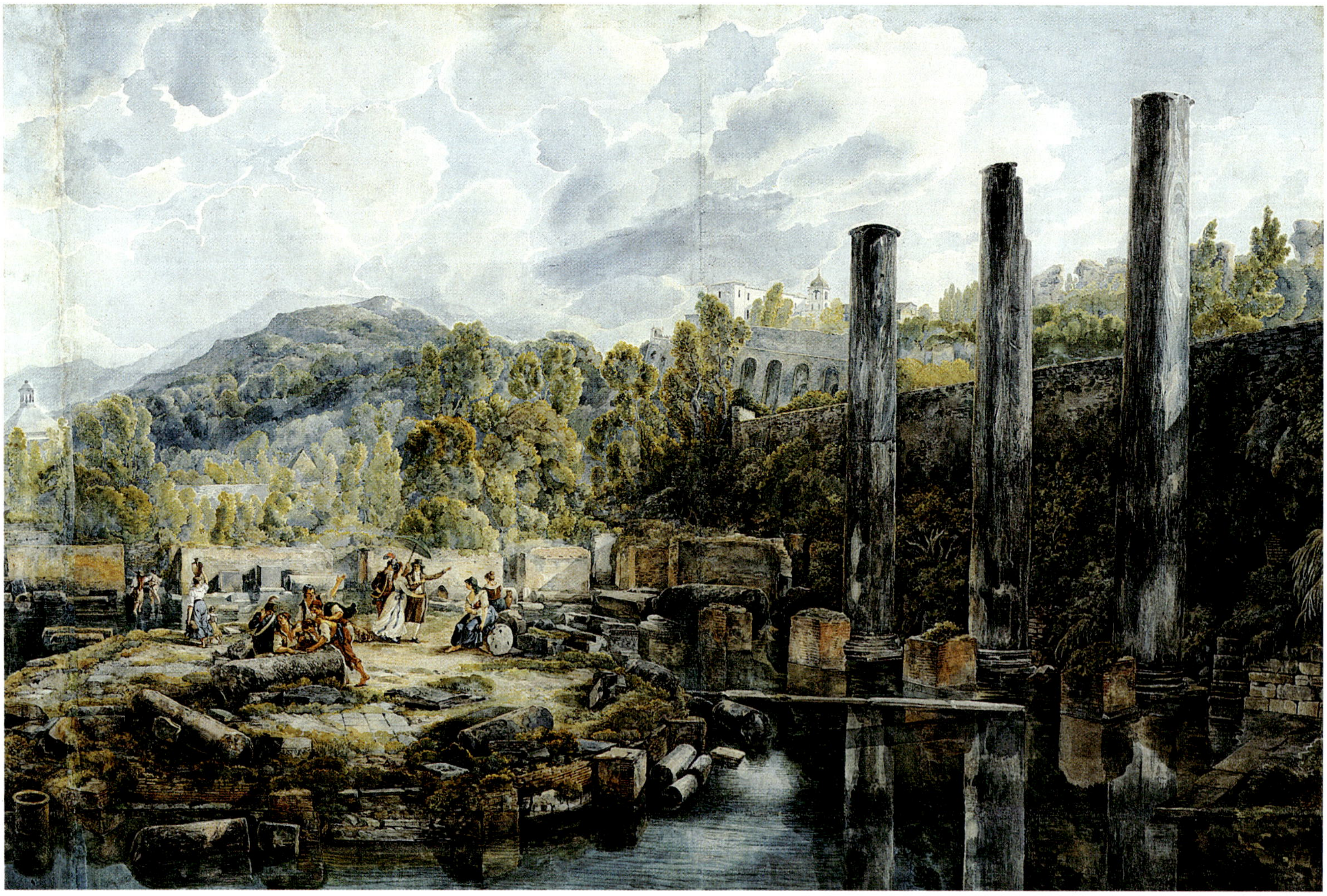

34. THE GROTTO OF POSILLIPO, 1794–1800

Pen and brown ink, watercolour, J Whatman papers laid down on canvas, 79 x 110 cm
Lausanne, Musée cantonal des Beaux-Arts
Inv. 822

Literature: Chessex 1982, ill. 8; Chessex 1984 (2), p. 76; exh. cat. London 1985, n. 33; exh. cat. Lausanne 1986, n. 72; exh. cat. Rome 1987, n. 66; Cusatelli 1987, p. 242; exh. cat. Florence 1994, pp. 37 et 46; Spinosa, Di Mauro 1996, pp. 142 et 203; exh. cat. Lausanne 1998b, p. 90

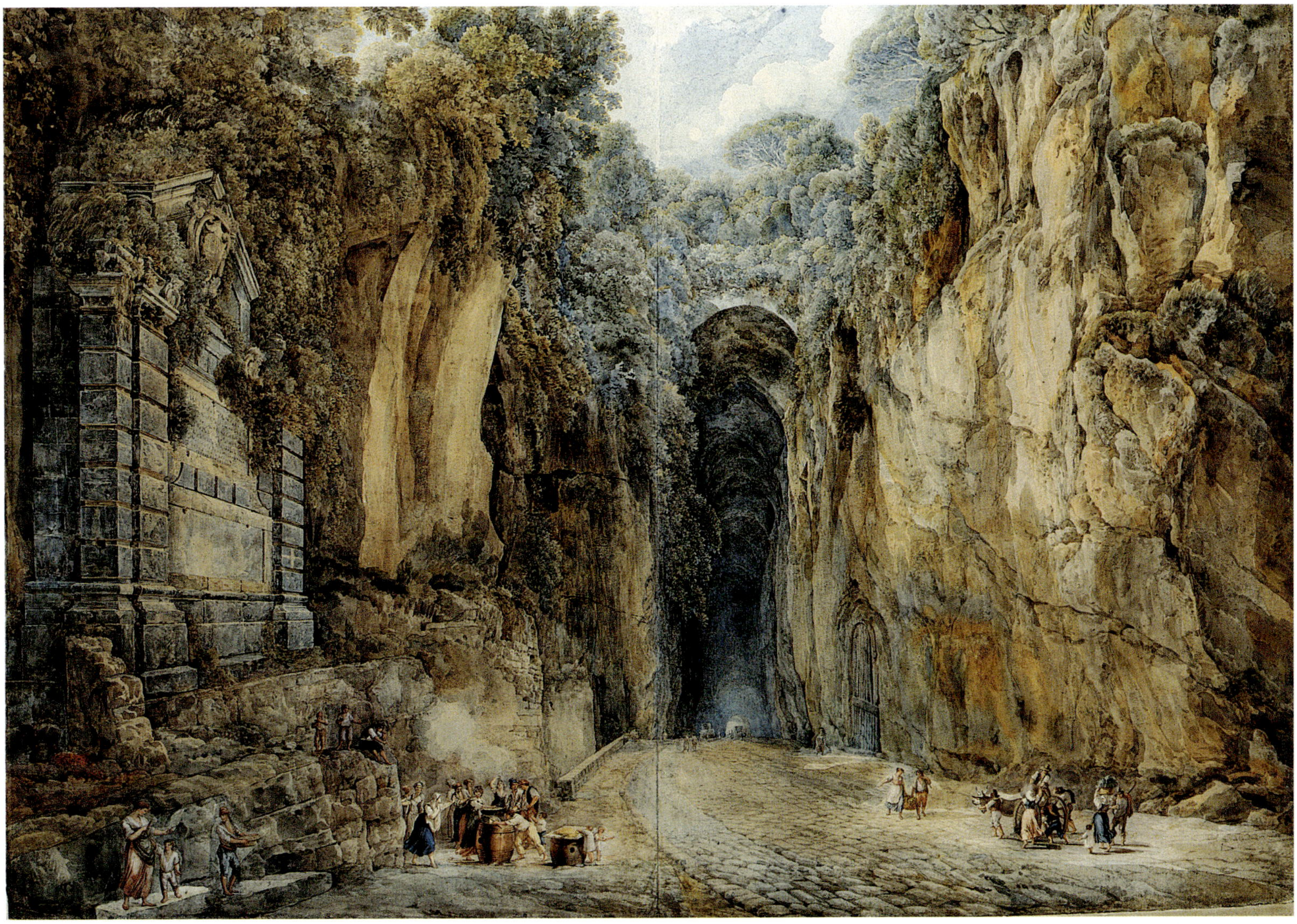

35. ERUPTION OF VESUVIUS BY MOONLIGHT, undated

Oil on paper laid on canvas, 75 x 104 cm
Lausanne, Musée cantonal des Beaux-Arts
Inv. 852

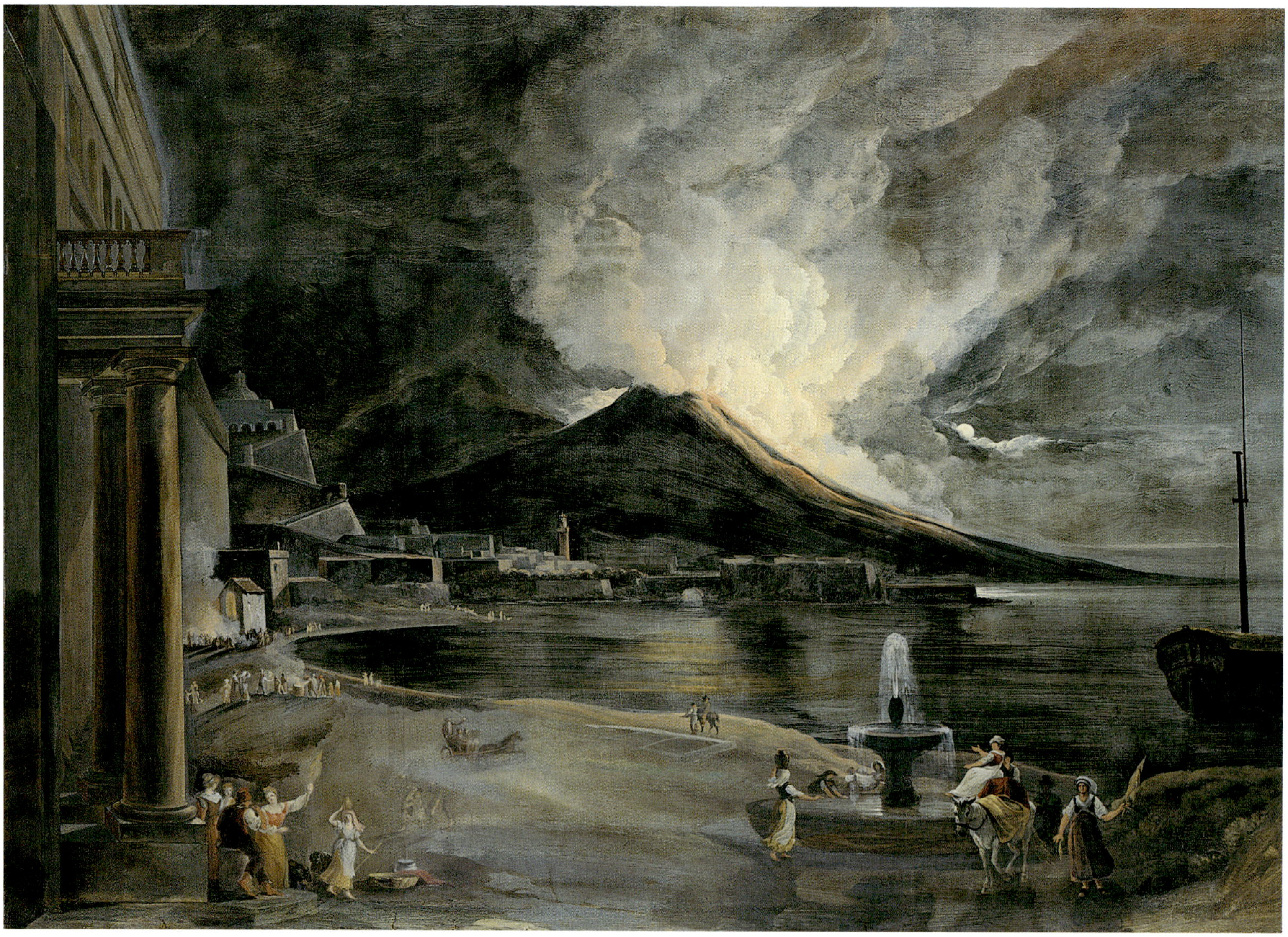

ABRAHAM-LOUIS-RODOLPHE DUCROS

36. ERUPTION OF VESUVIUS AND SHIPWRECK, c.1800

Watercolour, heighted with gouache and oil, remains of varnish, papers laid down on canvas, 103 x 72.7 cm
Lausanne, Musée cantonal des Beaux-Arts
Inv. 819

Literature: exh. cat. Berne 1810, n. 43; exh. cat. Lausanne 1953, n. 43; exh. cat. London 1985, n. 37; exh. cat. Lausanne 1986, n. 80; exh. cat. Rome 1987, n. 72; Chessex, exh. cat. Lausanne 1989, pp. 50–51; exh. cat. Berne 1991, n. 297; exh. cat. Lausanne 1998a, p. 37; exh. cat. Lausanne 1998b, p. 91

The so called "ash" eruption of June 1794 cast Naples and its environs into darkness for several days on end. The event gave rise to an abundance of images, first of all in response to the public fascination with the catastrophe, but also because there was a growing interest in volcanoes on the part of geologists and many fascinated amateurs who bought up the first publications on the subject.

This watercolour thus began with an event that the painter no doubt experienced directly (he is known to have been in Naples in early 1794). It is no simple documentary account of the eruption, but a partially imaginary view. Ducros stages the scene, with a big diagonal cutting across his composition. The right foreground has an emotional depiction of the desperate plight of the castaways, a clear reference to the storms painted by the French artist Claude-Joseph Vernet; the left background is used for the eruption and the lava flowing all the way to Torre del Greco. The dramatic lighting on the foamy waves and the broken mast thus stand in counterpoint to the black, eddying smoke from the volcano. It is hard not to see this unleashing of wild natural forces, dramatised by lightning, as a metaphorical expression of the political upheavals of this period of revolutions and wars, all the more so since Ducros's horizon was considerably darkened by his personal circumstances (exile, financial difficulties).

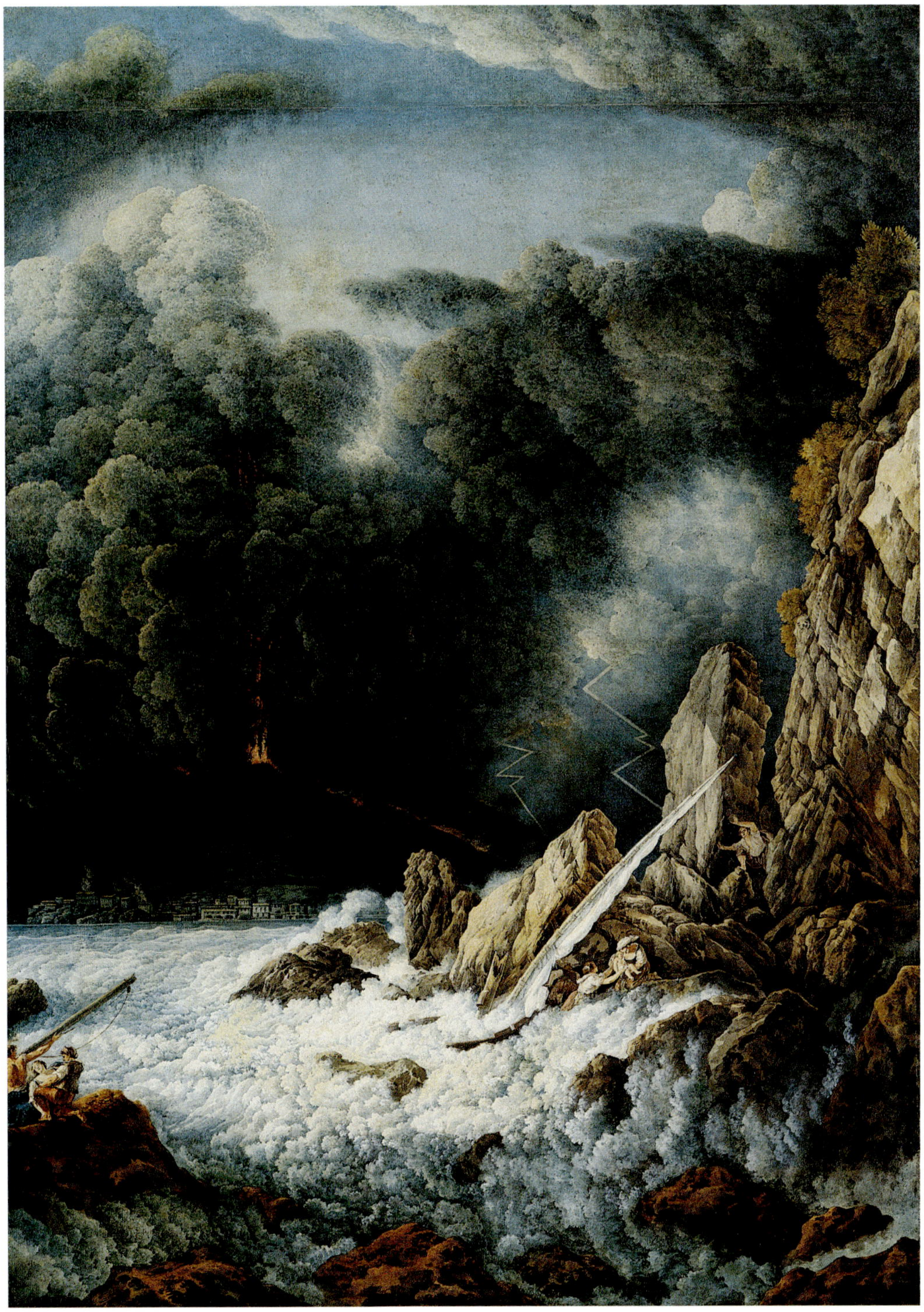

37. ERUPTION, undated

Oil on canvas, 91 x 122.5 cm
Lausanne, Musée cantonal des Beaux-Arts
Inv. 1282

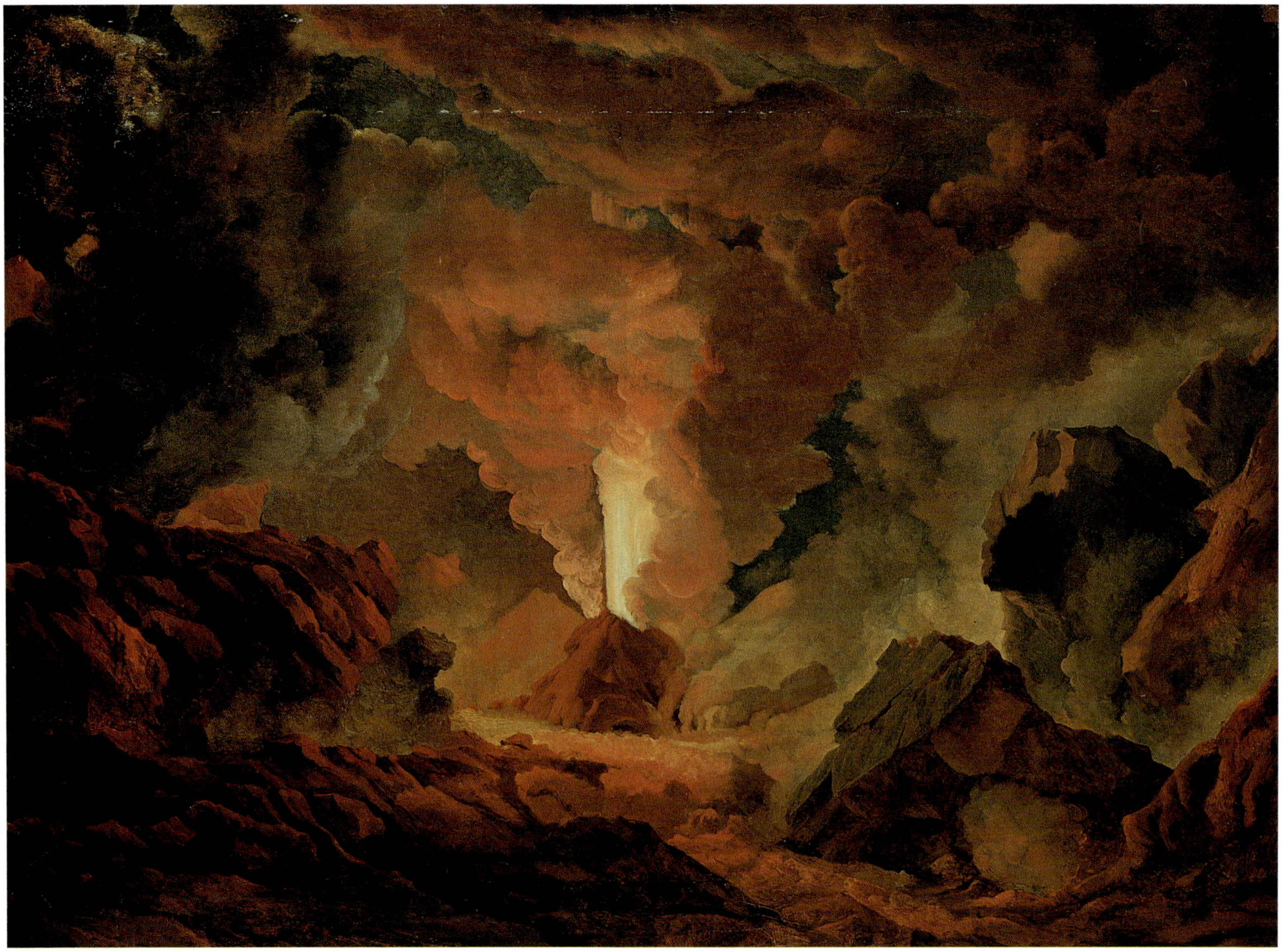

38. THE TEMPLE OF MERCURY, BAIA, 1794–1800

Watercolour, the figures heightened in gouache, D & C Blauw paper laid down on canvas, 67.5 x 104 cm
Lausanne, Musée cantonal des Beaux-Arts
Inv. 834

Literature: Agassiz 1927, p. 42; Chessex 1984 (2), p. 77; exh. cat. London 1985, n. 39; exh. cat. Lausanne 1986, n. 61; exh. cat. Rome 1987, n. 55; exh. cat. Atlanta 1988, pp. 72–73; exh. cat. Lausanne 1994, p. 12; exh. cat. Lausanne 1998a, p. 36; exh. cat. Lausanne 1998b, p. 89

Baia is located in the Gulf of Pozzuoli and is part of the Phlegrean Fields, an extensive volcanic area west of Naples. A renowned resort ever since Roman times, Baia was one of the great centres of Neapolitan tourism in the eighteenth century.

It was represented in many different ways, from extensive *vedute* (Antonio Joli) to studies of ruins of ancient monuments (William Pars, Jean-Baptiste Lallemand, Alexis Nicolas Perignon). Most artists concentrated on the topographical aspect, taking care to indicate the integration of the architecture into its immediate environment. The three most frequently depicted ruins – the Temple of Venus, the Temple of Diana and the Temple of Mercury – were always seen as part of a poetic vision in which we see the past being swallowed up by vegetation.

Ducros breaks with this tradition by taking the same approach as he applied to Tivoli when painting the interior of Maecenas's Villa. His skill lies in the avoidance of his contemporaries' literal transcriptions: the emphasis on the entrance portal, the thick vegetation around it and the play of sunlight slanting in from the open roof. First of all, Ducros takes a downward perspective, from half-way up the arch towards the visitors' entrance. At the same time, he considerably widens the angle of vision, which has the effect of removing any direct reference to the stabilising ground. The dwarfed figures heighten the sense of scale and make present in the image the memory of visitors, and the difficulty of gaining access to the permanently flooded temple. By breaking down our usual references, the painter manages to suggest a colossal space.

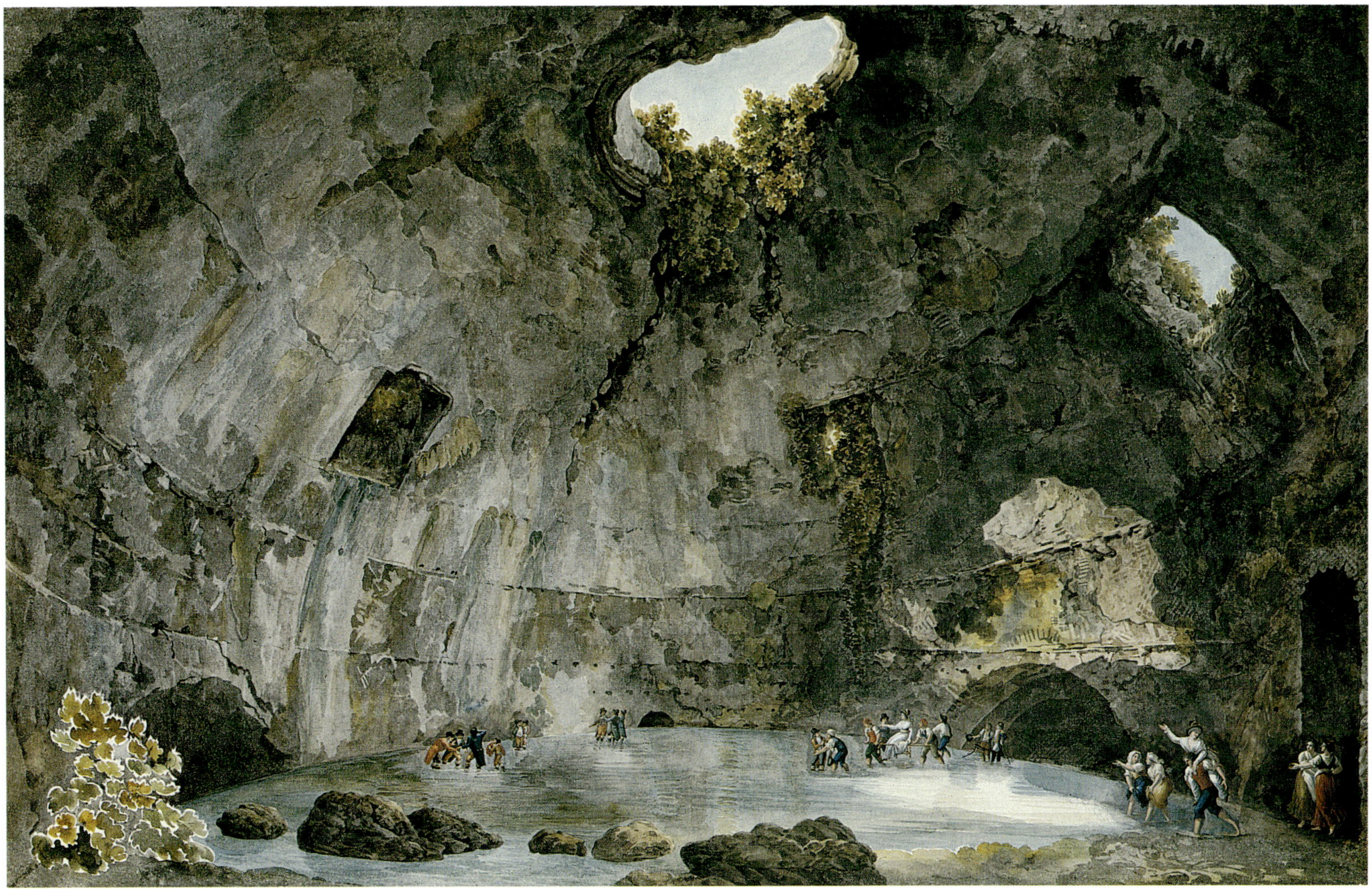

39. STORM AT NIGHT, CEFALÙ, c.1800

Watercolour, gouache and oil, papers laid down on canvas, 96 x 74 cm
Lausanne, Musée cantonal des Beaux-Arts
Inv. 812

Literature: Agassiz 1927, p. 44; exh. cat. Lausanne 1953, n. 60; exh. cat. Rome 1954, n. 42; E. Castelnuovo, 'Ducros, maître réputé du paysage pittoresque ou sublime' in *Encyclopédie illustrée du Pays de Vaud*, VI, Lausanne, 1976, p. 113; Zeri in *Storia d'Italia*, II/2, Torino 1976, ill. 96; G. Briganti, *I pittori dell'imaginario. Arte e rivoluzione psicologica*, Milan, 1977, ill. 35; exh. cat. Stockholm 1982, n. 176; *Museen der Schweiz*, Zurich, 1983, p. 170; Chessex 1984 (2), p. 78; exh. cat. London 1985, n. 41; exh. cat. Lausanne 1986, n. 86; exh. cat. Rome 1987, n. 75; Cusatelli 1987, p. 238; exh. cat. Atlanta 1988, pp. 76–77; Chessex 1992, p. 154; exh. cat. Lausanne 1994, pp. 12–13; exh. cat. Lausanne 1998a, p. 34; exh. cat. Lausanne 1998b, p. 105

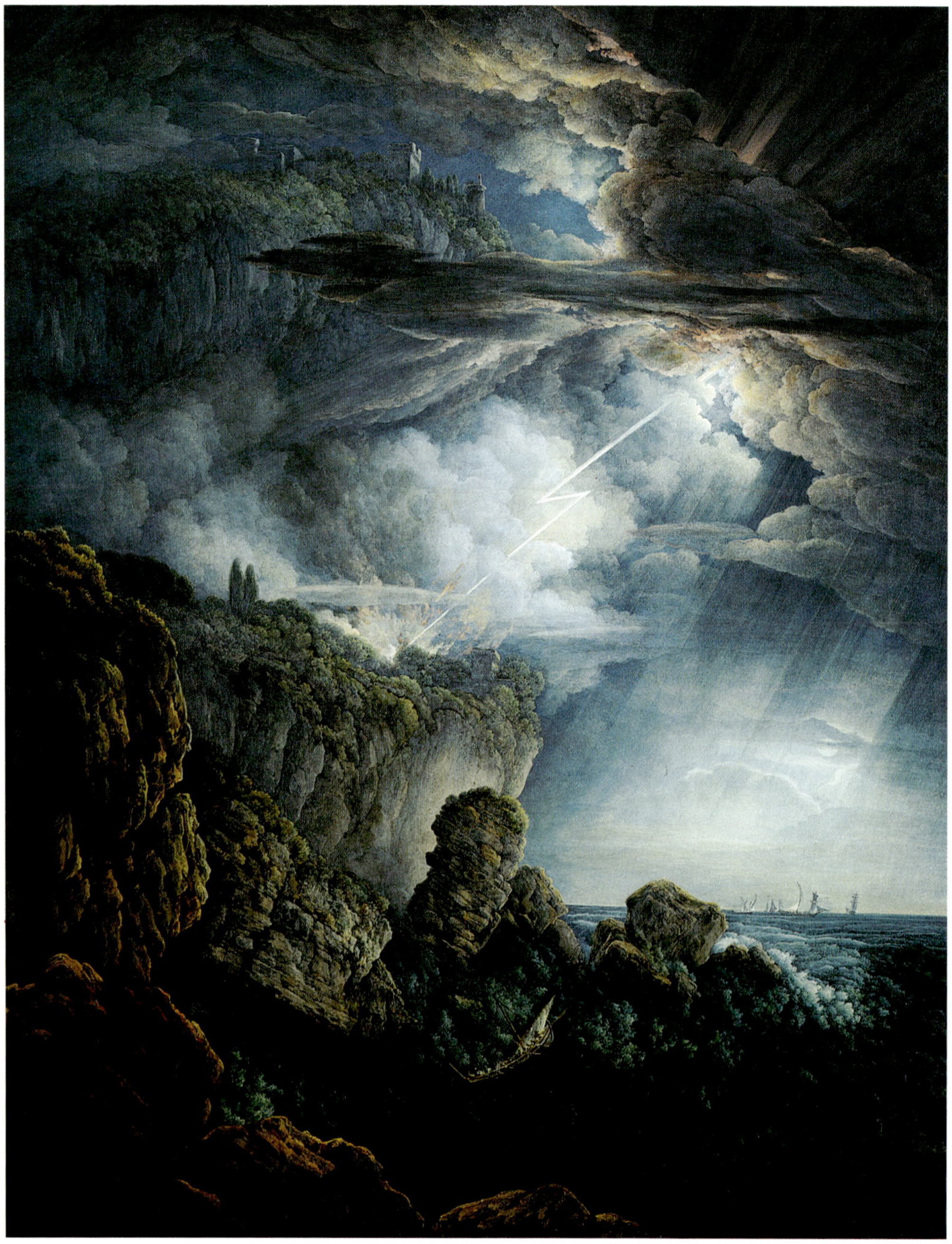

The absence of documents pertaining to the *Night Storm* means that we know nothing about the circumstances in which it was painted, the artist's intentions or, assuming there was one, the person who commissioned it. We know only that its style and technique belong to Ducros's late period.

This mysterious work made a big impression. It was part of the movement that was changing the way people looked at landscape at the turn of the nineteenth century. These artists evinced a new sensitivity to the effects of weather and filled their canvases with flashes of light, dark clouds and Gothic ruins, much as in the novels of the same name. This work means that we can link Ducros to painters such as Henry Fuseli and John Martin, who sounded the depths of the soul and the unconscious in their work. It is a kind of "freeze-frame" in which the lightning causing the building to explode, the boat in danger of sinking and the towers seemingly suspended above the cliffs suggest the imminence of a catastrophe whose causes and effects are unknown. Despite the initial impression of chaos, the work turns out to be highly structured. The composition is organised in four layers: the bottom one is bounded by the sea horizon, the top rests on the stratus and the two middle layers are separated by the median plateau struck by the lightning, whose point of impact constitutes the work's centre of gravity. The strong diagonals infuse the work with dynamism and the lightning connects the corners. Ducros plays skilfully on the transparency of watercolour and the opacity of the gouache and oil: dark brown transparent ochres highlighted with Naples yellow mixed with lacquer and other organic pigments for the cliffs; a colder Prussian blue for the sky and sea and effects of distance; Naples yellow and white mixed with lacquer for the pinkish tones of the rays of light, and the whole composition covered with gouache and organic pigments using the wash technique in order to reduce the transparency in certain areas. This highly complex technique enabled the artist to achieve effects that were more subtle than those of oil painting, effects that in 1822 prompted Sir Richard Colt Hoare to observe that the progress in watercolour painting was due to Ducros, whose works, he said, showed how much power and effect one can achieve using the immaterial substance of colours in water.

40. THE TEMPLE OF CONCORDIA, AGRIGENTO, SICILY, undated

Pen and India ink, watercolour on paper,
54 x 75 cm
Lausanne, Musée cantonal des Beaux-Arts
Inv. 2000–004

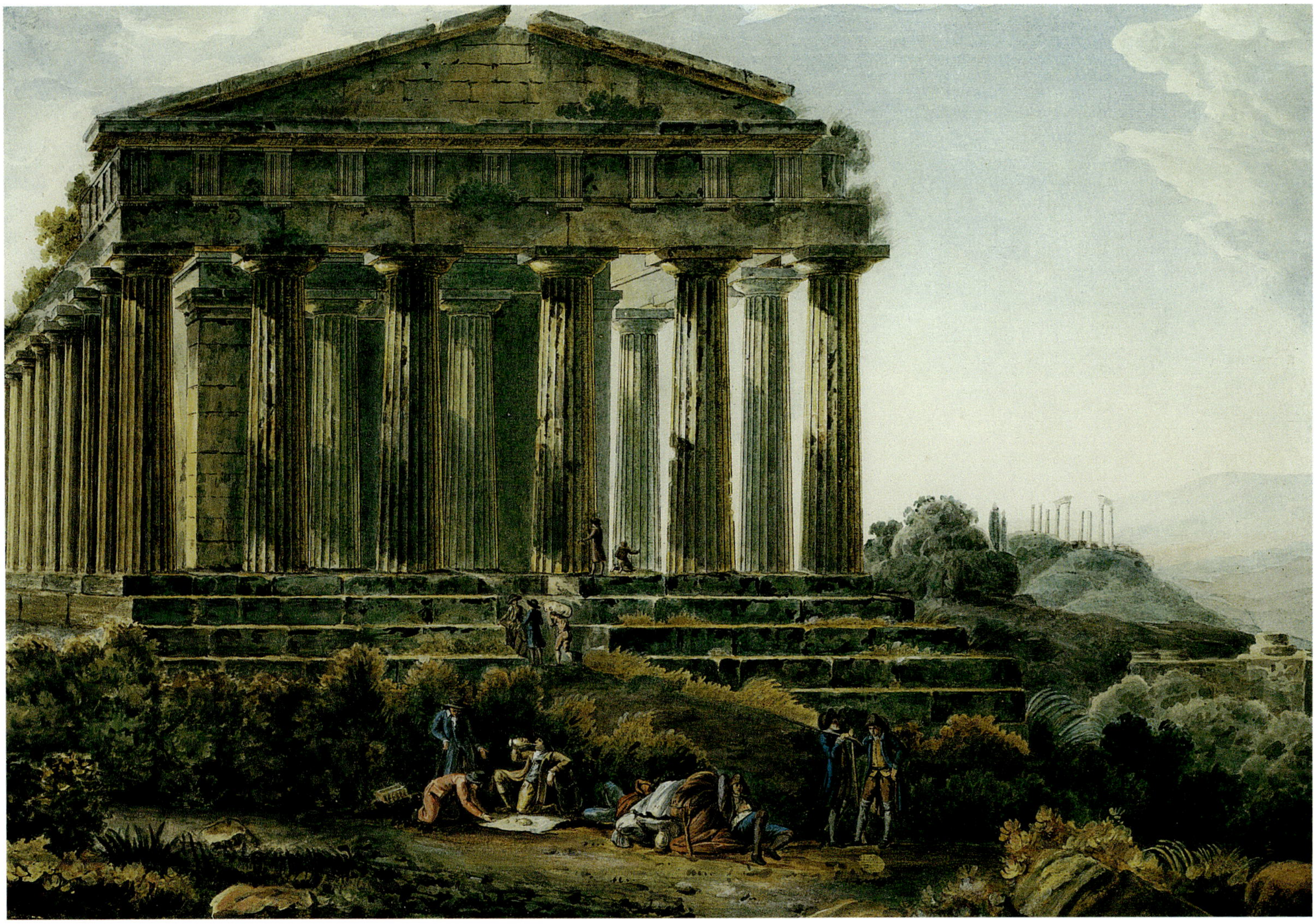

41. ENTRANCE TO MALTA BELOW THE FORT RICASOLI, undated

Pen and ink, watercolour on paper,
43.5 x 56.3 cm
Lausanne, Musée cantonal des Beaux-Arts
Inv. 776

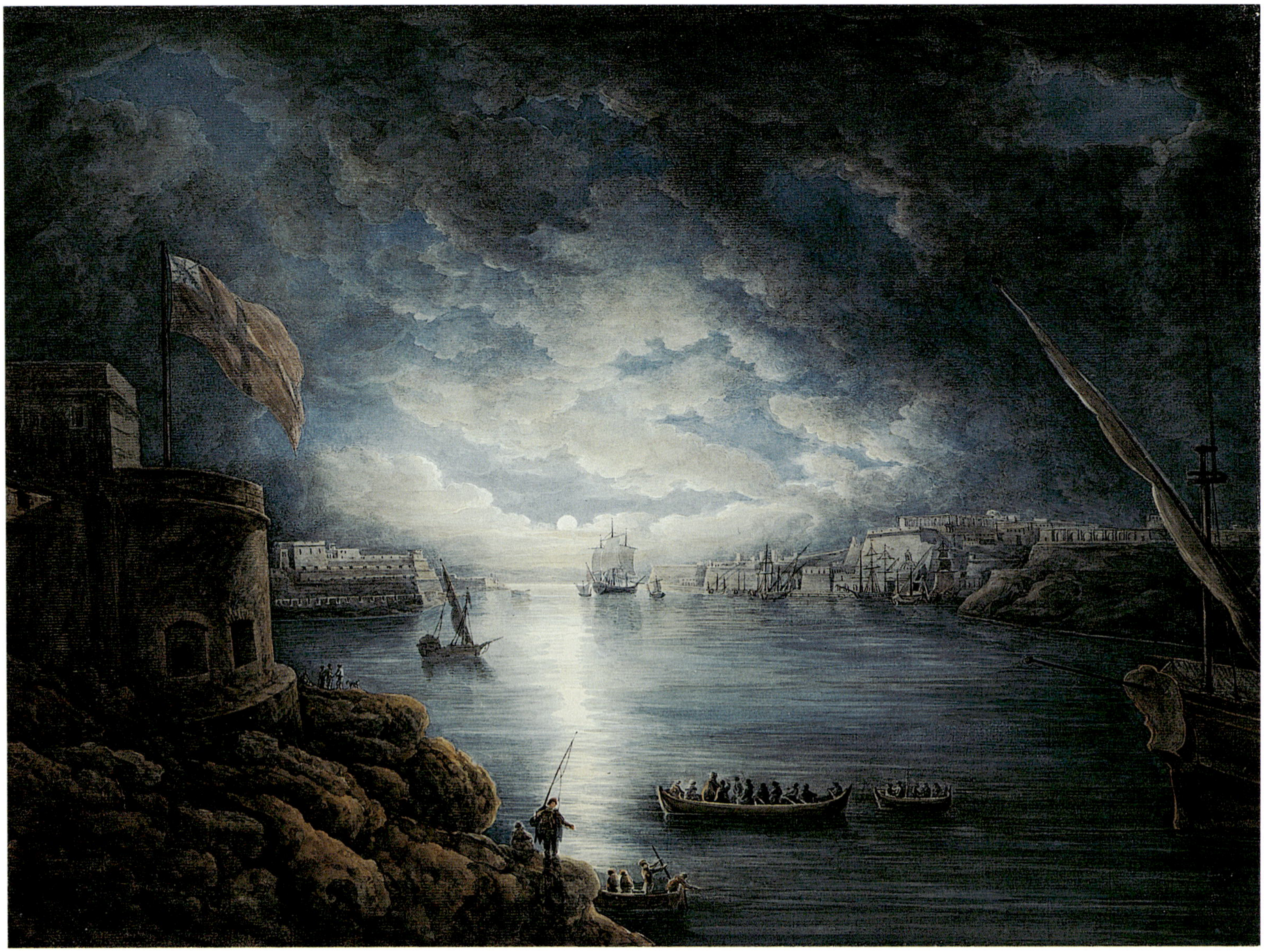

42. VIEW OF THE THREE CITIES FROM VALLETTA, 1800–1801

Pen and ink, watercolour, heightened with gouache, D & C Blauw and J Whatman papers laid on canvas, 88 x 159.5 cm
Lausanne, Musée cantonal des Beaux-Arts
Inv. 860

Literature: Agassiz 1927, p. 46; exh. cat. London 1985, n. 45; exh. cat. Lausanne 1986, n. 91

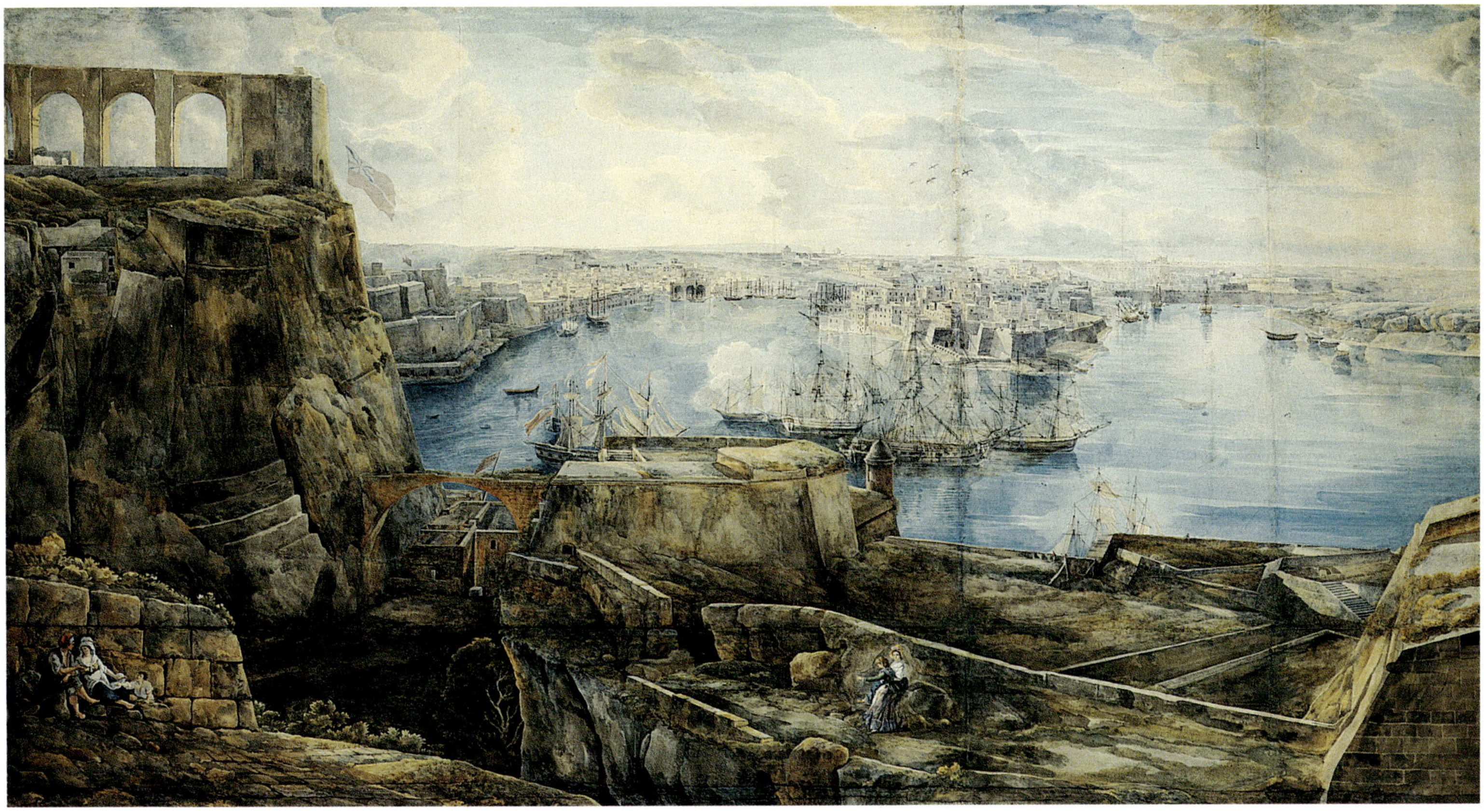

43. THE FOUNTAIN OF NEPTUNE AND FISH MARKET AT VALLETTA, c.1800–1801

Pen and black ink, watercolour, heightened with gouache, D & C Blauw papers laid down on canvas, 83.7 x 132 cm
Lausanne, Musée cantonal des Beaux-Arts
Inv. 805

Literature: Agassiz 1927, pp. 24 et 45; exh. cat. Lausanne 1953, n. 56; exh. cat. Rome 1954, n. 41; exh. cat. London 1985, n. 44; exh. cat. Lausanne 1986, n. 94; exh. cat. Rome 1987, n. 79; exh. cat. Valletta 1989, n. 7; exh. cat. Lausanne 1998b, p. 109

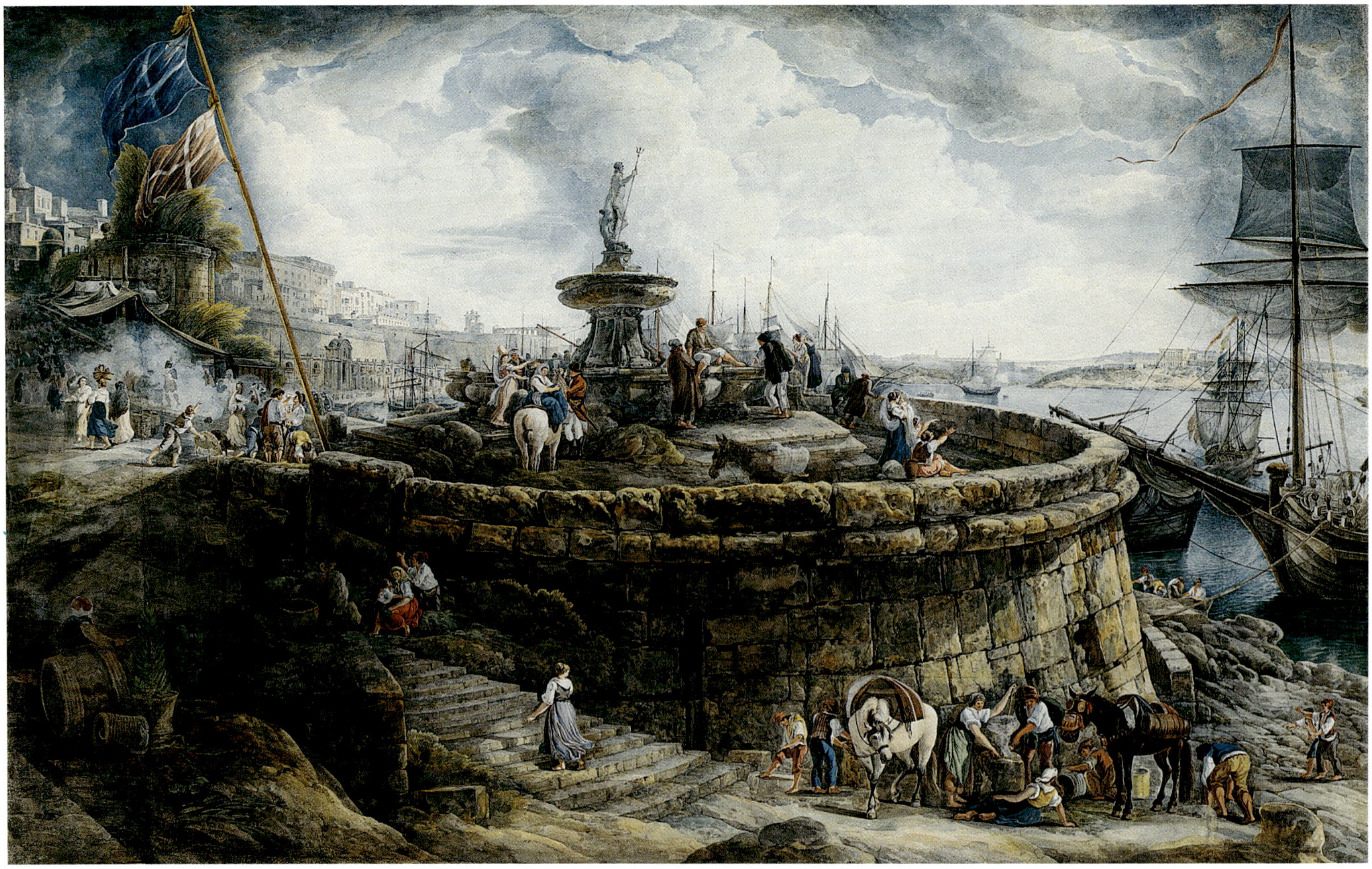

44. THE SQUALL BEHIND THE CUSTOMS HOUSE, VALLETTA, c.1800–1801

Pen and black ink, watercolour, heightened with gouache, papers laid down on canvas, 78 x 118 cm
Lausanne, Musée cantonal des Beaux-Arts
Inv. 795

Literature: exh. cat. Berne 1810, n. 41; Agassiz 1927, p. 39; exh. cat. Lausanne 1953, n. 53; exh. cat. London 1985, n. 46 (as 'Pavillion in the Grand Master's Garden, Valletta'); exh. cat. Lausanne 1986, n. 92; exh. cat. Rome 1987, n. 78; exh. cat. Valletta 1989, n. 5; exh. cat. Lausanne 1998b, p. 110

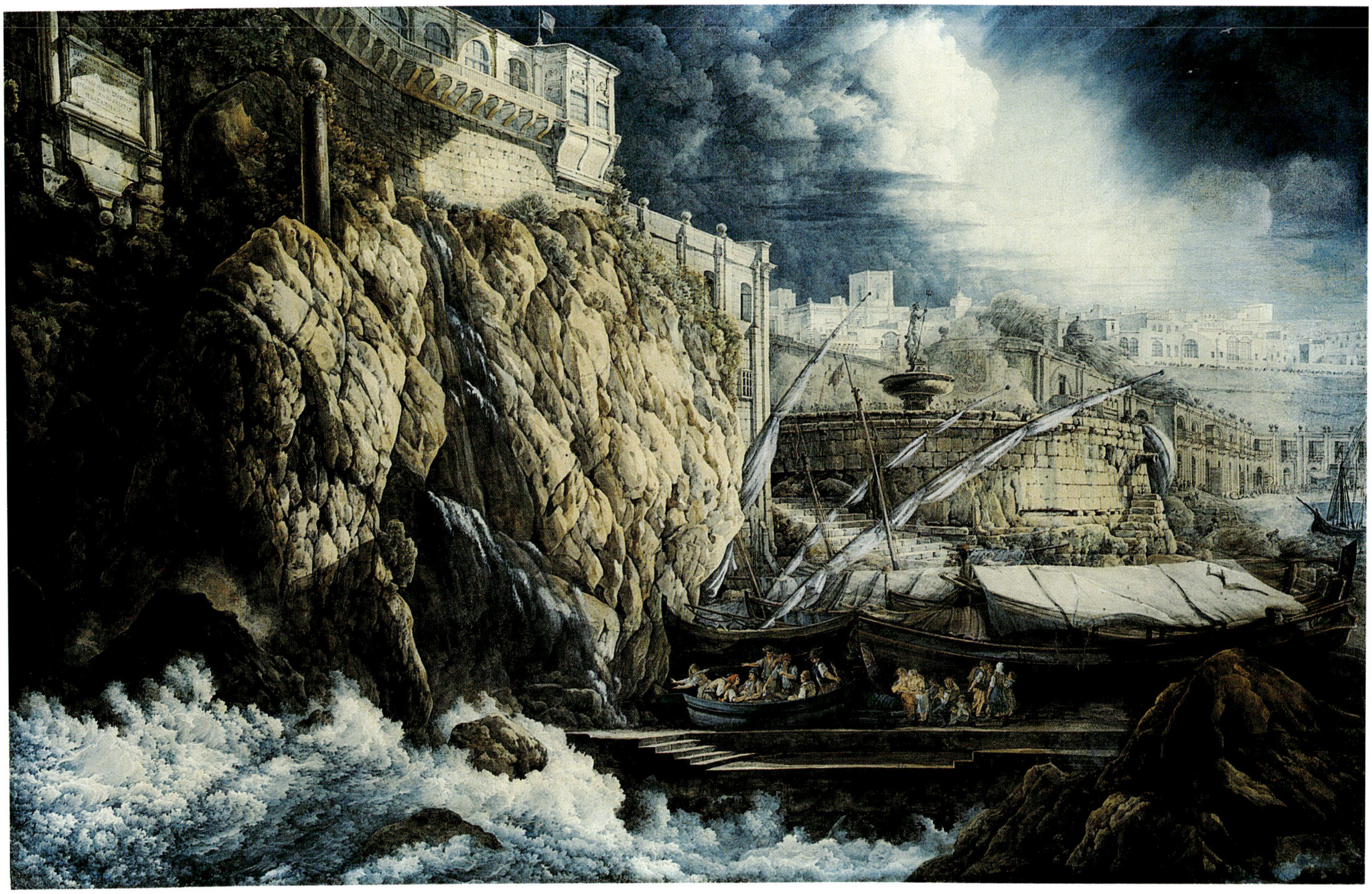

45. VIEW OF THE GRAND HARBOUR, VALLETTA, c.1800–1801

Pen and black ink, watercolour, heightened with gouache on papers laid down on canvas, 78.5 x 127.5 cm
Lausanne, Musée cantonal des Beaux-Arts
Inv. 802

Literature: Agassiz 1927, p. 45; exh. cat. Lausanne 1953, n. 54 (as 'Vue de Malte, de la Batterie Dükens'); exh. cat. Rome 1954, n. 38; exh. cat. London 1985, n. 43; exh. cat. Lausanne 1986, n. 88; exh. cat. Rome 1987, n. 76; exh. cat. Atlanta 1988, pp. 74–75; Chessex, exh. cat. Lausanne 1989, pp. 52–53; exh. cat. Valletta 1989, n. 1; exh. cat. Lausanne 1998a, p. 36; exh. cat. Lausanne 1998b, p. 107

This view down to the Grand Harbour at Valletta, with several English ships lying at anchor, was painted from a point above Upper Barracca, overlooking the Porta della Marina.

Ducros was in Malta from November 1800 to May 1801, shortly after the English army had captured the island from Bonaparte's French troops. He painted numerous views of Valletta, having obtained a commission from the commander of the conquering forces, Brigadier General Thomas Graham. He had plans to engrave a series of views of Malta which, in a letter to Sir Richard Colt Hoare, he described as "the boulevard of British power".

This view of the Grand Harbour is extremely detailed, showing the houses in Valletta, the Saint Barbara bastion with its sentry box, the distinctive arches of the Lower Barracca in the background and Fort Ricasoli closing off the harbour. Still, Ducros does introduce a degree of invention: the Fort Sant' Angelo on the far right has been moved in order to balance the composition. In reality, it would have been further out to the right, beyond even the wide-angle frame chosen by Ducros.

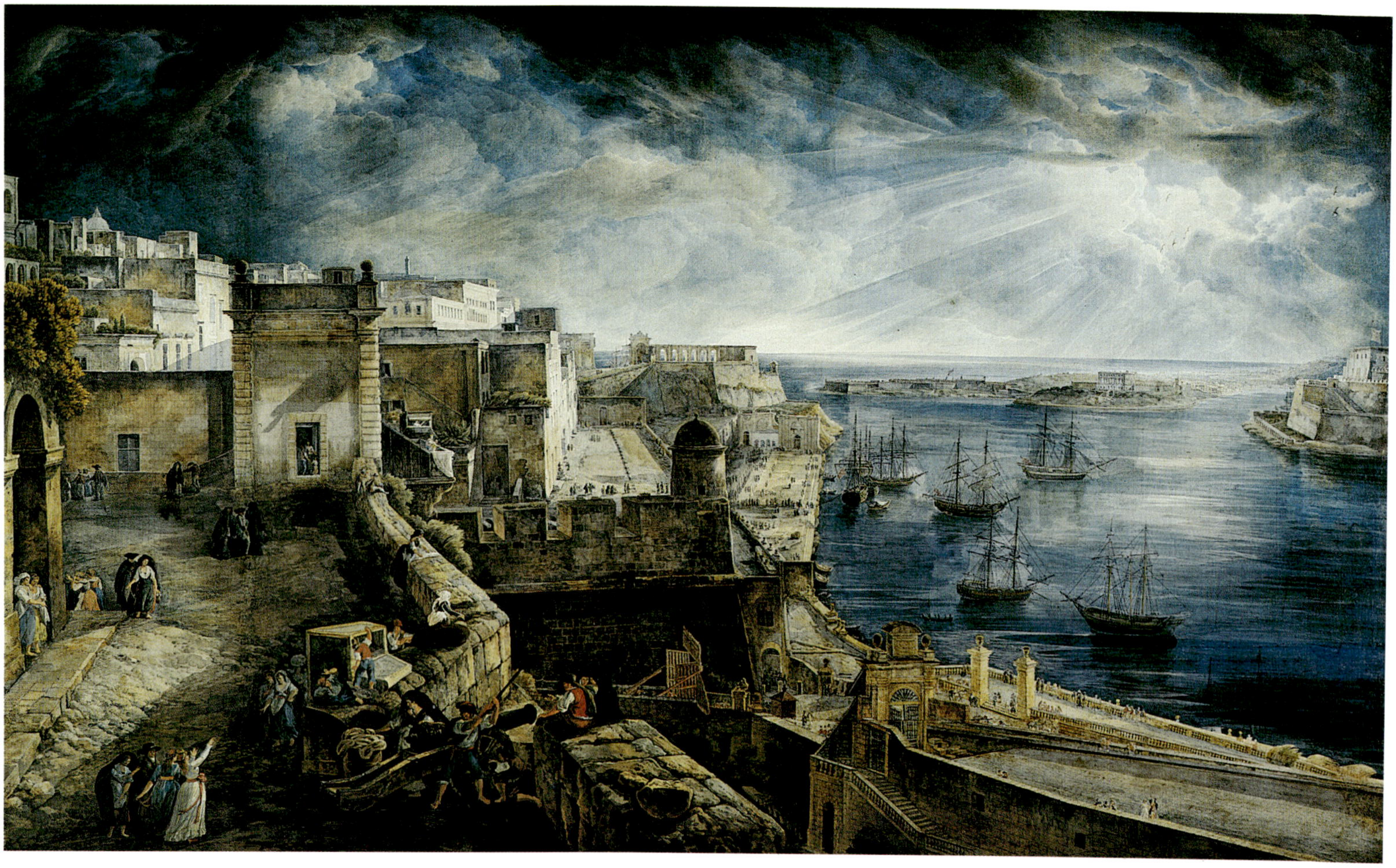

46. VIEW OF MALTA FROM THE PORTA DELLA MARINA, VALLETTA, c.1800–1801

Pen and ink, watercolour on paper laid down on canvas, 86.5 x 132.5 cm
Lausanne, Musée cantonal des Beaux-Arts
Inv. 813

Literature: exh. cat. Valletta 1989

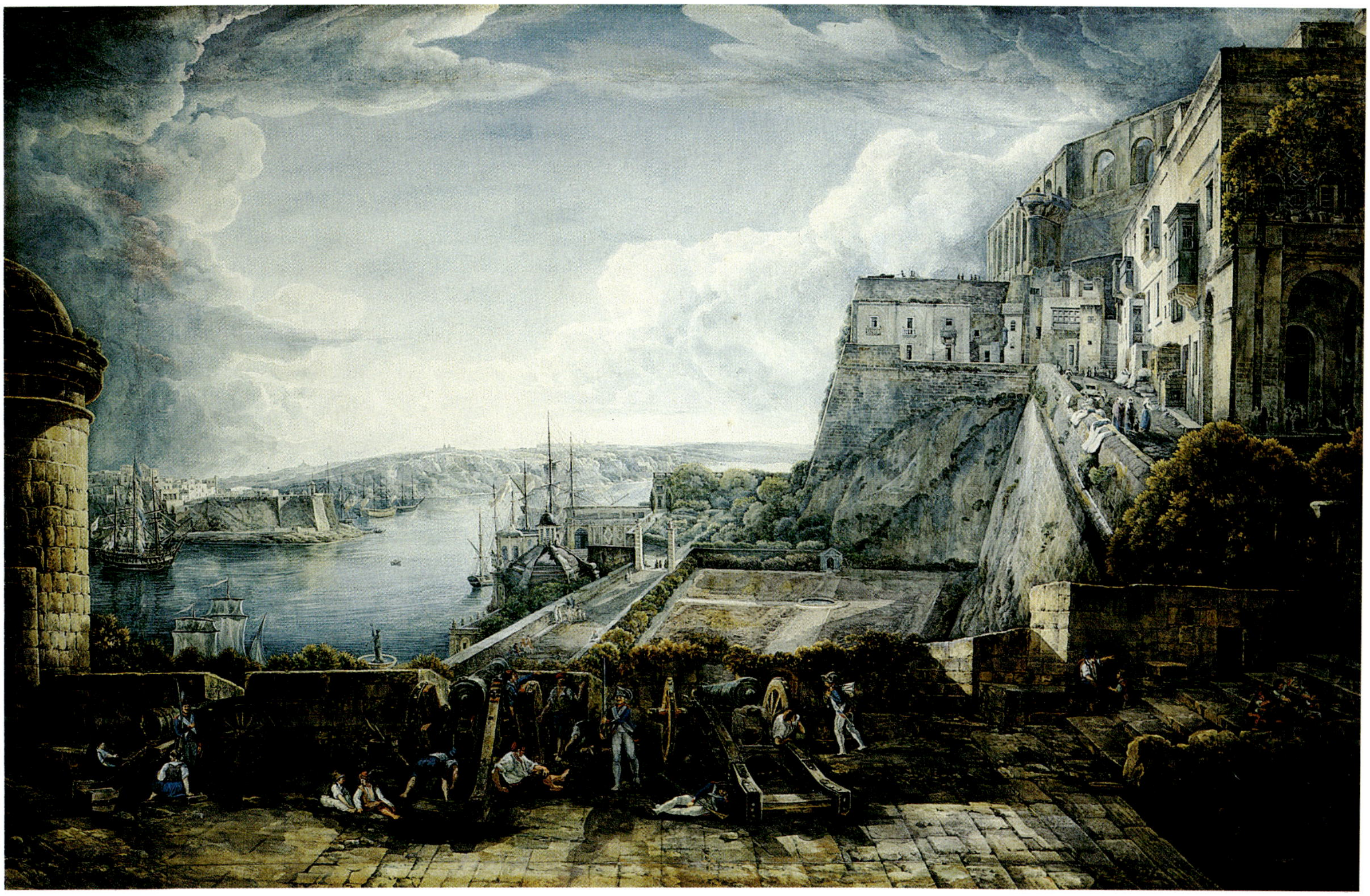

47. VIEW OF THE FORT SANT'ANGELO, VALLETTA, c.1800–1801

Pen and brown ink, watercolour, heightened with gouache, papers laid down on canvas, 77.5 x 107.5 cm
Lausanne, Musée cantonal des Beaux-Arts
Inv. 820

Literature: Agassiz 1927 p. 39 (as 'Porte de la Marine'); Chessex 1984 (2), p. 70; exh. cat. London 1985, n. 49; exh. cat. Lausanne 1986, n. 95; exh. cat. Rome 1987, n. 80; exh. cat. Valletta 1989, n. 8; exh. cat. Lausanne 1998b, p. 111

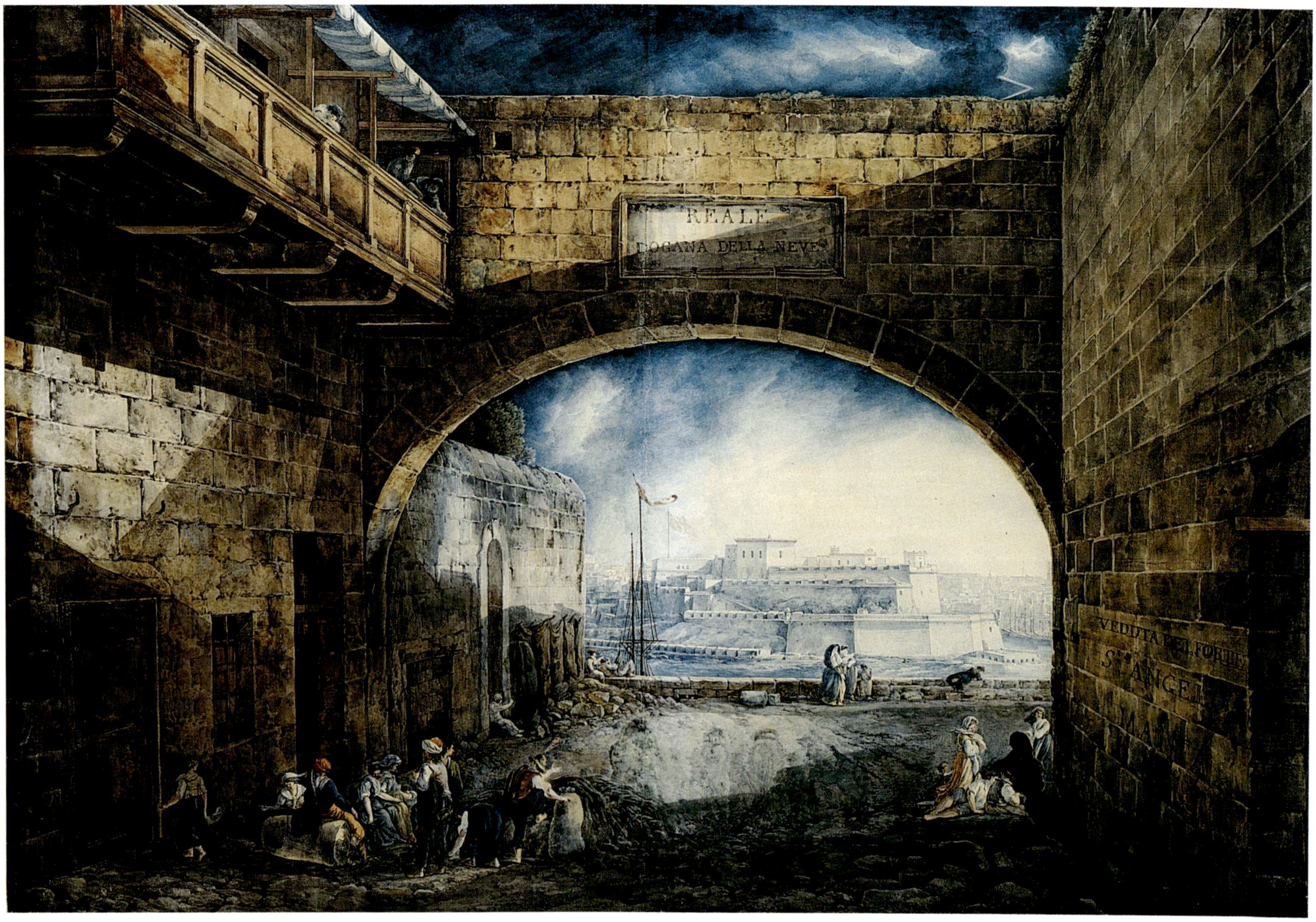